RED DEVILS
IN EUROPE

RED DEVILS
IN EUROPE

The Complete History of
MANCHESTER UNITED
in European Competition

ISBN 1 869914 04-X

Printed by: Toppan Printing Co (S) PTE.LTD
                      38 Liu Fang Road, Jurong Town, Singapore

Designed by: Osborn & Stephens Ltd

Typesetting by: Vigo Press

Origination by: Dot Gradation

ACKNOWLEDGEMENTS

The publishers of RED DEVILS IN EUROPE would like to thank their various collaborators, who have made possible the production of this book:

First and foremost Manchester United Football Club, without whom there would have been no book at all. Martin Edwards and his staff at the Club provided an endless stream of information and help; in particular Cliff Butler in the Museum and Fred Johnson, who gave access to his extensive collection of cuttings. I hope they feel the book does justice to the Club;

David Meek; who not only wrote much of the book, but also made his authoritative knowledge of the subject constantly available to the novice putting it all together!

The players and managers, past and present, who gave their time to be interviewed;

The *Guardian*, The *Daily Express*, The *Daily Mail*, The *Sun*, *The Times*, The *Daily Telegraph*, The *Daily Mirror*, The *Daily Herald*, The *News Chronicle* and The *Manchester Evening News*, who have allowed their match reports to be reproduced;

Syndication International, Associated Press, Popperfoto, Colorsport, Express Photos, Mirror Group Newspapers, The Photo Source, Andrew Varley, Sporting Pictures, Steve Hale, The Manchester Evening News; for providing an impressive number of photos and permitting a selection of them to be reproduced; and finally to W H Lane, who came up with the original concept!

We hope that RED DEVILS is both a comprehensive record in image and word of Manchester United in European competition, and a fitting tribute to the Club which took the first footballing steps across the Channel.

Ruth Bickersteth
COCKEREL BOOKS

FOREWORD

There is a magic about European football.

A clear winter's night, a big crowd, the floodlights shining on the stage, the atmosphere electric, strange foreign names lining up against us . . . it has never failed to thrill me.

I am sure I am not alone in my excitement for the big competitions in Europe. Certainly those of us who follow Manchester United, be it on the terraces or in the Board Room, feel a special affection for Continental combat.

It's not just that we can recall epic encounters over the years, but that we know our club led the way for everyone else in English football when the game in this country stood at the crossroads.

England had taken an insular stance when the concept of European club football was introduced on the Continent just over 30 years ago. The powers-that-be felt, for all kinds of reasons, that our clubs should not accept the invitations to take part.

Happily, Manchester United were made of sterner stuff, with a chairman and manager who had vision and ambition. Sir Matt Busby saw the possibilities and Harold Hardman, a former England international and a wise chairman, accepted the challenge with typical determination and enthusiasm.

In its day it was a bold, brave decision and I am proud to be associated with a club which played such a key role in widening the horizons of English football.

It was the right move at the right time. England at international level had suffered set-backs and were no longer the masters. The Hungarians had thrashed us 6-3 at Wembley in 1953 and showed it was no fluke by winning 7-1 in Budapest six months later.

England had even lost to the United States of America in a World Cup qualifier!

Then along came Manchester United in 1956, brilliant champions at home and suddenly successful on an international platform. They showed that all was not lost in the English game, with some handsome victories in the European Cup and those memorable matches against Real Madrid.

European football brought bitter tragedy for Manchester United of course with the Munich disaster in 1958. That sad story is woven inextricably into the history of Old Trafford.

Perhaps the memory of that unhappy time has added to the special relationship between United and European football. Certainly it was a story of inspiration and courage, which saw Matt Busby recover from the accident in mind and body to win the European Cup just 10 years later.

I think happily of that moment for my late father, Louis Edwards, the chairman who took the club into a new era with the resources to compete against the giants of Europe.

As I write now, English clubs are suspended from playing in the European competitions. I hope we will soon be allowed back in, because professionally we are losing ground.

This history of Manchester United in Europe has been written by David Meek of the Manchester Evening News, and there could be no-one better fitted for the task. He has shared for some 30 years in the great European adventure and I should imagine that, like the rest of us, he has enjoyed every minute of it.

Martin Edwards
CHAIRMAN – MANCHESTER UNITED FC
MARCH 1988

CONTENTS

LOOKING BACK WITH SIR MATT BUSBY

Manchester United blazed a trail for English football in Europe.

The Club defied the Football League in order to enter the European Cup in 1956.

It was a board decision firmly supported by the then chairman, Harold Hardman, an England amateur international winger in his youth, a small man in stature but independent and quietly determined.

The vision which broke the domestic, insular mould came of course from the manager, Matt Busby, a leader of men and ideas.

Europe 30 years ago was the grand adventure. It was a quest which led to the anguish and tragedy of the Munich air disaster before Manchester United became the first English club to win the European Cup in 1968.

In the dark aftermath of Munich, Busby may well have been tormented by the deaths and injuries to the splendid young men who suffered on the runway of Munich in the quest for success on Continental fields.

But you might just as well blame the inventor of the motor car for all road accidents.

English football as we know it today would itself have died had someone not had the courage and conviction to look to more distant horizons.

The knighthood he received soon after leading Manchester United to the European championship was awarded on many counts, not least the bold decision to enter Europe and change the face of English football.

The idea of European competition was born in 1927 with Henri Delaunay, secretary of the French Football Federation, one of the keenest supporters.

A proposal was put to the executive committee of FIFA but it came to nothing because, it was said, of the problems that would arise from the additional fixtures.

But after the Second World War, with the advent of improved air travel to reduce the time element and the arrival of floodlighting, it became a more practical proposition.

The French sporting magazine L'Equipe revived the possibility in an article in 1954. There was an encouraging response and the magazine took the initiative of proposing that the champion League club of each of the European Football Associations should take part in a championship of champions.

In April 1955, representatives of clubs from 16 nations met in Paris at the invitation of L'Equipe to launch a competition to be played in the 1955-56 season.

Chelsea, as champions in England for the first time in their history, entered but subsequently withdrew at the insistence of the Football League.

Congestion of fixtures was the reason given, and no doubt it was a genuinely held view.

The following season, Manchester United were invited by UEFA to take part and again the League objected.

Sir Matt Busby explained: "I was very keen on the idea and at one of our board meetings early in May 1956, Harold Hardman, the chairman, asked me if I thought it wise that the club should go in for the added commitment.

"My reply was: 'Well, Mr Chairman, football has become a world game.

"It no longer belongs exclusively to England, Scotland and the British Isles. This is where the future of the game lies.' 'All right,' said Mr Hardman, 'if that's what you really feel.' 'Yes, I do,' was my reply. 'Anyway, let's just try it.'

"It was at that point that a letter was received from the

Sir Matt Busby came out of the army to become manager of Manchester United in 1945 and soon tasted success. He won the F A Cup in 1948 and finished League runners-up four seasons out of five before capturing the championship in 1952. The following year he launched the first of his famous "Busby Babes" and qualified for the European Cup by becoming the 1956 champions, a devastating 11 points ahead of Blackpool.

United won the championship again the following season to earn a second crack at Europe, this time after finishing at the top of the First Division eight points in front of Spurs.

Sir Matt Busby

Tommy Taylor

Football League forbidding us to enter. At our next board meeting I again repeated my keenness on the challenge and once more proposed that if the Football Association were willing to accept and back us we should enter.

"This was duly forthcoming and at another board meeting on May 22 we decided to step into new waters.

"When I led Manchester United into Europe in 1956 in the face of League opposition some people called me a visionary, others a reactionary, while a few called me awkward and stubborn.

"Certainly I was eager to be part of this new European challenge and the reasons were many.

"There was money to be made for the club, there was a new kind of adrenalin inducing excitement for the players and there was an opportunity for spectators to enjoy the skills of Continental players.

"It also seemed to me to be the logical progression that the champions of England should pit their talents against the best of Europe. You cannot make progress by standing still.

"Looking back now I can see that our resolve to enter into European competition was a significant milestone in the history of the game.

"The pursuit of a challenge at the very highest level for clubs led down a road that has encompassed great glory and terrible tragedy.

"I need no reminding of the bitter sadness and suffering of Munich. I grieve still for my fine young players who lost their lives.

"For a long while the responsibility of urging us down that road to Europe weighed heavily on my mind, but of course no-one was to know the catastrophe that lay ahead. Like the rest of life we just have to do our best and do what seems right at the time.

"There was no alternative really in 1956 but to join the rest of Europe. It was inevitable at some stage with the forces at work which later were to make this country partners in the Common Market of Europe.

"Even after Munich we had to go on, if only out of respect for those who had perished in the cause of Manchester United. Ten years after the accident we had the great satisfaction of becoming the 1968 champions of Europe.

"The European path has not been easy in many respects. Different styles of play and culture, varying interpretations of the laws of the game by the referees and of course the glittering prizes at stake for success have seen some stormy encounters over the years.

"We had our share of controversy, especially when we played for the world club championship against Estudiantes. Other teams subsequently refused to play the South American teams.

"That was never my way. Despite all the problems I always felt that the only way we would reach a better understanding was to continue to meet and play.

"It's been done at national level competing for the World Cup, and even after the upset of Estudiantes, I was willing to try again had we qualified.

"European football was of course to bring us a second horror when Liverpool met Juventus in the final of the 1985 championship. A long history of crowd misbehaviour reached a tragic climax in Brussels in the pitifully inadequate Heysel Stadium.

"English clubs paid the ultimate penalty of being banned in disgrace from all European competition.

"But I don't want to strike too unhappy a note, because the Continental arena has brought pleasure and widened the experience of thousands of football followers.

"The excitement and electricity which flows at a floodlit evening game between two crack championship teams has an atmosphere and beauty all of its own.

"To take part in it is a rare privilege and certainly our hopes were high and our hearts were beating faster at the prospect of our baptism in Europe in 1956.

"Our very first game was against RSC Anderlecht of Belgium in the preliminary round. We played the away leg first and were quite pleased with a 2-0 win.

"I remember Duncan Edwards was missing through injury which was a big disappointment to us. In the event, Jackie Blanchflower played well in his place.

"We had an early fright when Mark Jones was penalised for handling and the Belgians had the chance to go ahead. Jef Mermans, their captain, hit the post with his penalty and Bill Foulkes cleared.

"Eddie Colman made the first goal for Dennis Viollet and Tommy Taylor got the other. It was a useful start but of course Europe was new to us then and no-one was sure whether a two-goal advantage was as commanding as we would regard it now.

"So we were all keyed up for the return match, and also a little anxious because we too were playing away from home. We had to stage the tie at Maine Road because Old Trafford did not then have floodlighting.

"The conditions were also a little unsettling. It had rained heavily and the pitch was covered in pools of water.

"We needn't have worried though. The boys won 10-0, an incredible score which possibly had some people assuming that Anderlecht were a poor side.

"But this was no little team from Malta or Iceland. Belgium,

Harry Gregg

Duncan Edwards

as now, was a strong soccer nation and Anderlecht were its champions.

"I have just got to say that we ran up what has to be regarded in football circles as a cricket score because we played darned well! I was becoming accustomed to see the great team of those days playing well, but they excelled themselves that night.

"It was in fact the finest exhibition of teamwork I had ever seen from any side either at club or international level. In spite of the score building up, I can still see young Eddie Colman running to collect the ball for a throw-in with only two or three minutes remaining as if we were losing and his life depended on it.

"His appetite epitomised the keenness of the whole team that night," said Sir Matt.

Colman's urgency was possibly inspired by the fact that, at that stage, the entire team were doing their utmost to get the name of David Pegg on the scoresheet.

Pegg was the only forward who didn't score in that match, and the fact that he didn't was no fault of his team-mates. They particularly wanted a goal for him because he had been the outstanding man with a devastating display at outside left.

He repeatedly turned the opposition inside out and was responsible for seven or eight of the goals which were scored by Dennis Viollet (4), Tommy Taylor (3), Billy Whelan (2) and Johnny Berry (1).

United broke the backs of the Belgians during a lethal 22 minutes after 20 minutes play, with a four-goal salvo.

On their previous visit to England, Anderlecht had beaten Arsenal at Highbury, a result to indicate the excellence of United's home debut in the European Cup.

The referee, Mervyn Griffiths of Wales, described it: "I have never seen football more deadly in execution."

Jef Mermans, the Anderlecht captain and international centre forward, said about their heavy defeat: "After United had scored their sixth goal, they still ran as hard as they had at the start.

"We have played against the best teams of Hungary and Russia – and never been beaten like this. Why don't they pick this team for England?" he asked.

The performance and result certainly vindicated United's decision to enter into European competition. There was no possibility of recriminations from the Football League.

A fuse had been lit and had caught the imagination of the public. A crowd of 43,635 had watched the match at Maine Road, a handsome enough start for any new venture.

By the time of the next round and a visit from Borussia Dortmund, the crowd had risen to an incredible 75,598 packing Maine Road.

A flirtation had become a romance which quickly developed into a full-blooded love affair. Like any long-lasting relationship it would be tested by many trials and tribulations, but it would be enduring.

Those early days in Europe were to play a significant part in creating a special glamour and stature about Manchester United which 30 years hence, despite an absence of trophies compared with one or two other clubs, still sees Old Trafford the best supported club in the country and perhaps the best loved.

The spirit of Sir Matt Busby still shines through Manchester United.

Jackie Blanchflower

From tragedy to triumph – European Cup Winners 1968

Association Football

MANCHESTER UNITED'S USEFUL LEAD

By an Old International

Anderlecht 0, Manchester United 2

BRUSSELS, SEPTEMBER 12.

Manchester United bore themselves nobly in the Belgian capital this evening and set about the Royal Sporting Club of Anderlecht at Astrid Park with all the fervour of a punitive mission   After

'fearsome shot" as the Belgians call him, tried for once a gentle flick and "fair made a mullock of it" as they say in Barnsley, but he may justly be forgiven. He was sternly shadowed throughout and was desperately unlucky to have a glorious scoring shot disallowed.

Events in the second half soon hotted up. A penalty was given against Jones when a b...

THE GUARDIAN, September 12, 1956

ANDERLECHT	0
MAN. UTD.	**2**

1956-57 EUROPEAN CUP, PRELIMINARY ROUND, FIRST LEG, MANCHESTER UNITED WIN 2-0

Manchester United's Useful Lead

By an Old International

BRUSSELS, SEPTEMBER 12

Manchester United bore themselves nobly in the Belgian capital this evening and set about the Royal Sporting Club of Anderlecht at Astrid Park with all the fervour of a punitive mission. After a display of football which had moments of real grandeur they won their preliminary round match in the European Cup competition 2-0 and in doing so added still more to the lustre of their reputation overseas. The return match will be played under floodlights at Moss Side Manchester, on September 26.

It would be difficult to imagine a prettier setting for what the Belgians advertised as this "Grand Match International en Nocturne" than the floodlit stadium at Anderlecht. Small, trim, compact – its capacity is only 35,000 – it makes up in the taste and finish of its appointments for what it lacks in size. Its grass-covered playing pitch was as close cropped and smooth as was Grigg Lane, Bury, in the old days. Its grandstands, or tribunes as they are called, with their cantilever roofs and no obstructing pillars, are a reproach to many clumsy old-fashioned erections at home. Its main stand, instead of presenting a blank wall on the outside, has the deep bow windows and inviting architecture of some old fashioned inn.

If one wants to feel British and proud of it travel round with Manchester United. The reverence with which their players are received in Belgium stems from the detailed knowledge of the club's achievements and its remarkable consistency over the past eight years. Happily the extravagant adulation poured over the players did not induce a mood of careless complacency. On the contrary, the Manchester boys seemed to sense the strong quality of the opposition and inspired by the esteem in which they are held gave of their best. What that means is already known to English readers. It may, therefore, be useful for future reference to run the rule over their Anderlecht opponents.

In tonight's encounter Anderlecht gave more than a hint as to why the club's assortment of amateur players and part-time professionals, under an English coach, has risen to the championship of Belgium. In fitness and stamina they stood little behind the English champions. In fire and fighting spirit they were worthy of a region strewn with famous battlefields. In ball control and tactical resource they were obviously based on the best continental models. And if they went under after a game struggle that is because they had to meet one of the fittest, fastest, and best balanced club sides in England.

Clever Ball Players

Their key men on this occasion were first Mermans – an attacking inside forward with something of the long leg reach of Charles Buchan and the speed of Viollet but happily not with the shooting power of Rowley. Next Lippens, right half; short, nippy, and clever with the ball. Then, too, Culot at left back, a player very much of the tall, slim build of Crayston, late of Arsenal. Three good players in short, the bony structure as it were of an enthusiastic and by no means negligible side.

It was a scene of unforgettable beauty as the game started with the pitch flooded in cool silvery light and the dark, beady eyes of the pink-faced hosts peering out from the stands and terraces. It all gave a peculiar sense of theatre. Nor had we long to wait for sensation to make its appearance on the stage. Mermans, the long streak, went through the middle like a runaway thief, but Wood, on guard, leapt beautifully to his right and all was well. United's counter to that, after 20 minutes of delightful give and take by both sides, in which Blanchflower, Jones, and Colman particularly shone, was a long, sinuous run by Viollet ending with a blistering scoring shot.

A second goal might have followed a brilliant shuttle of close interpassing by Berry and Pegg on the left wing. But Taylor, the "veritable colossus with the fearsome shot" as the Belgians call him, tried for once a gentle flick and "fair made a mullock of it" as they say in Barnsley, but he may justly be forgiven. He was sternly shadowed throughout and was desperately unlucky to have a glorious scoring shot disallowed.

Events in the second half soon hotted up. A penalty was given against Jones when a ball was driven hard against his hand. Lippens took the kick, hit a post, and as Vanden Bosch shot hard and true Wood made a wonderful lurch foward off all fours and saved magnificently. Anderlecht fought like wild cats; you can almost say their football had claws; but United held firm, with Blanchflower at right half one of the stars of the match. His judgement was impeccable and his long range shooting a sight to behold. Even Edwards was not missed. The gallantry with which Anderlecht were fighting a losing battle kept the excitement at fever heat; especially as Whelan bungled another rosy chance to forge ahead.

But better things were to come. Pegg floated across a superb centre from the right and Taylor, with a fine leap, butted the ball home. That, except for some strenuous and at times hot-tempered exchanges later settled the argument for the evening. Its resumption at Moss Side later on should not be missed.

Among the heroes of United's well earned victory Wood must be given the high place. He made three saves of superlative skill and importance. Blanchflower, as we have seen, covered himself with glory. Jones, too, at centre half rarely put a foot wrong and the Belgian folk must have thought he possessed as many heads as the hydra-headed monster so often did he get in the way.

Colman, in this high pressure football, had scarcely time to air his graces, but he fought gallantly nevertheless. Some of the forward moves tonight were exquisitely pretty; some devastatingly swift; and if Viollet, Taylor, and Pegg collected most of the honours this is not to say that Berry and Whelan, who are a little quieter, played badly. On the whole it was a triumph of team spirit and a credit to all concerned.

THE GUARDIAN, September 26, 1956

MAN. UTD.	10
ANDERLECHT	0

1956-57 EUROPEAN CUP, PRELIMINARY ROUND, SECOND LEG, MANCHESTER UNITED WIN 12-0 ON AGGREGATE

By an Old International

T he second leg of Manchester United's first round European Cup-tie against the Royal Sporting Club of Anderlecht was played on Manchester City's ground at Moss Side, Manchester, last night before an admiring crowd estimated at some 40,000. It ended, to the amazement of all beholders, in a fantastic

MANCHESTER UNITED SUPERB

Belgian Defence Shot to Pieces

BY AN OLD INTERNATIONAL

Manchester United 10, Anderlecht 0

The second leg of Manchester United's first round European Cup-tie against the Royal Sporting Club of Anderlecht was played on Manchester City's ground at Moss Side, Manchester, last night before an admiring crowd estimated at some 40,000. It ended, to the amazement of all beholders, in a fantastic

victory for United by 10-0. (They had already established a commanding lead by winning the first leg 2-0 in Brussels.) Thus an entrancing vista of exciting cup-ties both home and abroad opens up before our reigning champions.

The fact that Manchester United had made one change from the side that was at Anderlecht, the substitution of Edwards for Blanchflower, must have had a profound psychological effect on the Belgian players, for Blanchflower's display at left half in Brussels had been wellnigh faultless. Perhaps that accounted for their disappointing form this evening: that and the fatigue of travel. By contrast the Anderlecht team had been riddled with changes,

think, but on the whole it warranted it. It seemed as an appetiser for the splendid feast of football before us. The Belgians, already three down, had a hopeless task, for, prettily as they passed and repassed at times, they panted vainly at the heels of a team playing superlative football at an incredible pace. Amongst other virtues United showed swift powers of improvisation as when Taylor, seeing a ball drop

though the full significance of these will be apparent only to those more intimately connected with the club. But the removal of the tall Mermans from inside left to centre forward, presumably to harass Jones by his height, as well as by his speed and skill, did suggest one thing, that the nagging frequency and certainty of Jones's headwork in defence in the first leg had not been lost on Anderlecht's English manager, W. Gormlie. As things turned out he

BELOW: *Viollet (second from right) makes sure of United's eighth goal in the second leg of their match against Anderlecht*

need not have troubled. Jones, long before the end, might well have sent home for an easy-chair.

The First Fanfares

But all speculations and surmisals were swept away by the roar which greeted the entry of the gladiators. The Beswick Prize Band rose nobly to the occasion and gave a rendering of the Brabançonne more or less in line with the intentions of the composer. A bubbling sound at one period suggested a little water in the euphonium, but then it was raining heavily at the time and it has been a phenomenally wet summer. As soon as the teams got to grips the first Belgian attack revealed the presence of treacherous pools of water on the surface. Dewael, beautifully fed by Mermans, had the track to goal miraculously split open for him but as he darted along on his scoring mission he left the ball far behind him. It stopped dead as though held by glue. Nine minutes only of sparkling football had gone by when United produced one of the great goals of all time. Byrne cleared his lines with a superb volley and at the same time gave Pegg the sort of pass a winger dreams about. Pegg needed no second bidding. He ran off down the track, round his man like an eel and dropped his centre just where Taylor wanted it. A leap, a downward header, a shower of raindrops from the goal-net, and United were one up on the night, three up on aggregate.

Much ado about one goal, you may think, but

on the whole it warranted it. It seemed as an appetiser for the splendid feast of football before us. The Belgians, already three down, had a hopeless task, for, prettily as they passed and repassed at times, they panted vainly at the heels of a team playing superlative football at an incredible pace. Amongst other virtues United showed swift powers of improvisation as when Taylor, seeing a ball drop dead at his feet, toe-ended it instantly to the back of the net from the standing position: to be followed four minutes later by Viollet who fastened on a bungled clearance by the Belgian centre half back, skipped round the goalkeeper, and smacked the third goal home. Poor de Koster! He had hardly got over that shock when he tried a gentle back pass to his goalkeeper with Viollet in the vicinity! He wrung his hands as the fourth whistled home. As to the fifth, Viollet's hat-trick, no one was to blame. It followed a beautiful left-foot shot from the fringe of the penalty area.

No Respite

United, having done enough in the first half to rock the Chancelleries of Europe, might have been forgiven if they had eased up in the second. But their thirst for goals was insatiable and Taylor was soon adding a sixth following a muddle in the Anderlecht goalmouth. Others now stepped into the limelight, Viollet and Pegg having monopolised the stage in the opening phase: Colman, for instance, with his amusing "shimmy shakes" and body wriggles,

ABOVE: *Anderlecht despondent as another United goal goes in*

and Whelan with his subtle ball control and one glorious left-foot shot which the Belgian goalkeeper saved magnificently.

All very well, it may be argued, but where was the opposition? Apparently not at Maine Road. And yet this should not entirely detract from the merit of United's performance. There is a pitch of excellence which is absolute irrespective of the circumstances in which it is reached and United certainly had it this evening.

Whelan's seventh goal was as popular as it was long overdue. With twelve minutes to go and nine goals in the ditty box – seven in one evening so far – Byrne went forward prospecting, and from the right wing whither he had wandered, middled a ball so exactly that Viollet could not fail to score. Another soon followed from Berry, who had striven hard to get his name on the score-sheet. Then Whelan again, from Berry. Double figures at last! and if Pegg alone of the forwards failed to hit the target let him not worry. Of all the delights of a weirdly wonderful evening his first half display may well be the longest remembered.

Finally a word of thanks to the losers for their sportsmanship in circumstances which could not fail to be a little wounding to their self esteem. They received an ovation due to a gallant band of gentlemen.

Law (No 10) challenges for the ball in the first leg of United's semi-final tie against Real Madrid, April 1968

United against Real Madrid in their European Cup semi-final tie, April 1968

EUROPEAN CUP CHALLENGERS

Here are the players from whom Borussia Dortmund, the German champions, will select their team to meet Manchester United in next Wednesday's European Cup-tie at Maine Road. BACK ROW (left to right): Schanko, Burgsmueller, Wischner, Michallek. CENTRE : Kwiatkowski, Preissler, Bracht, Fluegel, Peters. FRONT: Kelbassa, Schlebrowski, Sandmann, Niepieklo, Kapitulski. All except Schanko, Wischner, and Fluegel were in the Dortmund team that won the German national title last June.

CRABBED AGE TESTS YOUTH

Borussia's Fine Display at Moss Side

BY AN OLD INTERNATIONAL

- United 3, Borussia 2 | snap and vigour about their passes, short, sharp, electric, and the same deadliness in ...ding off chances as when Viollet twice

THE GUARDIAN, October 17, 1956

BORUSSIA DORTMUND 2

1956-57 EUROPEAN CUP, FIRST ROUND, FIRST LEG,
MANCHESTER UNITED WIN 3-2

By an Old International

A nother great crowd of over 75,000 highly expectant football enthusiasts packed the stands and lined the terraces at Moss Side last night and watched Manchester United beat Borussia (Dortmund) 3-2 in the first leg of their first round match in the European Cup competition. The noise emitted when the contestants appeared guaranteed that the play would not lack vocal accompaniment of the shrillest kind.

The disparity of ages betweed the two teams did not escape comment. Before the match started one gathered the impression that the result could quite as easily have been arrived at by a comparison of the rival groups of birth certificates. One confident forecast of United's chances wrote off the Germans as "just a set of grandads – five minutes' chasing of the babes and they'll be sagging at the knees." But there were no signs of comparative senility about Peters, the German flyer on the right, Schmidt, another fleet-footed schemer at inside left, and Schlebrowski, a right wing half, with Byrne's own powers of recovery. Nor were their football brains lacking. And at the finish "crabbed age" was sticking it every whit as well as "ingenuous youth."

United's First Zest

Bees, it is said, will only work in the dark. Manchester United, on the other hand, seem to prefer the silvery sort of twilight produced by floodlighting on a mild October evening. As against Anderlecht, so against Borussia, the boyish English champions tore into their opponents with a zest amounting almost to voracity. Naturally, the inborn pugnacity of the Teutons reacted vigorously and soon both teams were locked in the opening phases of what was to be a delightful exhibition of clean, intelligent football. It made thrilling watching. The colours made a pleasant contrast; United in red shirts and white shorts, Borussia in shirts of golden satin and black shorts, and with a technique, be it said, as showy as their strip. After a brilliant opening during which the quick, agile movements of the German forwards made no small impression, Kelbassa, their centre forward, swept down the middle after a through pass at a speed which made even United's defenders appear slow! Luckily Wood was on the watch and timed his rescuing sortie admirably. The vast crowd's sigh of relief could be heard.

No doubt United's display against R.S.C. Anderlecht must be considered the zenith of their performances so far. We shall probably not see the like again. But tonight's exhibition in certain respects was not far below it. There was the same snap and vigour about their passes, short, sharp, electric, and the same deadliness in rounding off chances, as when Viollet twice flitted through the German defence like a wraith and put his side two goals on the way to victory in 27 rousing minutes. But if we say that there was not quite the same finishing in ball control as in the earlier match, when it was as dexterous as, say, a master violinist's fingering, we are merely stating a fact and not adopting the attitude of a pernickety perfectionist. That it was near enough to perfection for the peace of mind of Kwiatowski, the German goalkeeper, was shown by the way that splendid acrobat danced about his goal line like a cat on hot bricks. He was soon on excellent terms with the great crowd, which vastly enjoyed his two brilliant saves against Taylor and which doubtless accorded him a meed of sympathy when a sliced shot from Pegg was deflected through his own goal by a most crestfallen right back, Burgsmueller.

Viollet Injured

Just before the interval our pleasure was marred by a nasty accident to Viollet. Turning suddenly at speed he ran full tilt into Schlebrowski, and left the field in a dazed condition suffering from a severe blow on the cheek bone. It was rather a shock when United resumed with only ten men, but the panic was shortlived: Viollet was soon back, apparently none the worse. It was now Borussia's turn to press home some hot attacks, and but for the liveliness of Wood, who seems to have a cat's vision at night, and who made a glorious double-barrelled save at the foot of a post, United might have had part of their well-earned goal increment rubbed off. One felt that Borussia, playing in unwonted conditions for them, will be hard nuts to crack on their own pitch and in broad daylight. But imagine having to track down a ghost like Viollet, here one minute, gone the next, and all in a dim, hazy light. One of his dribbles through a spellbound defence was a masterpiece of swerves and delayed spurts. He just failed to score – but who cared? We had merely seen the flower without the fruit.

Then came a sensational change that sent United's spectators stamping homeward with vexation. First Byrne was guilty of seeming carelessness and gave Kapitulski an opportunity to score which he accepted: and then Schmidt, fired by this success, shot with such force that Wood could only palm the ball out to Preissler who scored exuberantly. For Germany this was a recovery that should set the Ruhr alight at the prospect of a rousing return match. For United it was a salutary reminder of the age-old truth that a footballer's chickens should not be counted before they are hatched.

BELOW: *Viollet (second from right) throws his arms aloft after scoring United's first goal in the first leg against Borussia Dortmund*

BORUSSIA WASTE THEIR CHANCES

By an Old International

Borussia .F.C. 0, Manchester United 0.

DORTMUND, NOVEMBER 21.

To-day, Wednesday, November 21, has been a national holiday in Western Germany, a day of repentance and prayer, but for Westphalian football lovers Manchester United added a touch of mourning this evening by making a goalless draw with Borussia at the Rota Erda Stadium, thus scraping through on the aggregate of 3-2.

A luxury hotel in Dusseldorf seemed scarcely the right sort of base from which to start a rigorous enterprise like the second leg of a first-round European cup-

nately for United at this stage Borussia, who were creating most of the chances, were mangling them with great regularity, and it was left to Taylor to create a welcome diversion at the other end by breaking clean away and bringing Kwiatowski to his knees. As Kwiatowski is a goalkeeper in the Trautmann class one felt that Taylor would have to get much closer for the kill than 35 yards.

As half-time approached play tended to settle in United's half, where Jones, Foulkes, and Byrne had to employ every weapon in the defender's armoury to peg back the speedy, virile, accomplished Germans. One felt glad that United had prepared for this contest by playing through two gruelling matches with Wolverhampton Wanderers and Leeds United previous-- ... ... stern

BELOW: *Byrne (left) wins the ball from Schmidt of Dortmund*

THE GUARDIAN, November 21, 1956

BORUSSIA DORTMUND 0

1956-57 EUROPEAN CUP, FIRST ROUND, SECOND LEG, MANCHESTER UNITED WIN 3-2 ON AGGREGATE

By an Old International

DORTMUND, NOVEMBER 21

Today, Wednesday, November 21, has been a national holiday in Western Germany, a day of repentance and prayer, but for Westphalian football lovers Manchester United added a touch of mourning this evening by making a goalless draw with Borussia at the Rota Erda Stadium, thus scraping through on the aggregate of 3-2.

A luxury hotel in Dusseldorf seemed scarcely the right sort of base from which to start a rigorous enterprise like the second leg of a first-round European Cup-tie, but the United players and their camp followers accepted this nuisance equably. A happier coach load could not be imagined than the one that left Dusseldorf this afternoon for Dortmund. Across the densely inhabited Ruhr region the coach threaded its way and the nearer it got to the Borussia ground the more the journey took on the aspect of a triumphal progress. But in view of the severe frosts here some of us felt a little apprehensive about the ultimate triumph.

Flood-lighting had been installed, and at great haste, for the match and it was excellent. It left the pitch entirely free from shadows and made the spectators on the stands and terraces across the ground easily identifiable as human beings and not just rows of eyes peering out of the grey mass like the black dots in frog spawn. The pitch itself was grass covered and well rolled and everything looked spick and span; altogether an attractive setting for the colourful ceremonial which ensued when the two teams appeared to a thunderous welcome.

Niepieklo Quiet

Remembering that Borussia had been without their pet marksman, the legendary Niepieklo, when they almost drew level with United in the previous leg at Moss Side after being three goals down, one craned forward with eagerness during the loosening-up exercises before the match proper to cast an appraising eye over this young goal-snatcher. He certainly looked the part, slim and slick-looking, and had a manner of addressing the ball rather like Broadis. But he did nothing to set the Rhine on fire.

At the end of the first fifteen minutes, by which time even the trees round the ground were festooned with bunches of human grapes, the outlook was rosy for both sides. Borussia's attempts to rush the Englishmen off their feet before they had got the feel of the frosty ground were foiled by the brilliance of Colman, who dropped right into his best style at once, and of goalkeeper Wood, who stopped two point-blank shots from Kelbassa and Preissler. At the other end Edwards, who was playing inside left in Viollet's absence, whipped a lovely ball clean across Borussia's goalmouth and both Taylor and Whelan muffed their attempts. Fortunately for United at this stage Borussia, who were creating most of the chances, were mangling them with great regularity, and it was left to Taylor to create a welcome diversion at the other end by breaking clean away and bringing Kwiatowski to his knees. As Kwiatowski is a goalkeeper in the Trautmann class one felt that Taylor would have to get much closer for the kill than 35 yards.

As half-time approached play tended to settle in United's half, where Jones, Foulkes,

and Byrne had to employ every weapon in the defender's armoury to peg back the speedy, virile, accomplished Germans. One felt glad that United had prepared for this contest, by playing through two gruelling matches with Wolverhampton Wanderers and Leeds United previously, for this was as stern a task as any they have so far confronted. As evidence of the pressure under which United were defending may be mentioned the fact that Jones once was obliged to leap high in the air like a fielder at long-on and pull the ball down one-handed as the only means of checking a wave of German forwards streaking into goal. But Jones took good care to see that he was well outside the penalty area at the time. The Borussian forwards in their eagerness fell repeatedly into United's off-side trap, much to the satisfaction of the British Tommies who were present in large numbers and highly vocal.

Fine Centre Halves

Were one to apportion marks for outstanding individual performances one would single out the respective centre halfbacks, Michallek and Jones, for major awards. United's forward line had been crude in the extreme and Taylor was heavily outweighted in the middle. Borussia fought on through the second half with a verve little short of ferocity, and if their forwards had had a vein of marksmanship to match their quicksilver mobility United's plight had been sorry indeed. Two superbly judged sorties by Wood held the ravening Germans at bay: one to brush the ball lightly off Schmidt's head and another to hoist it far into the crowd. A third made the English watchers thankful that another saviour had arisen whenever Jones, the Rock of Gibraltar, was passed. Here was history repeating itself: the Thin Red Line against the German hosts – or, if you prefer it, a spot of bother from the Old Contemptibles. Twenty-five minutes still remained for play when Kelbassa missed the sitter of a lifetime in the very jaws of United's goalmouth. After that we felt that even Wotan must be playing for England.

So, after many alarms and excursions, and a spate of incredible misses by Kelbassa and Preissler, ended a tremendous battle in which only United's perspiring defence came through with honours. Except in the matter of shooting, Borussia were easily top dogs.

THE GUARDIAN, January 16, 1957

ATLETICO BILBAO	5
MAN. UTD.	3

1956-57 EUROPEAN CUP, QUARTER FINAL, FIRST LEG, ATLETICO BILBAO WIN 5-3

Manchester United Two Goals Down To Bilbao

Wretched conditions affect play

From W. R. Taylor
BILBAO, JANUARY 16

Manchester United, after having most of the game against Bilbao Athletic in the first leg of the quarter final of the European Cup competition here today, were beaten 5-3, but should have a good chance of more than turning the tables at Moss Side on February 6. Conditions were vile. It was more like playing in a swamp than on a football pitch, for rain and snow had fallen for 48 hours and Byrne, the United's captain, said they were the worst he had ever played in.

Bilbao is a town of umbrellas. Young and old carry them, and the reason is obvious, but it makes walking a hazardous occupation. The sight on the popular side today would have been a joy to any umbrella-maker's heart. Before the match it resembled a field of toad stools through which no one could ever walk. A cloud of smoke rose above as though thousands of caterpillars were puffing away on thousands of hookahs on the top of them. And not one umbrella was coloured except by Nature. The black was gradually transformed by the snow. Between the kick-off and half-time the holders must have been soaked, but they grimly put them up once more during the interval, and again they changed from black to white.

In the stands were serried ranks of berets. There was not a cloth cap to be seen. There

RIGHT: *Carmelo saves at the feet of Taylor in Bilbao*

MANCHESTER UNITED TWO GOALS DOWN TO BILBAO

Wretched conditions affect play

FROM W. R. TAYLOR

Bilbao Athletic 5, Manchester United 3

BILBAO, JANUARY 16.

Manchester United, after having most of the game against Bilbao Athletic in the first leg of the quarter final of the European Cup competition here to-day, were beaten 5-3, but should have a good chance of more than turning the tables at Moss Side on February 6. Conditions were vile. It was more like playing in a swamp than on a football pitch, for rain and snow had fallen for 48 hours and Byrne, the United's captain, said they were the worst he had ever

⸻ of umbrellas. Young ⸻ ʼhe reason is ⸻

own half. The mainspring of the Bilbao attacks was Gainza, their captain and the most experienced member of the team. He wandered everywhere and always was very dangerous. He is a man with a great future in the field of mime if he is at a loss when he retires. His shrugs and swervings when penalised, as he thinks, unfairly, could not be more eloquent. United's defence had a hectic time and had a lucky escape when Colman brought down Marcaida in front of the goal and the kick was wasted by the Spaniards. Just before half time, after Wood had saved a beautiful swerving shot from Gainza, Bilbao increased their lead when Marcaida headed home from a corner taken by Gainza.

Uneasy silence

Bilbao had taken their chances, and United started ⸻ do so after the resumption. W⸻ ⸻ was

were, no doubt, a few in the ground somewhere, but anybody wearing one today could be recognised as coming from the greater Manchester area, certainly not from the Basque country.

The pitch, lightly covered with snow, was very green at the start, but turned into a sea of mud and slush, and after play had started the water came to the surface as though a heavy roller had been put on it, particularly on the wings, where the players at times seemed to be paddling.

In view of the conditions – there were complaints about frozen feet by players later – the match was always exciting and played throughout with spirit, but without any international incidents. The ball fell like a suet pudding, so heavy that it would have dropped through the bottom of almost any pan and after early attempts the goalkeepers never tried to bounce it again.

The light was none too good when Bilbao won the toss, in which there was little advantage; the United played in royal blue shirts and Bilbao in their usual red and white stripes. United promptly went into the attack but Viollet shot wide. The players slid all over the place at first, but Bilbao received a tremendous fillip in the second minute when Uribe scored after Jones had tried to pass back. This was the first of a series of back-passing which throughout the match must have given both sides some horrible moments.

Gainza's efficiency

Edwards sent Viollet through, but he was dispossessed by Garay with no ceremony at all and then United had an escape when Mauri hammered a powerful shot towards an open goal, but Byrne somehow managed to get his foot to the ball. Later United swung the ball twice across the goal but Taylor was unable to reach it, and then he had a chance when he received a pass from Colman, but Carmelo

came out of his goal and took the ball by sliding along the surface. A shot from Marcaida was well kicked around the corner by Wood and then, at the other end, Pegg beat one defender in a tackle and passed three more, but hit a post with his shot. Next Pegg was held on the goal line by Oruel, but the free kick was fisted out by Carmelo, who saved a powerful shot from Whelan seconds later. The ball was playing queer tricks in the swamp and dribbling was a chancy business, though in one movement Pegg and Whelan dribbled and passed together as though they were at Old Trafford on a warm Saturday in September.

United were having the better of things and it was against the run of the play when, after 30 minutes, Bilbao broke away and Uribe scored again when he shot through a ruck of players after the ball had been kicked into and out of the goalmouth three times. Pegg had the chance to reduce the deficit, but kicked well wide after he had been given time to tee-up the ball. After playing well for the first half hour and being two down for their pains, United were penned in their own half. The mainspring of the Bilbao attacks was Gainza, their captain and the most experienced member of the team. He wandered everywhere and always was very dangerous. He is a man with a great future in the field of mime if he is at a loss when he retires. His shrugs and swervings when penalised, as he thinks, unfairly, could not be more eloquent. United's defence had a hectic time and had a lucky escape when Colman brought down Marcaida in front of the goal and the kick was wasted by the Spaniards. Just before half-time, after Wood had saved a beautiful swerving shot from Gainza, Bilbao increased their lead when Marcaida headed home from a corner taken by Gainza.

Uneasy silence

Bilbao had taken their chances, and United started to do so after the resumption. Within

eight minutes the score was 3-2 and an uneasy hush had fallen on the sporting and hitherto very vocal crowd. Whelan forced a corner and Taylor scored from a pass by Viollet, and Viollet himself scored five minutes later. Colman tried shooting, and Taylor and Pegg tried heading without success, but Bilbao missed a golden opportunity when Artiche, with the goal at his mercy, blazed wildly over the bar. Colman was keeping his forwards moving and his persistence and control for such a light man on such a pitch was remarkable, as was the distances Edwards managed to kick the ball.

There were some mysterious free kicks awarded against United by the German referee, but they had nothing to do with the next Bilbao goal, which came from a corner and was scored by the centre forward when the ball stopped at his feet about two yards out. He could not have missed. A shot from Marcaida then dropped dead in the mud in front of Wood and this was followed by a piece of pantomime when the referee awarded a free kick which Edwards took very quickly and which was headed out by Itura; the referee had not even seen the kick taken and was rather indignant about the whole thing. Carmelo then had to stop a hard drive from Byrne who, with Foulkes and the wing halves, had a fine game, but Bilbao again went away on Gainza's wing and restored their lead of three goals when Artiche scored from a good centre.

The visitors still continued to fight and five minutes from the end Whelan reduced their deficit. The goal was the result of a fine individual movement during which Whelan beat three opponents before sending in a rising shot just beyond the reach of Carmelo.

Garay had a brilliant game for Bilbao. He is a heavy man, but kept his feet remarkably well. His backs played very square and shadowed the wings, but left wide gaps in the centre. There is another match to come, and surely United have noted this.

DAILY EXPRESS, February 6, 1957

MAN. UTD.	3
ATLETICO BILBAO	0

1956-57 EUROPEAN CUP, QUARTER FINAL, SECOND LEG, MANCHESTER UNITED WIN 6-5 ON AGGREGATE

Greatest Victory in Soccer History

By Henry Rose

GREATEST VICTORY IN SOCCER HISTORY

By HENRY ROSE Manchester United 3, Bilbao 0 (Aggregate 6—5) **RATING** ★★★★★

M**Y** hands are still trembling as I write. My heart still pounds. And a few hours have passed since, with 65,000 other lucky people, I saw the greatest Soccer victory in history, 90 minutes of tremendous thrill and excitement that will live for ever in the memory.

Salute to the eleven red-shirted heroes of Manchester United. The whole country is proud of you.

My hands are still trembling as I write. My heart still pounds. And a few hours have passed since, with 65,000 other lucky people, I saw the greatest Soccer victory in history, 90 minutes of tremendous thrill and excitement that will live for ever in the memory.

Salute to the eleven red-shirted heroes of Manchester United. The whole country is proud of you.

Hammering in my brain almost shattering my senses is the still-fresh memory of the spectacle of 11 brave, gallant footballers battering, pounding until they had them on their knees almost crying for mercy, a team of Spaniards ranked as one of the best club teams in the world.

Translated into calm, stereotyped language for the record book: Manchester United last night under the Maine Road, Manchester, floodlights, defeated Bilbao, the Spanish champions by 3-0 in the second leg of the European quarter-final Cup tie, won the tie on an aggregate of 6-5, and passed on to the semi-final.

I have never seen anything like it, and believe me, I'm not sure that I would welcome the experience again. It was almost just too much to bear.

LOOKING BACK WITH JIMMY MURPHY

Jimmy Murphy finished the war as the Army NCO in charge of a Services sports centre at Bari in Italy.

One day in 1945 he was talking in his usual Welsh, voluble way to a group of soldiers when he noticed a familiar figure on the fringe listening to his every word.

Says Jimmy: "It was Matt Busby and when I had finished he came over and shook hands. Then he said: 'If you fancy a job when you are demobbed, come and look me up at Old Trafford.'"

So was born one of the most enduring and successful partnerships in football management. They were as different as chalk and cheese in terms of personality, but in the game they were a perfect complement.

Matt was the headmaster, a little distant, authoritative, dignified, warm but absolutely respected.

Jimmy took the reserves and introduced them to the harsh realities of the game. He toughened them up. In practice games he used to make a habit of kicking Bobby Charlton because he thought the shy youngster needed more aggression.

Wilf McGuinness says he will always remember the pep talk Jimmy gave him on the eve of his League debut against Wolves.

Said Wilf: "Jimmy told me that I would be marking Peter Broadbent who would be doing his best to take the win bonus out of my pocket. He said that if that happened I wouldn't be able to take my mother a box of chocolates home.

"He wound me up to such a extent that when Peter, a nice man, came over before the kick-off to wish a young lad the best of luck, I told him to shove off and called him a thieving bastard."

Talk to the players who grew up at Old Trafford and each generation will tell you of the tremendous respect they had for Jimmy Murphy as they came up through the ranks.

Jimmy in turn will talk with great affection of the boys he helped fashion over the years. For Jim the sun is always shining, even if it is

hidden behind the clouds, and he is fond of telling you that it's from little acorns that the great oaks grow.

Watching the development of the youngsters and helping them was the great joy of his work. It was particularly hard for him after Munich because the crash destroyed the Busby Babes, the team coming into the full flower of manhood, the boys he had brought to the brink of great achievement.

"Even now if I close my eyes I can still see them playing," he says.

Of course he carried on after the accident. Matt Busby, lying critically injured in hospital in Munich had whispered: "Keep the flag flying, Jimmy."

And this he did, and he helped nurture more little acorns until, 10 years after Munich, he was there with Sir Matt to win the European Cup.

So many matches in a lifetime of football, so many players, but there will always be a special place in his heart for those cut down in their prime.

For Jimmy Murphy, Duncan Edwards is still the greatest, and those early European games are etched vividly in his memory.

"The future beckoned full of hope when we won the championship in 1955-56 by 11 points ahead of Blackpool. The team had an average age of under 23 and their success opened the gateway into Europe.

RIGHT: *Carmelo of Bilbao leaps to fist clear from Viollet (centre right) and Taylor (second from left) of United*

final Cup tie, won....

We're not licked yet—Busby

CHAMPIONS MAKE FINE RECOVERY

(Heading from News Chronicle Dispatch, Jan. 17)

3-5 BECAME 6-5
in Bilbao   in Manchester

HERE are the details of the two quarter-final matches in the European Cup:

FIRST LEG

BILBAO 5   MANCHESTER UTD. 3
Uribe 2, Marcida,   Taylor, Viollet,
Merodio, Arteche   Whelan   ...
                    h.t. 3-0   45,000

At San Mames Stadium, Bilbao.

SECOND LEG

MANCHESTER UTD. 3   BILBAO 0
Viollet, Taylor,
Berry   h.t. 1-0   65,000

At Maine-road Stadium, Manchester.

"Manchester United became England's soccer crusaders and there was a spirit of adventure about that first season in European competition," he explained.

"The boys played some dream football in the early ties, and then they showed their character in the quarter-final against Bilbao.

"The first leg in Spain was a nightmare. The pitch lay under a carpet of snow which continued to fall turning a forest of black umbrellas on the terraces into a white sheet.

"In the very first minute we should have scored, but a shot from Dennis Viollet stuck on the line. Worse was to come because the ball was cleared to Artiche who caught us on the break. Mark Jones slipped and he raced clear to score.

"By half-time we were three goals down and it seemed we would be out of Europe, but by sheer guts and flowing football we got back to 3-2.

"The Spaniards, who seemed to revel in the shocking conditions, turned on the pressure again to lead 5-2, and again our chances looked bleak.

"But just when everyone seemed to be flagging, Billy Whelan took the game by the scruff of the neck with only a few minutes remaining. He cut through the slush and beat five opponents by sheer brilliance and strength before hammering the ball high into the net from the edge of the box.

"How that boy found the strength to draw breath let alone shoot after that 40-yard run I will never know, but that goal kept us in the European Cup.

"We still had the daunting task of needing to win the return leg by three goals at Maine Road . . . but we had a centre forward called Tommy Taylor.

"Matt paid £29,999 to Barnsley for him to avoid a £30,000 price tag which of course was a big sum at the time. Tommy was extraordinarily shy. We had a hell of a job persuading him that he was good enough to play in the First Division. He really didn't want to leave Barnsley where everybody knew him. Matt's charm eventually won him over.

"He was an immediate success with his long, raking stride and superb heading ability. When he scored a goal he would stand with both arms raised aloft to salute the crowd.

"The second leg against Bilbao was Tommy's match. He played some of his best games in the European Cup and this was one of them. We had to score three goals, but by half-time we had pulled only one back through Dennis Viollet.

"I was sitting with Matt surrounded by a pile of half smoked cigarettes when, in the 70th minute, Tommy pivotted like a ballet dancer round Jesus Garay, one of the best centre halves in Europe, to smash a shot into the roof of the net.

"Now we were level on aggregate and nerves were jangling like mad when Taylor hit the post and the Spaniards just managed to scramble the ball away.

"Five minutes from the end with his black hair streaming in the wind, Tommy raced out wide to the right wing. He sped past Garay and was lining himself up for an angled shot at goal but paused and then casually flicked a pass into the middle for Johnny Berry to score.

"Although a lethal finisher himself, he was completely unselfish. This was even more evident when Bobby Charlton came into the side and he nursed the newcomer along like a veteran.

"The match against Bilbao was one of the great fight-backs of all time and it showed the mettle of a splendid side. Who knows what those boys might have achieved but for the terrible Munich disaster, and for the likes of Tommy Taylor with England as well?"

Jimmy Murphy's finest hour came a little later when he held the club together in the aftermath of Munich. The way he handled the almost impossible job brought him offers to manage in Brazil and at Juventus.

He turned down all approaches. Call it loyalty, or perhaps he did not wish to uproot his large and closely knit family, but I believe he had found his life's work and knew it.

He retired at Old Trafford as assistant manager in 1971 when Sir Matt Busby decided to step down. But he is still a familiar figure at Old Trafford dropping in with his weekly scouting reports . . . still working for Manchester United.

Women shrieked, strong men wilted, and at half-time even the "break" brought no relief. Hundreds in the crowd turned to their neighbours patting their hearts. "I don't think I can stand any more of this."

And when it was all over. Boy, oh boy! What a sight! What a sight!

Hats were thrown recklessly in the cold February air. MATT BUSBY, the triumphant manager, a Scot of impeccable social behaviour, leapt from his touch-line seat, grabbed JIMMY MURPHY, his assistant manager, in a rock 'n roll dance of victory.

Famous internationals all round chorused: "We've never seen anything like it."

Ex-England goalkeeper FRANK SWIFT: "I was ticked off for the first time in my life for swearing at a football match when I shouted to Dennis Viollet to shoot, adding something I shouldn't have.

JIMMY McGRORY, manager of famous Celtic, scorer of 510 goals; a record for British

football: "Phew. That's enough to last a lifetime."

SIR GEORGE GRAHAM, secretary of the Scottish F.A., due to retire in June: "That was something I'll never forget."

RAY WOOD the Manchester United goalkeeper, fully dressed: "My heart is still galloping."

THE REST of the valiant heroes could but blurt out yammering incoherent words of thanks.

Expensive

A READER rang me when I got back to the office: "I lost a 25-quid watch and had my head cut in the crush on the way out, but I couldn't care less. It was worth it." ... And another rang up: "Who scored? I was so excited there I didn't know or care."

From PIRU GAINZA, the vanquished captain: "Que muchachos 'tan magnificos," which freely translated means "These blokes are

magnificent."

But back to the match itself. For 42 minutes the Spaniards had carried out their avowed policy of putting up the shutters, clinging on grimly to what they had won in Bilbao. The play swayed chiefly down the middle, and that suited this iron curtain nicely.

A non-stop nerve tingler from the opening seconds, when centre half Mark Jones fell in a tackle. You could have cut the silence with a knife until he jumped up and into the fray; non-stop until the fading incredible seconds when the Basques made a final desperate effort to save the game.

That noise

No more silence. For the rest an uninhibited din that put the Hampden roar, the shouts from Elland Road and the Anfield Kop to shame.

Four minutes were left of what looked a goal-less half when a shot from Edwards hit

ABOVE: *One of United's three goals goes past Carmelo*

Mauri on the way, and VIOLLET, the on-the-spot man, was there to whip it home.

The break should have brought relief to jangled nerves. Not enough. From the restart it exploded into shattering action. Could United get those other two?

Disallowed

The invoice for a resounding "Yes" came within three minutes when United had the ball in the net twice, both "goals" being disallowed.

"I watched Mauri, kept behind him, and thought I'd scored a perfectly good goal," said Viollet.

"I would have allowed the second (this was also Viollet's) had Whelan not touched the ball into the net," said ALBERT DUSCII, a magnificent referee, who had a big share in the night's thriller.

WHAT AGONY! Agony, yes. But NOT despair. Dyed-in-the-wool Soccer managers, legislators from all parts of the country and Continent were to see what stuff these Manchester United players are made of.

Pegg, on the turn six yards out, shoots wide. Oh the groans of near despair. Eighteen minutes left and Tommy Taylor, playing the game of his life, and now having the measure of Garay, nearly the best centre half in the world, HITS THE POST. Still one to draw, two to win.

The mounting tension was unbearable. Then the Manchester skies were rent loose when little Eddie Colman, as quick-witted on as off the field, slipped a quick free kick to TAYLOR, and, oh joy! oh delirium! Tommy had rubbed one off.

ONLY SIX MINUTES left — 360 seconds; comes one of sport's greatest moments, the knock-out blow to a gallant opponent unable to take any more.

Tottering

Taylor, who has still not quite played out his big heart, swivels to the right, beats two of the tottering Basques, pushes back a short ball to BERRY, craftily moved to the centre.

It was in the net, and Manchester United had brought off one of the GREATEST SPORTING PERFORMANCES OF ALL TIME.

Take your curtain calls, Manchester United.

Take an extra one, Tommy Taylor. *SANTA CLAUS salutes you, beard and all.*

I was wrong in changing my mind. From Bilbao, when United lost 5-3, I sent an excited message to tell you that they would romp home here. I changed my mind on the eve of this game. I was wrong.

BUT, BOY AM I HAPPY.

THE GUARDIAN, April 11, 1957

REAL MADRID	3
MAN. UTD.	1

1956-57 EUROPEAN CUP, SEMI FINAL, FIRST LEG, REAL MADRID WIN 3-1

Manchester United Two Goals Down

Splendid effort by defence players

From an Old International

MADRID, APRIL 11

Real Madrid beat Manchester United 3-1 in the first leg of their semi-final tie in the European Cup Association football competition here today. Goals to Madrid came in melancholy succession in the sixtieth, seventy-third, and eighty-third minutes, Taylor's for United in the eightieth. The return match is at Old Trafford on April 25.

The root cause of the United's troubles early on was not so much Di Stefano as Gento, Real Madrid's stocky little outside left. Gento fizzes along the wing where other outside forwards just run, but he always has enough coolness and judgement in reserve to place his centres with deadly accuracy and three times he gave his other forwards, notably Stefano and Mateos, golden opportunities to score. Happily for the United, Wood, in goal, started in magnificent form, two of his saves were nothing short of heroic, while no praise is too high for the wit and grit of Colman, the astuteness of Byrne, the oak-tree strength of Edwards, and the dogged determination of Foulkes and Blanchflower. Except for isolated raids when Taylor missed one chance, a promising breakaway, through overrunning the ball, and made rather than missed another when he struck the crossbar with a header, all the United's best work undoubtedly was done in defence.

MANCHESTER UNITED TWO GOALS DOWN

Splendid effort by defence players

FROM AN OLD INTERNATIONAL

Real Madrid 3, Manchester United 1

MADRID, APRIL 11.

Real Madrid beat Manchester United 3-1 in the first leg of their semi-final tie in the European Cup Association football competition here today. Goals to Madrid came in melancholy succession in the sixtieth, seventy-third, and eighty-third minutes, Taylor's for United in the eightieth. The return match is at Old Trafford on April 25.

The root cause of the United's troubles early on was not so much [...]

Artistry sullied

This man Di Stefano now. Yes, he showed why he is the idol of the Latin races, the paragon of Continental footballers. His qualities are feline rather than tigerish, his ball control sleek and furtive, and his sudden, darting accelerations from a standing start something to behold. But this master of the side-step with the spring and agility that makes the matador did not dominate the proceedings in the manner to which he is accustomed. He executed some exquisite dummies and tricks it is true, and scored Madrid's second goal cleverly when Wood advanced from goal rather inadvisedly it seemed, but he lost his head and made, on Blanchflower of all people, the most squalid foul one remembers to have seen in either representative or cup-tie football. The pretence of a reproof conveyed to Di Stefano at the referee's insistance by his captain almost made one vomit at its cynicism. It seemed incredible that such an artist could trail his wings in the gutter in this way.

Manchester United soon lost whatever brief encouragement was given by Taylor's desperately scrambled header in answer to Stefano's goal, Madrid's second by the way. For three Madrid players went through like a pack of Rugby forwards and Mateo's demonstration showed that it was his toe and no one else's that kicked the goal home, and no excuses will be proffered in general terms. Rial had scored the first goal for Madrid after fifteen minutes of the second half.

Shreds and patches

The better team won and should have won more easily one thought, for the simple reason that it was the only team with an organised forward line. United's attack was very much a thing of threads and patches. Berry did little beyond being kicked off his feet in the penalty area without redress, Viollet was weak, Whelan was slow, and Pegg only found out in the last ten minutes of the match that he could beat his opposing back at will. As for the lion-hearted Taylor, never has that Barnsley lad stuck to a bitter task with a finer courage. He was kicked, pummelled, elbowed, shoved, held by the shirt, and generally man-handled in a way completely foreign to English notion.

If this sort of stuff is repeated at Old Trafford – and the referee has just described this as a "friendly game" remember – then the spectators may prepare themselves for something novel in the way of friendly football, but they'll see some superb stuff as well and if the United's five defending heroes play as they played today then as Trainer Curry said at the close of the match they'll "deserve gold medals as big as frying-pans."

TOP RIGHT: *Taylor (far left) scores despite the efforts of Real defender Lesmes (No 3) and 'keeper Alonso*

RIGHT: *Members of Manchester United leave for their tie against Madrid, left to right: Clayton, McGuinness, Taylor, Colman, Jones, Viollet, Wood, Byrne, Whelan, Bent*

THE GUARDIAN, April 25, 1957

MAN UTD	2
REAL MADRID	**2**

1956-57 EUROPEAN CUP, SEMI FINAL, SECOND LEG,
REAL MADRID WIN 5-3 ON AGGREGATE

Manchester United Bow to Real Madrid
Splendid fight back in vain

By an Old International

Real Madrid made themselves the toast of two hemispheres and Manchester United the toast of all English-speaking peoples when they drew 2-2 at Old Trafford last night in the second leg of their semi-final of the European Cup Association football competition. Real Madrid thus won the tie 5-3 on aggregate and will meet Fiorentina, the Italian champions, in the final in Madrid on May 15.

Bedlam after this will hold no terrors. One had thought that the notion that great deeds could be wrought by a vast concentration of noise had died with Joshua. But the Manchester dailies and the Manchester crowd had other ideas and if noise could have served their purpose United would have won hands down.

And as the match began with two trips and a case of a knee in the back of Taylor, besides several great clearances by Blanchflower to the obvious discomfiture of Di Stefano, the crowd had something to roar about. Nothing could have been more hair raising than the lusty give and take with which both sides opened out and nothing could have been more fortunate for United than the fact that the referee brought the ball back for a throw in on the half-way line just as Edwards floored Gento in the penalty area with a reckless tackle. Two characteristic thrusts by Di Stefano, one a terrific shot from the standing position and the other a flying header, sent a shiver of apprehension through the crowd. The white ghost was walking.

Two superb goals

Then the English crowd got a sample of Continental refereeing. Taylor was hooked by Marquitos from behind and fell on his face as flat as a flounder. This happened well inside the penalty area. The referee awarded an indirect free kick for obstruction, though how a player can be obstructed from behind is a matter which requires some explanation. But rumination on that point was soon cut short by a superb goal scored in the best Real Madrid manner. The move started with a silky back heeler by Di Stefano, who must have eyes in the back of his head. He rolled the ball through the only opening visible in United's massing defence and Kopa, darting through like a soul possessed, whipped the ball past Wood. United were three behind now with only 25 minutes gone, and eight minutes later it became four down, for Gento rounded off a glorious move

RIGHT: *Alonso punches over the bar to foil another United attack*

MANCHESTER UNITED BOW TO REAL MADRID

Splendid fight back in vain

BY AN OLD INTERNATIONAL

Manchester United 2, Real Madrid 2

Real Madrid made themselves the toast of two hemispheres and Manchester United the toast of all English-speaking peoples when they drew 2-2 at Old Trafford last night in the second leg of their semi-final of the European Cup Association football competition. Real Madrid thus won the tie 5-3 on aggre-

speed is as good as an extra man. He produced crisis out of the air, so to speak, by his rapid transit from place to place. Here was one who apparently could make bricks without straw. All honour to the Manchester defenders, who ran miles in the effort to overtake him. They reminded one of the Battle of Tippermuir when ten citizens of Perth are said to have burst themselves with running.

The lights came on aft the inte-

ABOVE: *Alonso punches clear from Taylor*

RIGHT: *Wood collects as Gento hovers*

BOTTOM LEFT: *United's Wood (far left) covers a shot from Real Madrid*

with a violent centre and the sheer pace carried the ball through Wood's grasp, and Mateos stood waiting gleefully to convert.

Now happily placed, Real Madrid spread their fine feathers to some purpose. They gripped the crowd's attention for a while by their resource, their understanding, and their ball-control. As for Gento, he soon made it plain that a forward with his speed is as good as an extra man. He produced crisis out of the air, so to speak, by his rapid transit from place to place. Here was one who apparently could make bricks without straw. All honour to the Manchester defenders, who ran miles in the effort to overtake him. They reminded one of the Battle of Tippermuir when ten citizens of Perth are said to have burst themselves with running.

The lights came on after the interval, but at first they brought no solution to United's problem. There, patrolling the middle was the gigantic figure of Marquitos, taking great sweeps at the ball, heaving his arms and legs about: the hardest tackler seen at Old Trafford surely since Barson had his day. As at Madrid, so here, Taylor worked and sweated like a collier at the coalface, but what was one among so many? There were so many times when he was outnumbered by at least three to one and this is not said to disparage his colleagues in the least. The other four forwards tore into the match in the middle period of the second half with a frenzy which would have cut most English sides to ribbons. But here was defence the like of which is rarely seen in these islands and only forward play of the highest class could hope to make any impression.

Recovery – but too late

Then, eleven minutes after half-time, the crowd had the solace it had been pining for. A fierce centre from Pegg roared into the goalmouth, appeared to strike Taylor on the shoulder, bumped against a post, and wobbled along the goal line until a figure in red, Whelan they say, belted the ball through. This was the fillip the Red Devils needed and wave after wave of impetuous attacks – one could hardly expect the reasoned variety in this holocaust – beat down on the Spanish goal. Now, at long last, the champions turned on the heat and but for Alonzo's agility in goal, a superb shot from Taylor and a later jab by Whelan, must have found their mark. At times one even had the unusual spectacle of seeing Real Madrid unashamedly kicking for touch. Five minutes from the end United pressed again and the heavens themselves must have heard the shout when Charlton scored the equaliser. Over some of the incidents that marked the final scene it would be better to draw the veil. Shabby tackles were made on both sides.

So with an aggregate of 5-3 against them United say goodbye to the European Cup, but the manner of their departure and the nature of the struggle they made in the second half will be the subject of song and story as long as the club exists. To have drawn level with Real Madrid after being two goals down stamps them undoubtedly as a great side.

The Busby Babes qualified for a second crack at the European Cup by winning the championship for a second crack at the European Cup by winning the championship for a second season in succession. They took the 1956-57 title eight points ahead of Spurs with a sparkling attack which scored more than a hundred goals.

Billy Whelan set the scoring pace with 26; Tommy Taylor bagged 22; Dennis Viollet picked up 16. A young Bobby Charlton made his debut and gave notice of great things to come by scoring 10 goals in 14 League appearances.

Busby's men were nearing perfection; in addition to reaching the semi-finals of the European Cup they missed a League and FA Cup double by a whisker.

They played Aston Villa in the final and lost 2-1 after playing most of the match without goalkeeper Ray Wood, who smashed his cheekbone in a collison with Peter McParland.

NEWS CHRONICLE, September 25, 1957

SHAMROCK ROVERS	0
MAN UTD	6

1957-58 EUROPEAN CUP, PRELIMINARY ROUND, FIRST LEG, MANCHESTER UNITED WIN 6-0

From Frank Taylor
DUBLIN, WEDNESDAY

Two great goals put United on victory trail

From FRANK TAYLOR: DUBLIN, Wednesday

Shamrock Rovers .. 0   M.

BILL WHELAN, the sm just down the road fre led this scientific slaug Rovers' European Cup shrieking Irish Soccer fan silence. Whelan has neve before in his native Dublin

This was murder for Sham timers, who ran out of steam long

Yet it could have been so different. gale behind them, were only one goal

Bill Whelan, the smiling Irishman, born just down the road from Dalymount Park, led this scientific slaughter of Shamrock Rovers' European Cup hopes. The 46,000 shrieking Irish Soccer fans were stunned to silence. Whelan has never played like this before in his native Dublin.

This was murder for Shamrock's team of part-timers, who ran out of steam long before the finish.

Yet it could have been so different. United, with a roaring gale behind them, were only one goal to the good at half-time, and Shamrock Rovers were ready to sweep England's champions right back into the Irish Sea.

Whelan had other ideas. He mastered the ball, he tamed the wind which threatened to make this match into a game of blow football.

He ignored the frightening roar of 46,000 Irish voices as he slapped in two magnificent goals in the 51st and 56th minutes which sank the good ship Shamrock without trace.

I shudder to think what might have happened to United in the second half if Whirlwind Whelan, the smiling executioner, had not stepped in and saved them. The aftermath of Hurricane Carrie swirled round the ground at the start, and it was lucky for United that Byrne won the toss.

The game began at a blistering pace and it was soon obvious that United were troubled by the conditions. Byrne kicked off the line

ABOVE: *The Manchester United team leave for their match in Dublin*

Action from the second leg semi-final tie between Manchester United and Real Madrid, May 1968

Action from the second leg semi-final tie between Manchester United and Real Madrid, May 1968

from Tuohy as Rovers roared into action.

United players could scarcely keep their feet. Bill Foulkes, particularly, had a slippery time trying to keep his balance and still deal with the deadly thrusts of the flying Tuohy, but Foulkes, like the rest of the United players, gradually found his feet.

Daring dives

Praise Roger Byrne for ice-cool captaincy and confidence when the game was finely balanced. Praise Whelan, the sorcerer, and his apprentice Johnny Berry.

But even so, United had a long time to wait for the opening goal which gave them the chance to play with more confidence.

The ball was swept upfield in the 36th minute from Berry to Pegg, and Tommy Taylor, with a magnificent chip, sent the ball over D'Arcy's head. The ball hit a post and trickled in.

D'Arcy, in his yellow jersey and yellow gloves, looked quite a character but some of his daring dives saved Rovers in the first-half.

There was only a two-minute break at half-time, and then Rovers, with the wind behind, sailed into action with Paddy Coad and Hennessey directing operations.

There was no doubt that United could have been in trouble, but then Whelan took command and the goals came with monotonous regularity in this sequence:

Whelan (51 and 56 minutes), Taylor (80), Berry (85) and Pegg, with a magnificent volley from a crossfield ball from Berry (86).

Late collapse

Looks easy, doesn't it, but I'm not forgetting that Wood made a magnificent save from Coad and Peyton hit the bar with a thrilling shot.

Only in the last ten minutes did Rovers cave in. At the finish United were rolling the ball around like true masters.

Freddie Goodwin, who came in for Eddie Colman, was a little out of position at first, but his passes throughout were models of accuracy.

It makes one wonder whether Rovers' journey to play the second leg at Old Trafford next week is really necessary – but you can take it from me that in that first half the whole defence was magnificent. They fought like tigers and they made United go all the way.

ABOVE: *Shamrock Rovers' keeper D'Arcy (right) strives in vain to keep out Whelan's goal*

THE GUARDIAN, October 2, 1957

MAN. UTD. 3

SHAMROCK ROVERS 2

1957-58 EUROPEAN CUP, PRELIMINARY ROUND, SECOND LEG, MANCHESTER UNITED WIN 9-2 ON

Shamrock Rovers put up a magnificent fight
Manchester United win by one goal

By an Old International

A t first sight it did not seem that even the glamour of a preliminary round of the European Cup competition could make Manchester United's 3-2 victory over Shamrock Rovers at Old Trafford last evening anything but a desultory formality. But in that we reckoned without our visitors.

Irish to the core and indifferent to the fact that they were starting this second leg of the preliminary round six goals down, the Rovers decided to approach the affair in a light-hearted, carefree frame of mind which added materially to the value of their performance. They lost the match but they left a grand impression behind.

It must have been as great a relief to the Irish players as it was a disappointment to the home crowd that two such artists as Edwards and Whelan had to stand down from the Manchester team and yield their places to McGuinness and Webster — persevering craftsmen though these characters are. Jones's introduction for Blanchflower at centre half was in a different class; one might almost call it a distinction without a difference; for when both are playing well there is scarcely a pin's point to choose between them.

D'Arcy's agility

The opening exchanges, in which Berry's trickery was prominent, suggested another runaway victory for United, for within five minutes Viollet had missed one sitter, through hesitancy, and had then explosively converted a second. Viollet's early goal, one off the Pegg as the saying goes, put the crowd into great good humour and they warmly applauded the agility of the Irish goalkeeper, D'Arcy, who realised that he was in for an extremely busy evening.

The difference between the two teams at first was most marked: coolness and precision from the full-time professionals, enthusiasm and boisterousness from the part-timers, with the clean sporting spirit on both sides making the entertainment a pure joy. That United had vast reserves of skill and stamina seemed obvious, but one felt that as long as the strength of the Irishmen held out this affair would be no repetition of the Anderlecht massacre and in view of the attractive bearing of the Shamrock players one fervently hoped that this would be so.

It seemed a little ominous, however, when Pegg in the twenty-second minute fastened on to a perfect opening provided by Viollet and though hustled by two defenders, managed to keep his feet and scraped the ball past D'Arcy. How the Irishmen survived the bombardment of the next five minutes would be a teaser to explain. But survive they did and launched at once a series of counter-attacks in which Peyton, their inside right, twice achieved prominence as the possessor of a useful turn of speed. In his second attempt Peyton breasted the ball down and tore past Byrne at top speed but he had the misfortune to over-kick the ball and a golden chance was lost.

Had that chance been taken the match

Shamrock goalkeeper Eamonn D'Arcy and right-back Burke look disconsolate as the ball rests in the net for Manchester United's third goal. It was Dennis Viollet's second goal.

SHAMROCK ROVERS PUT UP A MAGNIFICENT FIGHT

Manchester United win by one goal

BY AN OLD INTERNATIONAL

Manchester Utd. 3, Shamrock Rovers 2

At first sight it did not seem that even the glamour of a preliminary round of the European Cup competition could make Manchester United's 3-2 victory over Shamrock Rovers at Old Trafford last evening anything but a desultory formality. But in that we reckoned without our visitors.

Irish to the core and indifferent to the fact that they were starting this second leg of the preliminary round six goals down, the Rovers decided to approach the affair in a light-hearted, carefree frame of mind which added materially to the value of their performance. They lost the match but they left a grand impression behind.

It must have been as great a relief to the Irish players as it was a disappointment to the home crowd that two such artists as Edwards and Whelan had to stand down from the Manchester team and yield their places to McGuinness — persevering craftsmen

achieved prominence as the possessor of a useful turn of speed. In his second attempt Peyton breasted the ball down and tore past Byrne at top speed but he had the misfortune to over-kick the ball and a golden chance was lost.

Had that chance been taken the match would indeed have been set alight for at that point Shamrock Rovers were making United fight every inch of the way. Keogh, in particular, the Rovers' centre half, was standing up to Taylor magnificently and only once in a keen first half did the Barnsley boy break away. But what he did with that chance would not be believed in Barnsley!

Nothing livelier than the ten-minute rally of cut-and-thrust that immediately preceded the interval has been seen at Old Trafford for many a long day. Shamrock Rovers were out to show that if they achieved any success at all it would be through playing good football and good football only, and that they established beyond all doubt. United for their part had paid them the compliment of not easing up for an instant and the r...

would indeed have been set alight for at that point Shamrock Rovers were making United fight every inch of the way. Keogh, in particular, the Rovers' centre half, was standing up to Taylor magnificently and only once in a keen first half did the Barnsley boy break away. But what he did with that chance would not be believed in Barnsley!

Nothing livelier than the ten-minute rally of cut-and-thrust that immediately preceded the interval has been seen at Old Trafford for many a long day. Shamrock Rovers were out to show that if they achieved any success at all it would be through playing good football and good football only, and that they established beyond all doubt. United for their part had paid them the compliment of not easing up for an instant, and the result had been a first half far more entertaining than circumstances had led one to expect.

If ever three men slaved for the honour and glory of Ireland it was surely the Rovers' half-back line – Nolan, Keogh, and Coad. They had a double-barrelled duty of great difficulty to perform – to stay back and to keep an eye on United's frisky forwards for one thing and at the same time to keep their own forwards going with long through passes which had to be placed to a nicety to obtain any results. And sure enough in the 55th minute their reward came to the manifest delight of the home crowd. Little Peyton broke through United's defensive cordon and left Wood helpless. His success could not have been more generously applauded if it had been a goal signalling United's seizure of the Cup.

Jewel of timing

United's answer to Peyton's goal was itself worth the price of admission. It was a jewel of touch and timing as Viollet exquisitely side-footed a swift low pass from Berry wide of D'Arcy. That occurred in the sixtieth minute and some regarded it as the beginning of the end, the first rumble of the avalanche so to speak. But not a bit of it. Eight minutes later Hamilton cracked a second goal for Shamrock under Wood's falling body, and two minutes after that he forced Wood to stretch every muscle and sinew to pull down a glorious volley on the turn.

But the greatest save of all was surely D'Arcy's wide leap and one-handed slip catch to foil Pegg's superb header. It will live long in the memory as a symbol of the gallantry of these sporting Irishmen in a game splendidly controlled by A Alfteen of Belgium.

CZECHS COLLAPSE AFTER BLUNDER

By HENRY ROSE
Manchester U. 3, Dukla 0

RATING ★★★

MANCHESTER UNITED, those great ambassadors of British sport, are on the rampage again. With hearts and hopes high they go to Prague on Wednesday week in

DAILY EXPRESS, November 20, 1957

MAN. UTD.	3
DUKLA PRAGUE	0

1957-58 EUROPEAN CUP, FIRST ROUND, FIRST LEG, MANCHESTER UNITED WIN 3-0

Czechs Collapse After Blunder

By Henry Rose

ABOVE: *Cadek (right) challenges Taylor*

Manchester United, those great ambassadors of British sport, are on the rampage again. With hearts and hopes high they go to Prague on Wednesday week in the second leg of the European Cup first-round tie with a three-goal lead.

They achieved it, after much heartache, as the result of an electrifying spell of 12 minutes in the second half in the best Manchester United championship winning tradition.

It is a lead that looks a comfortable enough cushion on which to get through the round. But on the evidence of the first hour at Old Trafford last night, the valuable three goals insurance will be badly needed.

None of the 60,000 crowd could have had the slightest doubt, to be true to himself, that the Czechs were the better side up to that point.

United's orthodoxy could make nothing of a defence four-man deep, as fast as its forwards, and presenting as compact a covering as I have ever seen. In addition, the Czech forwards produced madly fascinating footwork with the end product, the shot in goal, nowhere in sight.

Then came a catastrophic 63rd minute that the Czechs will never forget. It reduced their defence to a complete shambles and put a revitalised United on the victory path.

Pluskal is, they tell me, the humourist of the side, but he will need all his sense of humour to see anything funny about it.

Either the goalkeeper or Pluskal could have cleared the ball. Neither did so, and Cardiff-born Colin Webster, who must be one of the greatest reserve players of all time, nipped in to score; glittering reward for fast, do-or-die following up.

Deflated

With the Czech defence deflated as surely as a flat tyre, United roared to the attack, and from Webster's centre Tommy Taylor burst magnificently in position, and rose like a bird to head the ball into the net off a post. A wonderful effort. Two in four minutes.

Eight minutes later and the probable safety margin for the return game had been reached when Pegg, from Whelan's pass found himself in front of goal unmarked by a defence that had seemingly deserted its post.

United's best friends cannot concede their being worth a three-goal victory, but there's no doubt that the better side won, taking the game as a whole.

In full-back Novak, 30 times capped, and Masopust and Pluskal, the wing halves, Dukla had three of the cleverest players on the field.

Superb

A great star in deep-lying centre forward Borovicka and in Dvorak, an inside forward, who might have set them on the victory trail in the first half but for the magnificent, brilliant, superb Edwards.

What a player! Once again he stood out as the best of his side.

Behind him, Byrne was immaculate, and it was good to see Eddie Colman back to his hip-wiggling best.

If the forwards did not play as well as a line as we know they can, they must be given full marks for snapping up their chances.

Irate Tommy Taylor fans assailed me as they passed the Press box at the end, but truth to tell Tommy's was not a five-star performance.

Tireless

He worked tirelessly without receiving the sort of passes a centre forward is entitled to, and took his goal superbly in a way that I honestly hope will help to restore his confidence when he steps out for England against France next Wednesday.

Not a great game; not a compelling one. Is the European Cup losing its glamour, or am I becoming an old grouch, I don't know. But I do know this game did not grip my interest as much as any one of the ties last season.

BELOW: *Pegg (centre) scores for United, watched by Cadek (second from left) of Dukla Prague*

NEWS CHRONICLE, December 4, 1957

DUKLA PRAGUE	1
MAN. UTD.	0

1957-58 EUROPEAN CUP, FIRST ROUND, SECOND LEG, MANCHESTER UNITED WIN 3-1 ON AGGREGATE

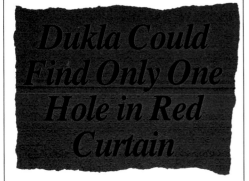

Dukla Could Find Only One Hole in Red Curtain

From Frank Taylor
PRAGUE, WEDNESDAY

E ddie Colman, the little lance-corporal from Salford, took the Czech army stadium on the hills above Prague by storm today, but United's shooting would not have frightened a goalkeeper in a junior girls' hockey match. That, briefly, is the European Cup story from Prague.

The top brass of the Czech army, generals, colonels, then down to the other ranks warmly applauded Colman's masterly display.

Colman was the little Caesar who conquered them all with his artistry. He, Roger Byrne and Mark Jones were the big three for United. Praise also Foulkes, Edwards and Wood for brave defence when the pressure was on.

Yet this was no blood-tingling performance by England's champions. They have won through to the quarter finals of the European Cup against Red Star, Belgrade, but they will need a better firing line than the forwards who played in Prague.

Colin Webster and Borovicka, the Prague inside-left, had their names taken by the referee for a duel which was not strictly according to the rule book.

Edwards stunned

Duncan Edwards, stunned in a heading collision, played well without being the dominant Duncan one expects. Mark Jones came off with

DUKLA COULD FIND ONLY ONE HOLE IN RED CURTAIN

From FRANK TAYLOR   Prague, Wednesday

Dukla 1   Manchester United 0

(Aggregate : Dukla 1, Manchester U. 3)

E DDIE COLMAN, the little lance-corporal from Salford, took the Czech army stadium on the hills above Prague by storm today, but United's shooting would not have frightened a goalkeeper in a junior girls' hockey match. That, briefly, is the European Cup story from Prague.

ABOVE: *Borovicka (centre) cuts off Pegg's attempted cross*

a swollen face caused in another heading collision. Not a dirty match by any means but not such a thrilling, sporting occasion as we had at Old Trafford.

Referee Treichel put his finger on the trouble when he said the play was too fast. It was a little naughty, too, for 10 minutes, while the players on occasions could not keep their feet on the slippery turf.

United created more chances, but the Czechs gave them a lesson in the finer arts of ball control. Did I say ball? It was more like a Christmas party balloon because it floated about the field, swerving in mid-air like a

Freddie Trueman outswinger. Nevertheless, the Czechs mastered it better than their opponents.

United, on this form, won't have much chance of shooting themselves further along the glittering road to European Cup success.

Dukla officials after the game told Matt Busby: "You have nothing to fear. Red Star have a better forward line than ours, and they use long passes, but their defence is very shaky. We have played them three times in the last two years and won all three."

This is happy news for United, but I must report that they never looked the part in this match.

Tommy Taylor foozled his way through the most miserable 90 minutes I have ever seen from him. Taking the charitable view, I suppose he must, despite his protests, have been feeling the effects of his knee injury.

Taylor was never in the match. Bill Whelan could not master the bouncy ball. Scanlon began in thrilling manner with fast runs and accurate centres; then he, too, fell into the general depression.

Progressive moves

Colin Webster, the Welsh firebrand, played as though he was wearing the red shirt of Wales, but his shooting has never been worse. This left David Pegg as the best and most dangerous forward of them all.

Dukla never revealed the skilful play they showed at Old Trafford, and their shooting was no better. It was rather like seeing a top class film, and then having to sit through a boring supporting programme.

For the opening ten minutes Dukla played brilliantly as United got the feel of the ball and the conditions. Then, for the only time in the match, we saw the real champions.

Nice progressive moves cut the Dukla defence wide open. Whelan missed two good chances, and Pegg created a third, but his final shot was blocked by Pavlis. Then the Czechs scored in the 20th minute. A long pass from Pluskal, and Dvorak, the only sharp shooter in the Czech army side, had whipped the ball into the net.

Dukla only two goals behind, 70 more minutes to play and the scene was set for a grand fighting game. Not on your life. It was cold, miserable Soccer with United defenders repeatedly breaking up the filigree work of the Dukla forwards.

Mind you, United could so easily have drawn this match. In fact, with 19 minutes to go, Taylor headed the ball in from a Pegg centre. The referee appeared to give a goal, and ran away from the protesting Czech players. Then he pointed dramatically, and gave a free kick. Taylor was offside, the official told me later.

Webster made a shocking miss from four yards when in the clear, but was unlucky with a header which hit the bar. The referee at first gave Webster offside, then rushed up, grabbed the ball, and gave a bounce up with no United player within 10 yards of the ball.

Needless to say, the Czech goalkeeper, Pavlis, grabbed the ball when the referee had dropped it.

Said referee Treichel: "I gave the bounce up because I realised I had made a mistake with an offside decision." It was that sort of a match.

NEWS CHRONICLE, January 14, 1958

MAN. UTD. 2

RED STAR BELGRADE ... 1

1957-58 EUROPEAN CUP, QUARTER FINAL ROUND, FIRST LEG, MANCHESTER UNITED WIN 2-1

Charlton mainspring of second-half rally

By Frank Taylor

Wakey, wakey, Manchester United! The crowd, and Bobby Charlton, have still left England's champions with a chance of staying in the European Cup. Can they now hold the Yugo-Slav champions in the return in Belgrade on February 5?

I think they can. But they'll need an iron curtain defence, and I fancy Matt Busby might have to call on some of his old European Cup squad for the return. David Pegg, for instance; and maybe room can be found for Johnny Berry.

Make no mistake, Bobby Charlton was the Bobby Dazzler of United's almost non-existent forward line last night. And it was the crowd's

thunderous roars which forced United into that furious fight back in the second half when they grabbed their two goals.

This was billed as a European Cup quarter final. In fact it turned out to be a game of shove Soccer. All I hope is that in the return the players forget all about sly elbow digs; I hope they use their shoulders fairly and squarely, instead of using the posterior so often as they did last night.

In the 90 minutes referee Lesquenes blew for 41 fouls. Twenty-four of them for Manchester United; and 17 for the Yugo-Slavs . . . and that doesn't include any for offside or hands.

It was a pity, because Red Star stroked and coaxed that ball on a tricky surface like true masters. Their defence was as impregnable as the Bank of England, and Beara, the ex-ballet dancer in between the sticks, lived up to his title of the "Black Panther."

United made a bang-crash beginning when first Charlton side-footed one narrowly wide and then Viollet nearly sneaked one in. But for the rest of the half England's champions were lost in the fog.

The Red Devils were just like red shadows of their true selves, whereas Red Star moved sweetly and with a polished poise when they attacked. It took them 33 minutes to score and it was a clanger by £23,000 Harry Gregg.

Gregg played a good game but he comes off his line when there is no need, and when Mitic, the Red Star right-half, beat two men Gregg came off his line inquisitively, although play was some 30 yards from him.

Held his head

The ball went to Tasic, who saw the opening, and lobbed the ball over Gregg's head with the master's case. United a goal down; and one must admit they asked for it.

At this stage it seemed only a thickening of

Charlton mainspring of second-half rally

By FRANK TAYLOR

Manchester United 2   Red Star, Belgrade 1

WAKEY, wakey, Manchester United! The crowd, and Bobby Charlton, have still left England's champions with a chance of staying in the European Cup. Can they now hold the Yugo-Slav champions in the return in Belgrade on February 5?

I think they can. But they'll need an iron curtain defence, and . . Matt

ABOVE: *Red Star's 'keeper Beara (leaping centre) clears from Charlton (far left) and Taylor (far right)*

the fog would have saved United, but obviously at the break Matt Busby told his men to move quicker to the ball and release it faster.

The assault on Beara's goal was almost monotonous; but the Black Panther made United's forwards look like kittens when it came to shooting. Three times in a frantic opening five minutes of the second half he came out and made three out-of-this-world saves from Charlton. Poor Bobby. He held his head in his hands like a man who was sure this was going to be Black Tuesday for him.

Fortunately, though United forwards dithered and passed and repassed against this superb Red Star defence, United's power men, Bill Foulkes, Roger Byrne, Mark Jones and Duncan Edwards, refused to let the initiative slip away.

The persistence of Edwards won the first goal. He roared past two men to put Scanlon in the clear with a pass which went as sharp as an arrow, and when Scanlon's low centre came over, Charlton at last found the target. Time: 65 minutes.

Beat three men

Ten minutes to go, and United were now in top gear. Viollet, on the right, beat three men on the bye-line, swung the ball into the middle, and Eddie Colman, who had had a very quiet game, stabbed the ball in.

In the dying minutes United just couldn't break through again. So desperate were Red Star that left winger Kostic was pulled up by the referee, who pointed dramatically to the dressing-room as though warning the Yugo-Slav, ". . . any more, and you are off."

This Red Star defence covered and fell back like guardsmen. Everyone was great. I'd give a medal to everyone, and then award an extra bar to Beara-the-great in goal: and Mitic, the captain, at right half.

But it was obvious that against a class side like Red Star, United need a little more ball play in the forward line, and that's why I fancy Matt Busby will have Pegg, Berry, and maybe even Bill Whelan standing by in case they are needed in Belgrade. Ken Morgans never gave up trying in last night's game, but one must remember he is only 18, and this was a tremendous match for one so young.

THE GUARDIAN, February 5, 1958

RED STAR BELGRADE 3

MAN. UTD. 3

1957-58 EUROPEAN CUP, QUARTER FINAL, SECOND LEG, MANCHESTER UNITED WIN 5-4 ON AGGREGATE

Manchester United through on aggregate

Excitement a-plenty in second half

From an Old International
BELGRADE, FEBRUARY 5

W ho would be a weather prophet? At Belgrade today in warm sunshine and on a grass pitch where the last remnants of melting snow produced the effect of an English lawn flecked with daisies, Red Star and Manchester United began a battle of wits and courage and rugged tackling in the second leg of their quarter-final of the European Cup competition. It ended in a draw, 3-3 but as the United had already won the first leg at Old Trafford by 2-1 they thus gained the right to pass into the semi-final round of the competition for the second year in succession on a 5-4 aggregate.

Much to the relief of the English party, and to the consternation of the 52,000 home spectators, Viollet had the ball in the net past a dumbfounded Beara in 90 seconds. It was a beautifully taken goal – a characteristic effort by that player – but rather lucky in the way a rebound had run out in United's favour. But, as Jones remarked, "You need luck at this game": and he might have added, "a suit of chain mail also would not have come amiss." A second goal almost came fourteen minutes later, delightfully taken by Charlton after a corner kick by Scanlon had been headed on by Viollet, but this was disallowed, because of offside, by the Austrian referee, whose performance on the whistle so far had assumed the proportions of a flute obbligato. That was due to the frequency

MANCHESTER UNITED THROUGH ON AGGREGATE

Excitement a-plenty in second half

FROM AN OLD INTERNATIONAL

Red Star 3, Manchester United 3

BELGRADE, FEBRUARY 5.

Who would be a weather prophet?

ABOVE: *United leaving for the second leg match against Red Star Belgrade*

with which fouls were being committed by both sides after Sekularac had set the fashion in shabbiness by stabbing Morgans on the knee. But in spite of the many stops and starts, events in the first half ran smoothly for United, on whose behalf Taylor led his line like a true Hotspur from centre forward. Other factors telling strongly in Manchester's favour at this time were the clean hands and sound judgment of Gregg in goal.

Charlton scores

Further success for United was impending. Charlton this time was the chosen instrument. Dispossessing Kostic about forty yards from goal, this gifted boy leaned beautifully into his

Their forwards flung themselves heatedly against a defence as firm and steady as a rock; even Sekularac, after a bright beginning in which he showed his undoubted skill, lost heart visibly and tumbled repeatedly. Nevertheless there was an upsurge of the old fighting spirit when Kostic scored a fine goal for Red Star two minutes after half-time. It

stride made ground rapidly for about ten yards, and then beat the finest goalkeeper on the Continent with a shot of tremendous power and superb placing. There, one thought, surely goes England's Bloomer of the future. Further evidence of Charlton's claim to that distinction was to emerge two minutes later. A smartly taken free kick got the Red Star defence into a real tangle. Edwards fastened on the ball and did his best to oblige his colleagues and supporters by bursting it (a feat by the way which he was to achieve later), but he muffed his kick this time and the ball rolled to Charlton, apparently lost in a thicket of Red Star defenders. Stalemate, surely. But not with Charlton about. His quick eye detected the one sure

MIC. MOBILE 7 shot from Charlton (right) AT Belgrade. best goal BEARA a CENTRE HALF SPAJE UNITED THIRD GOAL.

ABOVE: *Team line-up on the pitch in Belgrade*

LEFT: *Charlton (far right) scores United's third goal, Beara (far left) and Spajic (no 5) can do nothing to stop it*

BOTTOM: *Bobby Charlton, star of United's second leg match against Red Star Belgrade*

route through the circle of legs; his trusty boot drove the ball unerringly along it. 3-0 on the day; 5-1 on the aggregate. Nice going.

As was natural the Red Star players completely lost their poise for a while. Their forwards flung themselves heatedly against a defence as firm and steady as a rock; even Sekularac, after a bright beginning in which he showed his undoubted skill, lost heart visibly and stumbled repeatedly. Nevertheless there was an upsurge of the old fighting spirit when

Kostic scored a fine goal for Red Star two minutes after half-time. It ought to have been followed by a second one three minutes later when Sekularac placed the ball perfectly for Cokic. Cokic's terrific shot cleared the bar by a foot – no more. Next a curious mix up by Foulkes and Tasic, Red Star's centre forward, ended in Foulkes falling flat on top of Tasic and blotting him completely from view. According to Foulkes Tasic lost his footing, fell over, and pulled Foulkes over with him, but it looked

Viollet (front centre) and Taylor (second right) pressuring Beara, who punches clear on this occasion

bad, and the whistle blew at once with attendant gestures indicating a penalty. Tasic had the satisfaction of converting that one, although his shot only just evaded Gregg's finger-tips.

The score now was 3-2 and the crowd broke into an uncontrolled frenzy of jubilation and excitement. So much so that when Cokic failed to walk the ball into a goal that was completely unprotected – Gregg was lying hurt and helpless on the ground – a miniature repetition of the Bolton disaster seemed to occur at one corner of the arena. Down the terraces streamed a wild horde of excited spectators eager to help Cokic administer the final touch; and dozens of spectators hung limply along the concrete walls with the breath crushed out of their bodies, if indeed nothing worse had befallen them.

Anxious moments

A quarter of an hour from the end Red Star, with their confidence and self-respect restored, were wheeling and curveting, passing and shooting in their best style, and United's defenders had to fight their way out of a regular nightmare of desperate situations. It was significant hereabouts that United's inside forwards were not coming back to chase the ball as they had done so effectively in the first half, and this, of course, threw added pressure on the rearguard. As soon as this fault was rectified the Red Star attacks, though frequent enough, lost something of their sting. In fact, United began to pile on the pressure at the other end and once Morgans struck a post with a glorious shot. Then we saw as brilliant, and at the same time as unlucky a save as Gregg may

ever experience.

In dashing out and snatching the ball off Tasic's feet on the fringe of the penalty area, Gregg had the misfortune to roll forward still holding the ball, and so handle it outside the area. Kostic's free kick (according to Viollet) struck the side of Viollet's head and gained thereby such a tricky curve that Gregg could only palm the ball into the net. Three all. Yugoslavians' tails up now with a vengeance, and only one goal required to enforce the dearly sought replay. But only three minutes remained for play, and Jones, Foulkes, Byrne, Edwards, and Colman, who had played magnificently throughout, as had the rest, saw to it that that goal never materialised.

LOOKING BACK WITH ■ JACKIE BLANCHFLOWER ■

Jackie Blanchflower was a spectator for the last fateful European tie before the Munich tragedy.

It was a journey which cost him dearly as one of the players so badly injured in the air crash that he never played again.

The versatile Blanchflower, inside forward or centre half, had lost his place in the team through dropping out to play for Northern Ireland in a World Cup qualifying match against Scotland.

Competition for places was so fierce that season that going away to play international football was no guarantee of a first-team place back at Old Trafford.

"I played in the reserves against Barnsley just before the Belgrade trip and I think we had nine internationals in the team," mused Jack as he looked back on United's second season in Europe.

"The quality of the talent and the depth of it was frightening. But for the accident, I think Manchester United would have gone on to dominate English and European football like Real Madrid did for many years and Benfica after them.

"I believe England with Tommy Taylor, Roger Byrne and Duncan Edwards would have won the 1958 World Cup. Taylor had just scored a hat-trick against Brazil and was destined for great things internationally.

"If all those players who were killed and injured had been spared, the course of football history would have been very different.

"The quarter-final against Red Star illustrated the power of a club which was just getting into its European stride. It was such a young team,

but learning ever so fast.

"We had won the first leg in Manchester 2-1 with goals from Eddie Colman and Bobby Charlton. One goal was not a big advantage to take away, but the mood of the players was one of confidence. They had just beaten Arsenal 5-4 at Highbury while I was losing 6-5 in the reserves against Barnsley.

"We always felt we could go up a gear if it was necessary.

"I remember it was a pea-souper on the day we were flying out and I thought we would never get off, but the fog cleared.

"It was Bobby Charlton's first European trip and he had been kidded about the shortage of food in Eastern Europe. He packed his suitcase with biscuits and sweets.

"He might have been a kid, but there was nothing of the novice once the game had begun on a freezing cold day.

"We made a great start, with Tommy Taylor forcing an early error for Dennis Viollet to score after only a couple of minutes.

"I recall Sekularac as a danger, a busy little man who also chopped people. He got Kenny Morgans high on the thigh, but Charlton was

the star of the show. He scored with the kind of rocket which was to become his speciality and he also nicked in another to give us a three-goal lead and a 5-1 advantage on aggregate.

"It looked as good as over, except of course Red Star were a great team as well and they got back into it with a goal from Kostic, a penalty and a free kick from just outside the box.

"The match ended 3-3, but we were safe at 5-4 and celebrating a semi-final appearance for the second year running. It was the last match for so many, a long time ago now, but not so easy to forget for those of us still bearing the scars."

Jackie Blanchflower was grievously injured with notably a fractured pelvis and badly mangled arm. He wasn't able even to attempt to play again and not unnaturally it took him some time to come to terms with the harsh hand fate had dealt him.

But the cheerful Irishman is always joking these days. He lives just outside Manchester at Mossley with his wife Jean and their three grown-up children. He is a bookkeeper and a highly entertaining after-dinner speaker.

Jackie Blanchflower

MUNICH
25 YEARS AFTER

Daily Mirror

FORWARD WITH THE PEOPLE
No. 16,843

FRI
FEB 7
1958

SOCCER AIR TRAGEDY

Manchester United plane crashes

21 dead

AN Elizabethan air
charter to M
United football team,
lous "Busby Babes,
on take-off at Munic
Germany, yesterd
plunged the world
into mourning.

Among the twent
were United stars R
(captain), Tom
(centre forward), I
(centre half), Ed
(right half), Bill
(inside right), D
(outside left), Geo
back).

Also dead was
goalkeeper and
Frank Swift. Wh
last night fightin
was manager Ma
gave his name to
made it one of th
in football.

Twenty-three
passengers surviv
Among the de
Ledbrooke, the
ous Northern
His last big stor

● THE CRASH
Back Page and
● THE TEAM i
Centre Pages

Sport's
Day-By P
See F

THE END The chartered Elizabethan airliner shattered in a snowfield near
in which the Manchester United Munich. The pilot, Captain Jame
team was travelling home lies Thn n escaped through the roof.

THE BEGINNING This picture was Walter Crickmer secretary. Don Da
team, accompanied by Newton-town, boarded chester Directors Roger Byrne capta
the plane at Manchester on Monday. Left to can Edwards in Frank Swift tri
right, with known pictures starting with behind Scanlon in Frank Swift
airmen: Jackie Blanchflower', Billy Foulkes', Ledbrooke Da k Morre Geoff
Jones and Alf Clarke, Kenney

ABOVE: *Members of Manchester United arrive in Belgrade*

THE TEAM
IN THE PLANE CRASH
TRAGEDY

EDWARDS INJURED · FOULKES INJURED · JONES DEAD · WOOD INJURED · COLMAN DEAD · PEGG DEAD

BERRY INJURED · WHELAN DEAD · BYRNE DEAD · TAYLOR DEAD · VIOLLET INJURED

EVERY one a star! These are the eleven players who have made Manchester United League Champions for two years. This is what happened to them in yesterday's tragic crash:

DUNCAN EDWARDS. Left Half. He has broken his right thigh and fractured his ribs. He is also suffering from shock.

BILL FOULKES. Right Back. Escaped with slight injuries.

MARK JONES. Centre Half. Dead.

RAY WOOD. Reserve goalkeeper. Seriously injured.

EDDIE COLMAN. Right Half. Dead.

DAVID PEGG. Reserve Outside Left. Dead.

JOHN BERRY. Outside Right. Eye injury.

BILL WHELAN. Inside Forward and Eire international. Dead.

ROGER BYRNE. England Left Back and Captain of United. Dead.

TOMMY TAYLOR. England Centre Forward. Dead.

DENIS VIOLLET. Inside Left. Head injuries.

⤴ The last great match

THIS is a scene from Manchester United's last great match—just two days ago. Bobby Charlton is seen scoring goal No. 2 in the 3—3 draw in Belgrade, Yugoslavia.

Last night Charlton was injured and in hospital after the tragic air crash at Munich, Germany, as the team flew home.

● Harry Gregg was United's dashing young goal-keeper when this picture was taken in Belgrade on Wednesday. Last night he was recovering from slight injuries . . .

BUSBY *'little chance'*
Matt Busby, the great manager who brought Manchester United world fame, was "doing badly" last night. A doctor said he had "little chance."

SCANLON *head injuries*
Bert Scanlon, the local Manchester boy who made good, has head injuries. He recently established himself in the League side and was showing promise.

CHARLTON *head injuries*
Bobby Charlton, who is doing his Army call-up, has head injuries. Bobby is a nephew of famous former Newcastle forward Jackie Milburn.

GREGG *slight injuries*
Harry Gregg, the world's most expensive goalkeeper, was recently bought from Doncaster Rovers for £23,000. The crowds thought him worth it.

BENT *dead*
Geoffrey Bent, reserve full back, is dead. He was one of Busby's bright young men. He was all set to become a big star of the future.

BLANCHFLOWER *broken pelvis*
Jackie Blanchflower, Irish international centre half, has broken pelvis, rib injuries. He is a brother of Spurs' Danny Blanchflower.

MORGANS *injured*
Ken Morgans, Welsh outside right from Swansea. He has only just established himself in the League side, another Busby new boy of promise.

Aftermath of the disaster

In the papers the next day . . .

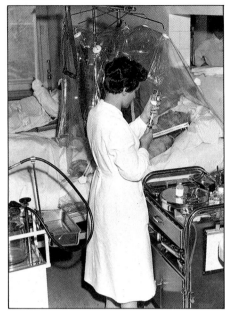

ABOVE: *Matt Busby in oxygen tent in a Munich hospital*

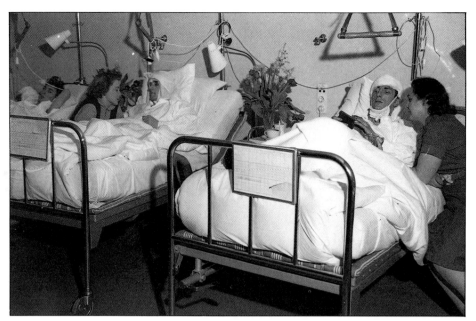

ABOVE: *Mrs Barbara Viollet (right) and Mrs Josephine Scanlon (left) visit their injured husbands*

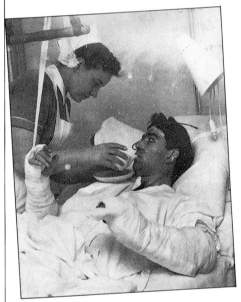

ABOVE: *Jackie Blanchflower and nurse*

ABOVE: *Sombre homecoming of United coffins*

ABOVE: *Staff members of the Munich hospital which nursed survivors arrive in Manchester at the invitation of the Mayor*

ABOVE: *Harry Gregg expresses his thanks to Sister Liselotte Pippig*

Manchester United and Benfica take to the Wembley turf for the 1968 European Cup Final

Charlton lifts the trophy for Manchester United

United show their teeth

PENALTY WINNER STARTS UPROAR

By TERENCE ELLIOTT: Manchester U. 2, Milan 1 **RATING**

I HAVE never seen ~~~~~~~~~ ~~matic as the climax to this European

DAILY EXPRESS, May 8, 1958

MAN. UTD.	2
AC MILAN	**I**

1957-58 EUROPEAN CUP, SEMI FINAL, FIRST LEG, MANCHESTER UNITED WIN 2-1

United show their teeth

Penalty winner starts uproar

By Terrence Elliott

I have never seen anything as dramatic as the climax to this European Cup semi-final at Old Trafford last night. I have never seen a player react in such anguished manner to the forfeiture of a penalty than did Milan centre half Cesare Maldini with 11 minutes to go.

And I have never seen a crowd set alight with the flame of victory as this Old Trafford when little Ernie Taylor's penalty rocketed into the net off the underside of the crossbar. They threatened to uproot the whole structure, rising as one man to greet the victory goal.

It was a tremendous second half for Manchester United, climaxed by a scene one will find difficult to forget.

Dennis Viollet hared down the right with the ball at his toes. Centre half Maldini raced out to meet him. But the dark-haired Munich survivor Viollet suddenly decided to round his man and go straight for the target.

The two of them raced shoulder to shoulder ... the Italian found he couldn't beat Viollet and hustled him off the ball.

As Danish referee Helge pointed to the spot, Maldini flung himself to the ground in anguish and the referee was surrounded by protesting Milan players.

But little Ernie Taylor, still ice-cool when all around had erupted into scenes of indescribable excitement, placed the ball carefully and flashed home the winner.

BELOW: *Gregg leaps to save from Schiaffino (No 9) of Milan*

Easy goal

Milan missed their way in the first half. Outside left Cucchiaroni and star turn inside right Bredesen dribbled the ball with such precision that United looked set for a beating.

Only defensive work saved United, only lion-like courage and ferocious tackling saved them in those dangerous moments when it was all Milan.

And it was all so easy for Milan when they took a lead in the 24th minute. Bredesen intercepted a pass from Crowther to Greaves.

The inside right slammed the ball through to Schiaffino, who glided it easily round Gregg.

But five minutes from half-time Viollet put United back in the fight, hurtling in to snap up a half-chance when Maldini mishit a back pass.

Some of United's first-half tackling made me wonder how these Milan boys could take it without retaliation.

Tottered

But in the second half when Schiaffino, wearing a large-sized strip of plaster over a cut eye following a collision with Gregg, was not nearly so effective, United showed the football we know they can play.

They really went to town . . . simply stormed into Milan with all they had. They were playing the football, too, and Milan tottered.

Buffoni made great saves from Goodwin and Taylor . . . Webster shot high over . . . and then came that penalty which overshadowed all else in this game of fighting fury.

Well done, United. Now you go to Milan with a chance to reach the final after all.

And I think you may yet achieve another feat verging on the impossible.

Was referee Helge right to award a penalty? Milan said an indirect free kick was all the offence warranted.

But to their great credit they walked off the field with handshakes all round . . . after being on the receiving end of some of the toughest tackling I have ever seen.

LOOKING BACK WITH BILL FOULKES

A total of 23 people lost their lives as a result of the air disaster at Munich on February 6, 1958.

Eight were Manchester United players, eight were journalists, three were club officials, and then there were two crew and two supporters.

There were 21 survivors, and they included nine players. Jackie Blanchflower and Johnny Berry were so badly injured they never played again.

Bill Foulkes, and Harry Gregg, hardly hurt, played immediately. Bobby Charlton, Dennis Viollet, Ray Wood, Ken Morgans, and Albert Scanlon all returned at different stages.

The last act of the team destroyed at Munich was to put Manchester United through to the semi-finals of the European Cup.

England unsympathetically deprived them of Charlton's services by taking him on a pre-World Cup tour, but Foulkes, Gregg, Morgans and Viollet played in both legs against A C Milan . . . and suffered heavy defeat.

"I think we had run out of emotional steam," says Bill Foulkes now.

"The team, brought brilliantly together by Jimmy Murphy, had performed marvels. Considering the devastating circumstances we had held our own reasonably well with a few draws in the League to finish ninth.

"We had put everything into our F A Cup ties to win through to Wembley. But we had lost that final against Bolton and by the time the European semi-final had come round I think a lot of us were pretty well drained.

"We did very well to win the first leg 2-1 at Old Trafford with a penalty from Ernie Taylor and a goal from Dennis Viollet, but we collapsed 4-0 in Milan.

"To be quite honest it's a match which for years I have tried to shut out of my mind. It was a terrible experience to lose by four goals and I have wanted to forget all about it.

"The Italian crowd, about 80,000 of them, didn't show us much sympathy. As we walked out we were bombarded with vegetables. I remember being hit by cabbages and the biggest bunch of carrots I have ever seen. They hurt, too.

"I think we battled well in the first half but it was very hostile in the giant San Siro Stadium with all the flares and fireworks.

"Milan had a good team, too, with players like Schiaffino and Liedholm, and they crushed us in the second half. I believe most of us were glad in the end to settle for 4-0.

"It was a sad end to a horrific season, but inevitable when you think about it. Emotion and spirit had kept us going for a time, but after a while it was not enough.

"I know I was happy just to rest and count my good fortune that I was at least playing football while so many of my old team-mates and friends hadn't made it."

Bill Foulkes was born at St Helens and left mining to join the club in 1949 as a part-time professional. He became a full-time player who gave great service until 1970 when he became youth team coach at Old Trafford.

He won four League championship medals, played in three F A Cup finals and of course became a European champion in 1968.

He has been a successful manager in the United States and Norway. He is presently back in the Manchester area with his wife Teresa and three grown-up children looking to break into management or coaching in English football.

Such is the esteem of his old playing colleagues that he was voted the first chairman of the newly formed association of former Manchester United players.

DAILY EXPRESS, May 14, 1958

| AC MILAN | 4 |
| MAN. UTD. | 0 |

1957-58 EUROPEAN CUP, SEMI FINAL, SECOND LEG, MILAN WIN 5-2 ON AGGREGATE

United take it on the chin

Dirtiest game I've seen

From Terence Elliott

MILAN, WEDNESDAY

TWO-MINUTE GOAL PUTS MILAN

United take it

DIRTIEST GAME I'VE SEEN

Manchester United were blasted out of the European Cup in the most foul-studded game it has been my misfortune to see.

And so was my hitherto high regard for German referee Albert Deutsch.

MANCHESTER UNITED were blasted out of the European Cup in the most foul-studded game it has been my misfortune to see.

---From TERENCE ELLIOTT: Milan, Wednesday---

Milan 4, Manchester U. 0

(Aggregate: 5—2)   **RATING** ★★★

officials and players when he clashed with Fontana.

Pearson was no more than enthusiastic — and certainly not vicious.

The crowd—100,000 I reckon—were out to needle United from even before it.

. . . so was my hitherto

out, it appeared that United were in the game again with a chance when disaster hit them again with seven minutes of the second half gone.

Milan's attack surged down in a line and Gregg ran out to meet the challenge. He was beaten when Schiaffino shot, and Cope, who . . .

sporting

particular, full marks for tremendous courage.

Down in the dressing room Jimmy Murphy agreed with me when he said United had no excuses—but he also said : "The referee gave us nothing."

Ernie Taylor was even more outspoken : "This was the worst referee I have seen in 17 years of football."

Herr Deutsch said if he had not used the whistle so much the game might have got out of hand.

The most astonishing incident in a match in which every United kick was greeted by a screaming crescendo of whistles short . . .

Play was far too rough on both sides for my stomach.

But I can find no excuse for some of Herr Deutsch's goings on.

Three times Milan officials ran on to the field to gesticulate with him.

He stopped the match to run along the line and warn them about their conduct.

But he capped the lot and made even the frenzied Italian crowd laugh when he gave a free kick in the penalty area after Colin Webster had been grabbed round the neck by

centre half Zannier, swung round and then flung to the ground in a rugby tackle.

On the other side of the fence Mark Pearson was warned three times and Colin Webster was surrounded by a group of Milan officials and players when he clashed with Fontana.

Pearson was no more than enthusiastic — and certainly not vicious.

The crowd — 100,000 I reckon — were out to needle United from the start — aye, even before it.

The leading evening sporting paper here, La

Gazzetta Dello Sport, said before the game: "Although the battle will be hard, Schiaffino and the rest of the forwards go out with the bayonets gripped in their teeth like the Fascists of old."

Screams

That must have been the big idea of the 100,000 fans who screamed and whistled at United from the moment they walked out.

Two minutes after the kick-off United were a goal down.

It was Schiaffino, the £75,000 Uruguayan centre forward, who put that ball into the net.

But even that was not the end of hope for United. With Ronnie Cope playing brilliantly and all the defence desperately holding out, it appeared that United were in the game again with a chance when disaster hit them again with seven minutes of the second half gone.

Milan's attack surged down in a line and Gregg ran out to meet the challenge. He was beaten when Schiaffino shot, and Cope, who had fallen back on the goalline, kicked the ball

clear, but only after it had bounced and hit his hand.

Maybe he was handicapped in his effort to clear by a photographer's flash bulb which blazed out in that vital moment, but it was a penalty according to the referee and Leidholm made no mistake.

It was all over for United when outside right Danova, a last-minute choice for Milan, beat Gregg again with the greatest of ease from close range after the great Schiaffino had carved a way clean through.

Schiaffino made it four ten minutes from the finish when Danova reciprocated by beating Foulkes to make it easy for the centre forward to crash the ball into the roof of the net.

I hand Pearson, Webster, Cope, Morgans and Goodwin, in particular, full marks for tremendous courage.

Down in the dressing room Jimmy Murphy agreed with me when he said United had no excuses – but he also said: "The referee gave us nothing."

Ernie Taylor was even more outspoken:

"This was the worst referee I have seen in 17 years of football."

Herr Deutsch said if he had not used the whistle so much the game might have got out of hand.

The most astonishing incident in a match in which every United kick was greeted by a screaming crescendo of whistles came shortly before the interval.

Minute's silence

With United fighting back the referee suddenly stopped the game.

We stood with the rest of the crowd for one minute's silence with out thoughts on Munich. But I now learn that that minute which put United out of their stride was in memory of an Italian F.A. official.

Now it is Milan v Real Madrid for the final in Brussels on May 28.

But United, I understand, are to be invited to compete again next season.

Manchester United eliminated from European Cup

Outclassed and outplayed by Milano

FROM HAROLD MATHER

A.C. Milano 4, Manchester Utd. 0

MILAN, MAY 14.

A.C. Milano won the right to meet Real Madrid in the final of the European Cup competition in Brussels on May 28 when they won the second leg of their semi-final with Manchester United here to-night 4-0; and so won 5-2 on aggregate.

Every team has an off-day. United had one recently in the F.A. Cup Final and it therefore was hoped that to-night they would be at their best. In the event they were outclassed and outplayed by a faster, more skilful, and more enterprising team. The combination of Schiaffino and Danova was so good and the footwork of both so deceiving that often wide gaps were woven in the visitors' defence, gaps, which, in spite of some fine work by Greaves, Gregg, and Goodwin were never really plugged.

On attack the United forwards were a second best and were not helped that often they had to forage could begin a

bar from a range of twenty yards. Relieved, Milano hit back hard. Cucciaroni shot over the leaping Gregg and also over the bar, and after a United attack during which Buffoni cleared a well-placed free kick by Greaves. Cucciaroni shot across the face of the goal after being put away by Schiaffino.

It was now all Milano again, but they were helped not a little by some strange decisions by the referee, especially with regard to supposed handling offences and to tackling by the United defenders. But United withstood the pressure and just before half-time forced their first corner, on the right, from which a header by Taylor was saved. So at the interval, United, though having had much the less of the play, still had a fighting chance.

This chance disappeared only four minutes after the restart, for a Milano attack swept up the middle. Schiaffino lobbed the ball over the head of Gregg, who may have been blinded by the flash of photographers' bulbs, and Cope, standing on the line, coul` only at th expense `m gai

THE GUARDIAN, May 14, 1958

AC MILAN	4
MAN. UTD.	0

1957-58 EUROPEAN CUP, SEMI FINAL, SECOND LEG, MILAN WIN 5-2 ON AGGREGATE

Manchester United eliminated from European Cup

Outclassed and outplayed by Milano

From Harold Mather

A.C. Milan won the right to meet Real Madrid in the final of the European Cup competition in Brussels on May 28 when they won the second leg of their semi-final with Manchester United here tonight 4-0, and so won 5-2 on aggregate.

Every team has an off-day. United had one recently in the F.A. Cup Final and it therefore was hoped that tonight they would be at their best. In the event they were outclassed and outplayed by a faster, more skilful, and more enterprising team. The combination of Schiaffino and Danova was so good and the footwork of both so deceiving that often wide gaps were woven in the visitors' defence, gaps which, in spite of some fine work by Greaves, Gregg, and Goodwin were never really plugged.

On attack the United forwards were a poor second best and were not helped by the fact that often they had to forage for the ball before they could begin a movement. Taylor and Webster tried hard and Viollet had his moments, but even so, Buffoni had not one hard ground shot to save in the match – and he is good against anything in the air. So United went down. Perhaps their play was affected by the shrill whistling of a vast crowd of some eighty thousand, perhaps by many of the decisions of the referee, A. Deusch, of Germany, perhaps it was all the result of a long, wearying season. Whatever the cause they were beaten comprehensively, their finishing being particularly weak.

Milano could not have made a better start for the game was only three minutes old when, after a move on the left by Cucciaroni and Liedholm, Schiaffino beat Gregg. As was perhaps only to be expected after such an early setback, United were all at sixes and sevens for the next twenty minutes or so. Milano won corners on the right and then the left; a mix-up in the United goal resulted in the ball bobbing about there for several seconds before it was cleared; and then Danova, given a fine through pass by Bredesen, who bobbed up in all kinds of positions, shot just over the bar from twenty yards out.

Hereabouts United gradually began to pull themselves together. Webster, being tackled from behind, shot wide; Viollet shot over the bar; and then, after 30 minutes, United had a good chance which, alas, went begging. Webster made the running, passed to Morgans and, from the latter's cross, Taylor blazed over the bar from a range of twenty yards. Relieved, Milano hit back hard. Cucciaroni shot over the leaping Gregg and also over the bar, and after a United attack during which Buffoni cleared a well-placed free kick by Greaves, Cucciaroni shot across the face of the goal after being put

away by Schiaffino.

It was now all Milano again, but they were helped not a little by some strange decisions by the referee, especially with regard to supposed handling offences and to tackling by the United defenders. But United withstood the pressure and just before half-time forced their first corner, on the right, from which a header by Taylor was saved. So at the interval, United, though having had much the less of the play, still had a fighting chance.

This chance disappeared only four minutes after the restart, for a Milano attack swept up the middle, Schiaffino lobbed the ball over the head of Gregg, who may have been blinded by the flash of photographers' bulbs, and Cope, standing on the line, could save only at the expense of handling. Liedholm gave Gregg no chance with the penalty. In the next minute Milano almost scored again, Greaves clearing off the line after Danova had screwed the ball round the back of Gregg. No matter how they tried United could not find their feet. They were, it seemed, troubled by the grass which,

at least on the wings, was long. Certainly passes went astray frequently and, as a consequence, the forwards never really were in the picture as an attacking unit.

Some of the referee's decisions still remained strange, but there was no doubting which was the better side. Taylor once was unlucky with a hard shot which beat the leaping Buffoni but passed over the bar, and once Webster might have been awarded a penalty against Beraldo after his header had been saved by Buffoni at the second attempt. But the speed, the beautifully controlled quick passing, and the fine positional sense of Milano was telling its tale.

Thus, it came as no surprise when Schiaffino paved the way for a goal by Danova and then scored himself, the goals coming within seven minutes of each other. Some fifteen minutes still remained but United now were a beaten team. Their players never gave up, but they never worked smoothly. Positional changes forward had no effect and at the end Milano were well on top.

The Munich air crash of 1958 had plunged Manchester United into tragic turmoil and a desperate period of rebuilding.

But Sir Matt Busby, displaying his great managerial gifts of patience, vision and judgement, gradually pulled the club back into shape. He went boldly into the transfer market for players like Albert Quixall, David Herd, Maurice Setters, Denis Law and Pat Crerand before being rewarded with the FA Cup in 1963 with a team skippered by Noel Cantwell.

A 3-1 victory at Wembley against Leicester City launched the Reds into the European Cup Winners Cup in 1963-64. This was the season which saw George Best make his debut to help the team finish second in the League to win entry into the Inter Cities Fairs Cup.

United were in full flow now and with winger John Connelly added to the team they won the 1965 championship to keep their European run going with entry again in the European Cup.

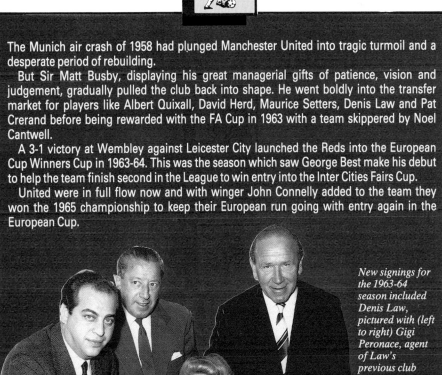

New signings for the 1963-64 season included Denis Law, pictured with (left to right) Gigi Peronace, agent of Law's previous club Torino, Jimmy Murphy, Matt Busby

DAILY TELEGRAPH, May 29, 1963

MAN UTD.	3
LEICESTER CITY	**I**

1963 F.A. CUP FINAL, MANCHESTER UNITED WIN 3-1

Busby's New Team Match His Former Babes

Law and Crerand Baffle Leicester in Continental Style

By Donald Saunders

Manchester United, who only a few weeks ago had fallen so far from glory that they looked like slipping ignominiously out of the First Division, will be back in Europe next season as worthy representatives of British football. A thoroughly-merited, handsomely-achieved victory over disappointing Leicester at Wembley on Saturday has earned United, the first English team to follow the European Cup trail, a place alongside Spurs in the Cup-Winners' competition.

And no one who saw them rise brilliantly to the challenge of Saturday's big occasion will doubt their ability to make Manchester United as great an attraction on the Continent as they were in the 50's.

A series of spiritless, unenterprising performances spread over a number of years had convinced me by Saturday morning that United were a poor side, content to live on the glittering reputation of their predecessors. By teatime that same day such thoughts seemed ludicrous.

As Cantwell led his troops on a lap of honour, everyone knew that here were a team of spirit, pride, skill and intelligence, a team, indeed, of true thoroughbreds, that fully deserved to climb up beside the Busby Babes of the 40's and 50's.

Despite the failure of Leicester to move out of their defensive shell, this was one of the better post-war finals. Our thanks for that go entirely to United.

HIGHEST LEVEL
Comparable artistry

The football they played suffered little in comparison with the artistry of Milan and Benfica which had pleased us at this same stadium only four days earlier.

Even Rivera and Eusebio, the bright young stars of European soccer, did nothing on Wednesday that Law did not equal on Saturday. No Italian or Portuguese half-back showed greater intelligence or craftsmanship than did Crerand. And the teamwork which won Milan the European championship was no sounder than that which earned United the Cup.

It was United's possession of this last quality that most surprised me. They have long been renowned for their collection of brilliant, if temperamental, individuals. On Saturday, for the first time, this expensive talent blended perfectly to produce a superb team effort.

Matt Busby, United's patient Scottish manager, must take a major share of the credit, for it was he who kept faith with these men despite disappointment after disappointment.

It was he, too, who decided on bringing Law and Crerand to Old Trafford, a move which had looked like proving to be a rash gamble.

WISDOM CLEAR
Determined to succeed

But Mr. Busby's wisdom is now clear to all. His two compatriots, themselves inspired by a great Wembley occasion, in turn acted as an inspiration to their collegues.

I have never seen Law play better. Audacious, slippery as an eel, driven to greater and greater effort by a very Scottish determination to succeed, this volatile young man unravelled Leicester's defensive web and cast it contemptuously to the winds.

At his elbow always was his fellow-Scot, Crerand, a half-back often praised for his skill but, since crossing the border, consistently accused of slowness. Crerand soon found the pace of this game and exercised arrogant

BUSBY'S NEW TEAM MATCH HIS FORMER BABES

Law and Crerand baffle Leicester in Continental style
By DONALD SAUNDERS
Manchester .... (1) 3   Leicester .... (0) 1

Pat Crerand, with (left to right) Les Olive, United club secretary, Matt Busby, Jimmy Murphy

authority in midfield. Leicester could neither frustrate nor counter this canny Scotsman's determined probing.

Charlton, the wayward genius, again looked every inch an international winger and on the other flank Giles at last fulfilled the promise of his early days. In the middle, Quixall, the forgotten "golden boy" of yesteryear, gave a new generation some indication of why he was once thought to be the answer to all England's inside-forward problems.

Meanwhile, Herd, by snapping up two goals made all Arsenal supporters regret, perhaps for the first time, his departure from Highbury to Old Trafford.

Setters, too, made an important contribution to victory by keeping a firm grip on his fiery temperament and giving a sensible, restrained performance of defensive and attacking football as Crerand's partner.

Foulkes, like Charlton, seeking his first winner's medal in three final appearances, was as sound and solid as ever, and Cantwell and Dunne played Leicester's much-vaunted wingers, Riley and Stringfellow, out of the game.

Even Gaskell, clearly the most nervous player on the pitch, ultimately conquered the jitters and responded ably to the few calls made on his services.

OVER THE TOP?
Seemed stale

But now the tumult and the shouting have died we are still left to wonder what happened to Leicester, the club who were once set for the double yet ended the season with neither Championship nor Cup.

Were they "over the top"? I think so. Physically and mentally they seemed stale. From time to time one was given glimpses of the modern, intricate pattern that made them the most discussed side of the season.

Rarely did we see them break quickly from defence, a move which had won most of their victories. Where once it had been difficult to separate Leicester's defence from attack, this time there were two entities, with nothing and no one to link them.

Leicester so badly needed a dominant character, a Law or a Crerand, to turn a wan-looking, one-pace, defensively-minded team into a lively force. Young Cross, a tireless worker, tried so hard to do this but as yet lacks the experience for the job. So Leicester, unable to raise the game and hit back at United, eventually went quietly to defeat.

LEFT: *Passport to Europe – United captain Noel Cantwell tosses the FA Cup high after his team's 3-1 victory over Leicester City. Behind him (from the left) are Tony Dunne, Charlton, Crerand, Quixall, Herd*

BELOW: *Triumphant homecoming to Manchester with the FA Cup*

IN THE BALANCE
Banks drops centre

Possibly things would have been different had they snapped up one of several early chances, instead of allowing United to snatch the lead. That all-important first goal came in the 29th minute, following an interchange of passes between Herd and Law, which left Charlton with the chance to hammer the ball goalwards.

Banks smothered the shot and it was cleared towards a sadly out of touch Gibson, who allowed Crerand to beat him to the ball. Crerand's accurate, low cross was taken on by Law with his left foot, then thumped into the net with his right.

A half-hearted second-half rally by Leicester was brought to an abrupt end with another United goal. Again Charlton let go one of his thunderbolts, Banks could only parry the shot and Herd put the rebound over the line.

A well-taken, diving header by Keyworth revived Leicester's hopes briefly near the end. But in the 85th minute Banks horrified every England player and official in the stadium by dropping a high centre from Giles and allowing Herd to ram it home.

So once again a team whose progress to Wembley had been admirably consistent lost their touch at the wrong moment while their opponents found their true form when it was most needed.

Manchester United held to a draw

From ALBERT BARHAM: Willem II 1, Manchester U 1

Rotterdam, September 25
Willem II of Tilburg, the lowly Dutch team of part-time players, live to fight again in the European Cupwinners Cup. Tonight in the Stadion Feijenoord, they ˡᵉˢᵉʳᵛᵉᵈˡʸ held Manchester

proved that point; so too did Timmermans and Koopal, but behind all their efforts there seemed just too much eager anticipation. A great many long clearances not seemingly meant for anyone in particular were thumped hopefully inˡᵒ ᵗ Manchᵉ

THE GUARDIAN, September 25, 1963

WILLEM II TILBURG	1
MAN. UTD.	1

1963-64 EUROPEAN CUP WINNERS CUP, FIRST ROUND, FIRST LEG, DRAW 1-1

Manchester United held to a draw

From Albert Barham
ROTTERDAM, SEPTEMBER 25

Willem II of Tilburg, the lowly Dutch team of part-time players, live to fight again in the European Cup Winners Cup. Tonight in the Stadion Feijenoord, they deservedly held Manchester United to a draw 1-1 and can only

hope Manchester United play as uninspiringly when they next meet in the second leg of the first round at Old Trafford, on October 15. To crown a thoroughly unhappy evening for Manchester, Herd was sent off by M. Tricot, the French referee, after a foul on Brooymans, after 80 minutes.

This was not a match of great skills. Willem's defence was too determined for that to be allowed and United scarcely could seem to find even the necessary inspiration to outwit it. Yet Manchester, although they have been out of European competitions for the past five years, have used their many friendly matches against Continental teams to keep them abreast of the trends, particularly of massed defences.

Manchester United have been affectionately remembered in Holland, looked upon in fact, according to the programme notes, as the personification of football. How far they fell below that standard last night. In this vast, grey upturned bowl, there were great acreages of empty seats. For all the affection, few apparently wanted to witness an expected massacre of this Dutch Second Division team. How wrong they all were: in fact Willem rescued the match from its drabness with a spirited attempt in the dying minutes which almost brought them success.

Hit a post

Inexplicably, United made very heavy weather of the match. The confidence and the expected overwhelming superiority was, to say the least, dormant. There were just a few arching leaps from Law, and a shot which hit a post 15 minutes from time, to remind one that it was there at all. It took a snap goal in the tenth minute to bring the game to life, if only briefly, and against all the odds it was Willem, who scored. Koopal, a little older now than when he played for Holland, used all his old cunning to draw Foulkes, slip a pass to Louer and the wing-forward cut in to the centre to flash the ball past Gregg.

That moment seemed to set the pattern of the game and possibly taught Manchester United that they proved that point; so too did Timmermans and Koopal, but behind all their efforts there seemed just too much eager anticipation. A great many long clearances not seemingly meant for anyone in particular were thumped hopefully into the Manchester half and eagerly the Dutch forwards chased the improbable in search of the seemingly impossible, for Dunne, Foulkes, and Cantwell were seldom caught again.

It is all credit to Willem, who, from the tenth minute, developed a rugged defensive barrier in which van Dormalen, playing his first senior game, and Vriens, another of the younger players, quite competently contained all Law's inventiveness and Chisnall's shrewdness, and seemed to overwhelm young Sadler.

Instead of the expected easy United victory, the match became one of increasing raggedness and a grim struggle in midfield. It was just as well that the night was a warm one, for the goalkeepers had little to do. Gregg, especially, for at least Dijkmans had a couple of shots from Law to deal with and he saw another fly off Law's knee past a post. Perhaps the greatest shock was reserved for the final 15 minutes when Willem came out of their defensive shell long enough for Louer to burst through, and many thought that his shot had crept under Gregg's falling body over the line. But it was not to be, and in the almost desperate minutes which followed Herd was sent off the field. This was not by any means one of Manchester's better days. No doubt they will right things at Old Trafford.

RIGHT: *Law (centre) flicks in his second goal in United's second leg tie against Willem II Tilburg*

SIX-GOAL BARRAGE SINKS THE DUTCH

By RONALD CROWTHER

Manchester U. 6, Willem II 1

MANCHESTER UNITED cruised gaily on last night to round two of the European Cupwinners' Cup tournament with a second-leg victory which gave them a 7—2 aggregate over the Dutch Second Division team.

DAILY MAIL, October 15, 1963

MAN. UTD.	6
WILLEM II TILBURG	**1**

1963-64 EUROPEAN CUP WINNERS CUP, FIRST ROUND, SECOND LEG, MANCHESTER UNITED WIN 7-2 ON AGGREGATE

Six-goal barrage sinks the Dutch

By Ronald Crowther

Manchester United cruised gaily on last night to round two of the European Cup Winners' Cup tournament with a second-leg victory which gave them a 7-2 aggregate over the Dutch Second Division team.

It was almost with the ease of men strolling through a field of tulips that they disposed of the obscure little team from Tilburg. It is doubtful if United could ever hope to have it as easy in any competitive game.

For the humble Dutch part-timers who were so strangely out of touch after their game of a lifetime in the drawn first leg in Rotterdam three weeks ago, the dikes burst after only seven minutes when Maurice Setters slammed United into the lead.

After that it was always clear it was just a matter of time before the flood of red-shirted raiders burst through.

Barrage

Dennis Law, bounding back to dominate the scene after his lay-off through injury, had a hat-trick. It was he who sank the Tilburg team with two goals in the 12th and 31st minutes. Then, in an exciting four-minute barrage in the second half, Bobby Charlton, Phil Chisnall, and Law, ripped home three more.

It could have been a six-goal lead for United even before half-time if only three clear-cut openings created by the clever, unobstrusive worker Chisnall had been turned to advantage.

In any case, Law should have had a penalty when the desperate Dutch goalkeeper, Dijckmans, grabbed him by the legs – Rugby style – just before the break.

Pathetic little Willem, sporting to the last kick and scrupulously clean in all their desperate chasing and tackling, didn't even score their goal. It was the gift of United captain Noel Cantwell in the 37th minute when, without warning to goalkeeper Harry Gregg, he turned and cracked the ball past him into the net.

Before a 42,672 crowd that grew strangely silent at times, the game sagged for lengthy stretches as United tended to treat it purely as an opportunity to put on an exhibition of individual ballwork and over-elaborate passes.

THE TIMES, December 3, 1963

SPURS	2
MAN. UTD.	**0**

1963-64 EUROPEAN CUP WINNERS CUP, SECOND ROUND, FIRST LEG, TOTTENHAM HOTSPUR WIN 2-0

Small error with big consequences

Spurs half-way home against Manchester United

From Our Association Football Correspondent

Tottenham Hotspur and Manchester United, after a tense hiatus of a week, last night got through the first leg of their European Cup Winners' Cup tie under the floodlights of White Hart Lane. Spurs, with two goals in the bank, may regard themselves as half way home, for there is one important point to be taken into consideration. This is that today Law, the master of United, may well find himself suspended for his recent behaviour which could keep him out of the second leg at Old Trafford next Tuesday. This could be a decisive point.

Yet two-thirds of the way through last night's match Manchester themselves were half way home, and perhaps even more than that, for it was not until 67 minutes had gone that Tottenham at last burst through the solid, red barn door that had been put up in their faces by a magnificent Manchester defence. It was Mackay, in a scintillating move with Jones down the left, who finally crashed down the barrier. And even then, with only four minutes left and a single goal separating the two sides, United must have felt their chances bright of stepping farther into Europe again.

Transport of delight

But disaster struck them as the last grains of time were sliding away. Dunne who, until then,

had made scarcely the semblance of a mistake at right back, tried to pass back to Gaskell, his goalkeeper. It was a half stabbed pass; the ball never reached his colleague. In a flash Dyson had slipped in to whip the ball home and send Tottenham into transports of delight. That small error may yet decide things. But football is its own master and, even should Law be missing, United are a great club with a great fighting spirit and many other fine players who may yet see them out of the wood.

White Hart Lane last night, with its 60,000 crowd a heap of expectation – and a heap of £30,000 in the till – was roofed in by a dark, cloudy sky. One had expected Manchester to adopt the formally accepted pattern of defence away from home, switching to offence at home. That is the way these two-way European Cup-ties are played. It is the side that can produce the best of both these worlds over three hours that usually emerges the victor.

ABOVE: *Gaskell leaps, but is beaten by Mackay's shot as Tottenham score in the first leg match*

SMALL ERROR WITH BIG CONSEQUENCES

◆

SPURS HALF-WAY HOME AGAINST MANCHESTER UNITED

From Our Association Football Correspondent

Tottenham Hotspur 2, Manchester United 0

Tottenham Hotspur and Manchester [United] after a tense hiatus of a week,

always conscious, too, of the fact that behind their backs there was always a threat of Law darting through

Defensive screen

Stiles, at inside right, was expected to employ himself largely in a defensive screen around Gaskell, a young goalkeeper playing only his second senior match of the season after a broken thumb. If ever there was a hero on the field it was Gaskell. By a series of courageous and often finely timed saves he kept hauling Manchester back into life. Ahead of him, too, there were Cantwell, his captain, Setters, a terrier at wing half, and on the other flank Crerand, the dynamo of midfield. Still, up to half-time, Stiles played an attacking role, probing where he could and nudging when he could the dynamic Law into action.

So Tottenham, as the minutes unwound, found the problem of beating this mobile Manchester side increasingly difficult; always conscious, too, of the fact that behind their backs there was always a threat of Law darting through in his exciting fashion on the long Manchester cross passes. Once or twice Tottenham found themselves against the ropes, covering up momentarily as Law and Charlton flashed in their darts. But mostly it was Tottenham, without the guiding finger and the logic of Blanchflower behind them, who kept trying to find the combination to unlock Manchester's defence.

Tottenham had one great chance early on to do just this and it was Greaves, of all people, who let it slip. He was set free by a chip from Mackay, Mackay the warrior who was here, there, and everywhere from the first whistle to the last. Greaves was now clear, hardly a quarter of an hour had gone by. He moved left, took aim, steadied and hit the side net. He had had too much time to think. If only he had reacted as he had done right at the start, when he angled home a beautiful shot from White's pass instinctively, only to find himself offside! Once, too, the brave Gaskell somehow or other palmed away a flick by Dyson from Mackay's cross and so the Tottenham bombardment left them still blank to half-time.

Now it was that Stiles withdrew his horns into defence. Manchester United, it seemed, had set their plans upon a quick goal, or if not that at least holding the opposition to half-time and then crowding them out. Up till midway through the second half they succeeded. It was a man's match and in the vast crowd, swaying and surging like a sea, there was a concentration of anguish.

Flying Heels

But Tottenham in the end, had forces too powerful within them to submit, Mackay drove them on relentlessly, and though the flying heels of Jones were clipped splendidly by Cantwell's positional play there was Greaves flitting from point to point, trying to find a gap. There was Smith hurtling his huge frame, trying to make the gap, like some human torpedo.

At last it came. With 23 minutes left a flowering move down the left between Dyson and Jones enabled Jones to draw a red herring across United, execute a perfect back heel, and Mackay, thundering behind him, was through the gap to send a thunderbolt to the top corner. Mackay thereupon did a double somersault to show his own feelings as the crowd exploded. Still, there was always Law, now the central spearhead of Manchester's long-range attacks.

Twice Brown tipped over the bar from him and once, as Brown and Norman hesitated, Law, quick as light, was between them only to flick the ball inches too high. That was Manchester's last gesture of the night. Within seconds at the other end came Dunne's wretched error, something that he must now accept as part of a personal burden.

BELOW: *Activity in the Manchester goalmouth as Tottenham put pressure on Gaskell*

DAILY HERALD, December 10, 1963

ABOVE: *Herd's header hits home – second leg against Tottenham*

| MAN. UTD. | 4 |
| SPURS | 1 |

1963-64 EUROPEAN CUP WINNERS CUP, SECOND ROUND, SECOND LEG, MANCHESTER UNITED WIN 4-3 ON AGGREGATE

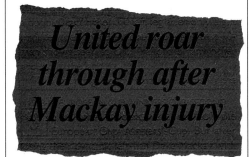

United roar through after Mackay injury

By Peter Lorenzo

Spurs, the holders, are out of the European Cup Winners' Cup. But after losing their dynamic left-half Dave Mackay with a double fracture of the left leg after only eight minutes they produced one of the greatest 10-man shows seen at Old Trafford or any other ground in the land.

Two snorting Bobby Charlton goals in the last 13 minutes – the winner, to give United a 4-3 aggregate triumph, coming just three minutes from time, – left Spurs without any tangible reward from their gallant display.

United go on to maintain English interest in the European competition, yet unquestionably it was the spirit, bravery, and unflinching determination of Spurs that demanded the lion's share of the credit here last night.

The sickening injury to Mackay came in the eighth minute just two minutes after David Herd had dived full length to head United's first goal, from a neat cross by young David Sadler. It was a complete accident, yet a risk that was ever present to such a courageous player as Mackay, who doesn't know the meaning of the word fear.

Sadly but characteristically it was from a 50-50 chance that the swashbuckling Scot was hurt. The ball had spun loose out to the left of the penalty area following a Spurs raid.

It was from a similar position that Mackay lashed in his thunderbolt goal last week. But this time as he swept in so did United left-back

MAN. UNITED 4
SPURS 1

Noel Cantwell and down the pair crashed.

Mackay still got in his shot ... the ball was deflected for a corner ... but although Cantwell was on his feet in a flash, Mackay lay there unmoving. Cantwell took one look at him and waved frantically for the stretchers.

With a characteristic show of defiance and courage Mackay refused to lay down as the ambulancemen carried him off.

Despite the handicap of losing such a driving, dynamic player, despite the non-stop roaring of the 48,639 crowd who could now sense victory for United so close to hand ... Spurs refused to submit, or even wilt.

Setters shows the way

In the first-half Maurice Setters tried hard to infuse method and calmness into his side. He showed the way himself with a terrific 35-yard shot that snapped against the bar.

And it was the stirring Setters who did most of the work, for United's second goal in the 54th-minute to restore the aggregate score to 2-2.

From Quixall's corner the towering Norman headed out, but Setters promptly headed back and the ball was bouncing for goal before Herd made sure.

Spurs' immediate answer was a crisp four man move featuring Dyson, Smith, White, and Greaves. From White's left-wing cross Greaves scored to make it 2-1.

The tension and the fury mounted. In a jarring clash Maurice Setters cut his head badly. He was helped off, had six stitches put in the wound, then returned after 13 minutes to play as furiously as ever.

Ron Henry was limping with cramp and fatigue as the battle raged. Then two minutes after he had blazed over an open goal, match-winner Bobby Charlton bobbed up in the inside-right position and cracked in a rocket left-foot volley from a long pass by Pat Crerand.

Bitterest blow to come

Spurs were very nearly spent ... but the bitterest blow was still to come. From another crisp Crerand pass, Charlton, again lurking in the inside-right position, smashed in a storming right-foot shot which Bill Brown could only push harder into the back of the net.

It was all over. Spurs out. United go marching on ... but this is a match that will be remembered for the courage and fighting spirit of a footballing team who played football until the last gasp.

DAILY HERALD, February 26, 1964

MAN. UTD. 4

SPORTING LISBON   **1**

1963-64 EUROPEAN CUP WINNERS CUP, QUARTER FINAL, FIRST LEG, MANCHESTER UNITED WIN 4-1

Lion-tamer Law

Busby boys need that killer touch

By Steve Richards

Generous Manchester United, lacking the ruthlessness of a really great team, needed two Denis Law penalties to grab a three-goal advantage in the first leg of the European Cup Winners' Cup quarter-final at Old Trafford last night.

The echo of their incredible goal misses may be heard in the second leg in Lisbon next week, even though the dusky Portuguese didn't look well enough equipped to pull back such a deficit.

Their flimsy imitation of the offside trap was smashed into unrecognisable pieces by United's creative work. This was often brilliant. The finishing, I regret, was sometimes pathetic.

I cannot over stress the value of Law's hat trick against the lions of Portugal, and the daring goalkeeping of David Gaskell which plugged gaps that opened alarmingly in the first-half.

BELOW: *Law (far left) watches the first of his three goals hit the back of the Sporting Lisbon net*

ABOVE: *Referee Martens of the Netherlands is besieged by protesting Lisbon players in the first leg tie with United*

At first it looked like being the most kind-hearted United act since they threw a splash banquet after the F A Cup final in May.

Two passes by Law and George Best dynamited the offside trap. They made two glorious chances for Bobby Charlton and Nobby Stiles. But each guilty man finished sloppily.

Deceived

Law was needed to show them how. He did.

Sometimes he was so fast he deceived the linesmen into thinking he was offside when he wasn't really.

But in the 22nd minute he timed his dart for Charlton's through ball intelligently, side-stepped two recovering, stumbling defenders and sidefooted the ball away from goalkeeper Carvalho's left hand.

After he had had a shot deflected on to the bar, Charlton struck in the 39th minute with a deceptive shot from the edge of the penalty area. It was stronger than it looked, Carvalho half-stopped the ball, but it still sped over the line.

Law had provided the final pass, and pushed the score along to 3-0 with his first penalty after he – of all people – had unbelievably headed wide almost from off the goal-line.

This 59th minute spot kick glided the ball away from the goal-keeper's right hand after Stiles had been upended. Few Portuguse protests here, but when Charlton was felled 14 minutes later the unexciting Portuguse became over excitable and both linesmen had to rush onto the field to protect the threatened referee.

Dutch referee Johann Martens, nearly 6½ft tall – and bald – nearly toppled over as he back pedalled from the angry Lisbon lads who had been given a flash of hope in between the penalties by right-winger Silva's superb 25 yard drive which reduced the lead to 3-1.

Carelessness

But the storm ended and Law forced the ball into the other corner with this spot kick. No more scoring, but the unforgiveable careless-ness in the target area continued.

The Portuguese complained about the re-feree, but honestly, they could not have been more kindly treated than by United's rusty shooting.

Vigorous Maurice Setters shot over in the 81st minute when he didn't seem to realise Law was better positioned to score.

Even in injury time this non-stop United produced yet another opportunity, but Charl-ton shot the wrong side of the post when I thought a pass to the waiting Law would have been more beneficial.

Law's speed of thought and movement was beyond the Portuguese but I am sure that – perfectionist that he is – he'd be the first to agree with me United were just not ruthless enough, and this could trip them up against more formidable opposition.

MANCHESTER UNITED GAIN POSITION OF STRENGTH

From Our Association Football Correspondent

Manchester United 4, Sporting Club of Lisbon 1

Manchester United, unless they do something foolish, virtually have one foot in the semi-final round of the Euro-···nners' cun. ¹ast night

THE TIMES, February 26, 1964

MAN. UTD.   **4**

SPORTING LISBON   **1**

1963-64 EUROPEAN CUP WINNERS CUP, QUARTER FINAL, FIRST LEG, MANCHESTER UNITED WIN 4-1

Manchester United Gain Position of Strength

From Our Association Football Correspondent

M anchester United, unless they do something foolish, virtually have one foot in the semi-final round of the European Cup Winners' Cup. Last night, before a baying 60,000 crowd at Old Trafford, they built up a lead of three clear goals over Sporting Club of Lisbon and now go to Portugal a week hence able to speak from a position of strength.

The gap, indeed, might have been wider. United were helped in the second half by two penalty kicks, granted by a referee from the Netherlands, and, although the second seemed to make some sense, the first was rather like double Dutch. Certainly one felt very sad for the Portuguese at such a blow at such a moment when Stiles was tackled in the penalty area. But that is the way things go and, in fact, had not the United forward line, Law apart, been in one of its more prodigal moods, the Manchester total might well have been seven without any help from the referee.

At Close Range

Three times within the first quarter of an hour before they opened their score Charlton, Stiles, and then Setters should have hit the back of Carvalho's net at close range; and was who set Manchester United on their way. And, needless to say, it was a sudden long through pass from Charlton that cut open the sensitive Portuguese heart. Going twice in the closing moments Setters again and then Herd should have widened the gap. As it is, though, the Portuguese seem to be on the rim of defeat.

The fact was now that these Portuguese, for all their subtle close forward play and their moments in attack that bubbled like champagne, had no defence up to the task of putting handcuffs on Charlton and Law, who proved once more to be the terrible twins through the middle. The Lisbon defence, in fact, appeared complete strangers to the long through pass, and it was here that Law and Charlton, time after time, caught a defence trying to play the off-side game and, in the process, standing far too square, with Gomes and Hilario hugging the flanks and leaving their centre half, Baptista, like an unshorn lamb in the middle.

The real difference, indeed, was that United played along the lines of longitude and aimed at this central desert and achieved a reward that should have been greater. In contrast the clever little Portuguese replies were worked too often across the lines of latitude and though much of it looked pretty enough in attack their whole effort in the end was stunted. If there is to be any rescue for the Portuguese then they will have to think, and think quickly, and redraft their whole defensive plan when they take the field on their own stadium in the district of Alvalade in the suburbs of Lisbon.

But all things being equal it seems that the whole tie is now beyond them. Law once again was the dominating figure. Even at a distance one could almost see his eyes ablaze with excitement; his speed was that of a humming bird's wing. He vibrated with danger. He was mischievous, eager and in everything he did he offered a sharp and shining cutting edge to his play.

Law was like some circus performer glittering in the giant spotlights that bathed him from the edge of the stadium. He it was who set Manchester United on their way. And, needless to say, it was a sudden long through pass from Charlton that cut open the sensitive Portuguese heart. Going like the wind, Law nodded the ball down, beat one man, held off another who could get no closer than his elbows, drew out the goalkeeper, slipped the ball home into the top pocket, as it were, and wheeled away in exultation.

By half-time, the Portuguese had switched back to a usual formation with Mendes and Carlos swopping places, Mendes having begun at inside right instead of right half with the intention of playing as a defensive inside forward. But it made no difference, and as half-time came it was now Law's turn to return the compliment to Charlton. Again there was the sudden long through pass sweeping behind the square defence. In roared Charlton, his right foot was too hot to handle and the ball rolled over the line, in spite of Carvalho's brave effort to parry the rocket.

At the change of ends, with the Old Trafford crowd chanting and baying for more goals, there was almost another glorious consummation as Law leap-frogged over Batista to head Charlton's cross from the left just past the post. There was soon also a tremendous save by Carvalho to a lobbed shot by Best, a flowing, promising young winger of the future. But with half an hour to go came the Dutch decision that might well have cut the heart out of the Portuguese. Stiles was tackled as he tried to reach Charlton's long cross pass and a penalty that seemed harsh indeed, was the sentence dealt out. Law calmly stroked the ball past the goalkeeper's right side.

Finest Shot

One could almost hear the sighs of the Portuguese supporters who had made the long journey. But far from immediately cutting out the Lisbon heart, Figuetredo a clever centre forward full of glances and flicks, sent Silva through the middle and the finest shot of the night, from 25 yards, went past Gaskell to his top corner like a streak of light.

United now for a spell went ragged but Law and Charlton – with little help let it be said from Stiles and Herd – recaptured the rhythm. Best sent Charlton in, he was downed and there was another penalty. The Portuguese protested vigorously but the Dutch official stood his ground firmly and Law, now picking his spot past Carvalho's left, scored his third goal in a match for the seventh time this season. That was the end though there could have been more in the kitty for United before the whistle.

Still United are riding their tricycle in the Football League, the F.A. Cup and now the European Cup Winners' Cup firmly enough. They may wobble a bit on Saturday against Sunderland unless Herd, Stiles and Crerand can find the form that eluded them last night.

THE TIMES, March 18, 1964

SPORTING LISBON	5
MAN. UTD.	0

1963-64 EUROPEAN CUP WINNERS CUP, QUARTER FINAL, SECOND LEG, SPORTING LISBON WIN 6-4 ON AGGREGATE

Manchester Disunited

Overwhelmed by Lisbon XI

LISBON, March 18

Manchester United's hopes of keeping the European Cup Winners' Cup in England crumbled in an avalanche of goals at the Alvalade Stadium here tonight.

United were but a shadow of the side that tore the heart out of Sunderland just one week ago. Crerand and Setters were completely unable to get to grips with Silva and Geo and the Sporting attack, which had seemed so inept, even naive, at Old Trafford, suddenly burst into life. They were two goals up in the first nine minutes and although United still led on aggregate by the odd goal, 4-3, at the interval, three goals in the opening nine minutes of the second half sealed their fate.

Lisbon achieved just the start they must have been hoping for when Silva pulled back a goal only two minutes after the start. Manchester United were under severe pressure and when Dunne handled the ball the referee had no hesitation in awarding a penalty, whereupon Silva exacted due retribution from the penalty spot.

Manchester, took fleeting command, and Setters went close with a header from a corner, but the match was still only 12 minutes old when Silva, this time, without the protection of the penalty spot, wove his way skilfully through and beat Gaskell.

Manchester were a sad sight, vulnerable in defence and disjointed in attack. Well as they were doing, Lisbon would have gone still farther ahead, even at this stage, had their finishing measured up to the approach work.

Out of their Depth

Sporting dominated entirely, with Law and Charlton reduced to nonentities. Best tried one or two runs on the left wing, but was easily checked, and the United forwards looked wholly out of their depth until the thirty-eighth minute, when Law, suddenly finding himself with a loose ball, hit a post. The ball was scrambled clear.

United's tackling in defence drew whistles from the crowd, and on one occasion they came near to conceding a penalty through a robust tackle. Law incurred the displeasure of the crowd when he crashed into the Portuguese goalkeeper just before half-time, but the referee ignored a plea for an infringement.

At half-time Sporting led 2-0, having reduced their deficit to only one goal. They had looked much the better side, with United a disorganized force and Law and Charlton hardly evident.

Off Balance

United badly needed a goal when the second half started, but within two minutes Sporting had levelled the overall scores. Geo, the former Brazilian player, scored.

The Manchester defence was caught off balance as the Portuguese attacked down the right wing, and clever short passing by Silva and Mascarenhas left Geo with a good chance which he took with skill and calmness.

The 50,000 crowd were really on their toes, and they exploded as Morais, the winger, seized on a pass from the right and scored to put Sporting ahead on aggregate. This was a remarkable setback for United, who showed little talent against this fastmoving Lisbon side. It was not long before Sporting went further ahead. Silva scored from close in seven minutes after half-time to make their lead 5-0.

Poor Shadow

United were a poor shadow of the team of the past weeks, and Mascarenhas nearly put Sporting farther ahead with a grand shot which scraped the post after he had beaten three men.

The United attack was innocuous, and the defence sluggish and ready prey for the lightning Portuguese forwards. Carvalho, in the Portuguese goal, had little to do. The nearest Manchester came to a goal was after 67 minutes, when they were awarded a free-kick just outside the penalty area. The ball was slipped to Charlton, but he shot just wide.

THE GUARDIAN, September 23, 1964

DJURGARDENS IF	1
MAN. UTD.	1

1964-65 INTER CITIES FAIRS CUP, FIRST ROUND, FIRST LEG, DRAW 1-1

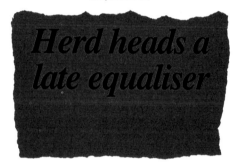

Herd heads a late equaliser

LOOKING BACK
■ WITH PAT CRERAND ■

Sir Matt Busby was renowned for his dignity and cool head ... but he did have his more volatile moments, and one of them was undoubtedly in Portugal following a 5-0 defeat against Sporting Lisbon in the European Cup Winners Cup.

"Matt ranted and raged, he went off his head with us," says Pat Crerand as he looked back on Manchester United's only humiliation in Europe.

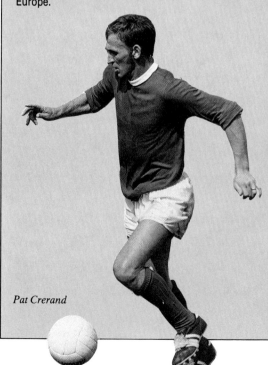

Pat Crerand

Manchester United slithered to a 1-1 draw in their Inter-Cities' Fairs cup-tie against Djurgardens on a rain-soaked pitch here tonight.

The United should move into the second round when they meet the Swedes in the second leg at Old Trafford on October 27. But tonight Djurgardens were in control for most of the first half, and their goal in the eighth minute by B. Johansson warmed the 6,537 specatators, who braved the chilly night wind.

It was not until the second half that Manchester settled down to give a splendid exhibition of teamwork in the tricky conditions. They constantly attacked, with Charlton prominent in many of the raids. But Djurgarden's defences held out until three minutes from the end, when Herd headed in the equaliser from close range, after a perfect cross from Connelly.

Right wing threat

Djurgardens, lying second in the Swedish First Division, went on the attack from the start and had the United Defence at full stretch for a time. Most of their raids developed on the right wing, and it was from one of these that the Swedes took the lead. Andersson broke through and crossed accurately. Johansson shot the ball into the corner of the net.

When United did get going, their attacks soon floundered against the tough Swedish defence. The only time they did look like scoring was in the 35th minute. Best got the ball into the net, but was ruled offside.

United attacked with more spirit after the interval, and showing splendid cohesion they threatened the Swedish goal.

"What he was going to do to us was nobody's business. He said our performance was an insult to the people of Manchester and that we had let him and ourselves down badly.

"We were in disgrace all right and there were dire warnings about what was going to happen to us when we got back home to Manchester.

"I think we made matters worse by trying to drown our defeat afterwards and coming back to the hotel a bit late. I know he said he was going to fine me and about five or six of the others as well.

"Matt was normally such a great acceptor of defeat, always calm, and even when he was angry he never lost his temper.

"But he did that night, and I can't say I blame him. We really did make a mess of it after winning the first leg in Manchester 4-1.

"It should have been a cakewalk, and taking that attitude was probably our big mistake. But the game at Old Trafford had been so easy for us. I remember thinking what a poor side they were!

"Denis Law had scored a hat-trick with the help of two penalties and Bobby Charlton had got the other.

"What we didn't appreciate in those early years in Europe was how the Continental teams could vary so much home and away. Playing away sometimes they didn't seem to offer much resistance. They weren't as tough as British teams in their mental attitude.

"We could easily have doubled our score in the first leg. I think we even missed a penalty.

"Over there it was a different story, added to which I think our goalkeeper froze at the start and we were two goals down before we knew what had hit us.

"I don't blame the goalkeeper unduly because the rest of us didn't get going either. We made another bad opening immediately after the interval to concede another couple of goals.

"Silva completed his hat-trick after an hour to make it 5-0 and we never looked like pulling anything back.

"Really I am ashamed to talk about it, even now, and it remains a nightmare memory. I can only plead that we had had a very exhausting lead-up to the game in Lisbon.

"We had been involved in three FA Cup ties against Sunderland, drawing home and away before settling our quarter-final issue at Huddersfield.

"We won 5-1 in the final game with the help of a hat-trick from Denis Law against his first club, but the grounds had been wet and heavy.

"We were in everything that season right to the death and it was an extremely busy period. We crammed ten games into the month of March including three in four days.

"The Lisbon match fell in a bad week. It came just four days after losing to West Ham in the semi-final of the FA Cup, which I suppose didn't help our manager's mood when we crashed so heavily in Europe so soon afterwards.

"We were still chasing the championship, though, and faced a tough fixture on our return against Spurs in London. We pulled ourselves together and got a great 3-2 win.

"I recall we were all invited to the House of Commons that night for a dinner, and Matt, so pleased with the result at White Hart Lane which kept us the title trail, said we had made amends.

"He told us to forget the fines, and he actually apologised for losing his temper. That was a

measure of the stature of Sir Matt Busby. In actual fact we deserved every stinging thing he had said about us and we finished in second place, four points behind Liverpool.

"Harold Wilson said that a week was a long time in politics. It can be just as dramatic in football. One moment we were sailing along in three competitions . . . and then nothing. It was a shattering experience, especially the fiasco in Lisbon."

Pat Crerand joined United from Glasgow Celtic to pass the ammunition for Denis Law. Busby had Law, David Herd and Bobby Charlton up front, but too often the ball didn't reach the explosive trio with any quality of pass.

So the United manager paid £56,000 in 1963 for a perhaps slow moving but always perceptive and creative wing half. With Crerand's arrival it was like fitting the last piece of a jigsaw and it came to be a by-word . . . when Pat Crerand plays well, Manchester United play well.

He won an FA Cup winners medal three months after his arrival and went on to collect two League championship medals as well as the European Cup winners medal in 1968.

In all he was just short of four hundred League and Cup appearances in nine seasons at Old Trafford.

After retiring as a player he went on to the junior coaching staff, was assistant to Tommy Docherty for a while and then tried management himself at Northampton Town.

His heart very much remains at Old Trafford, though, and he is a familiar figure at the ground on match days, working for sponsors with their guests, as well as running a pub in nearby Altrincham.

GOAL-KING LAW A SPREE!

By FRANK CLOUGH

MANCHESTER UNITED 6   DJURGARDENS 1

No wonder Denis Law is smiling as he leaves the field at Old Trafford. The Scot went on a goal spree against Djurgardens, hitting three of Manchester United's six. Here he is being congratulated by Swedish left-back Arnesson.

MERCURIAL Manchester United stripped this Stockholm side of all the grandeur and glory that should have accompanied their "champions of Sweden" label in this one-sided mockery of a Soccer match last night.

It was billed as an Inter-Cities Fairs' Cup fight. It was about as fair as matching Wythenshawe Wanderers — if there is such a team—against Inter Milan or Real Madrid.

Four shattering goals in 10 minutes finally splintered the backbone of defence that was the only thing Djurgardens had to offer.

But even as the excitement built to a new crescendo with every goal, I was still nagged by thoughts of the first half when this stuttering, spluttering United had made stormy weather of their one-goal lead.

Maybe you think it's churlish to criticise a team that wins so convincingly. But the...

THE SUN, October 27, 1964

| MAN. UTD. | 6 |
| DJURGARDENS IF | 1 |

1964-65 INTER CITIES FAIRS CUP, FIRST ROUND, SECOND LEG, MANCHESTER UNITED WIN 7-2 ON AGGREGATE

Goal-king Law A Spree!

By Frank Clough

Mercurial Manchester United stripped this Stockholm side of all the grandeur and glory that should have accompanied their "champions of Sweden" label in this one-sided mockery of a Soccer match last night.

It was billed as an Inter-Cities Fairs' Cup fight. It was about as fair as matching Wythenshawe Wanderers — if there is such a team — against Inter Milan or Real Madrid.

Four shattering goals in 10 minutes finally splintered the backbone of defence that was the only thing Djurgardens had to offer.

But even as the excitement built to a new crescendo with every goal, I was still nagged by thoughts of the first half when this stuttering, spluttering United had made stormy weather of their one-goal lead.

Maybe you think it's churlish to criticise a team that wins so convincingly. But the fact still remains that until they exploded open the gallant Stockholm defensive fighters, United had looked a long way from Cup or title challengers.

The ultra-purists might even have made the point that the more skilful football up to the half-time break had come from the visitors, spasmodic though it was.

Certainly the individual skills of some of their players were a delight to watch. But they lacked drive and speed and insisted on trying to work everything to a plan. Consequently their football was slow and stereotyped.

United, enigmatic, erratic and individualistic as ever, went in front with a gem of a goal. Bobby Charlton rolled a short free kick to David Herd, he turned it behind the defensive wall and there was that fire engine called Law streaking past the ball, but recovering to flick it past the 'keeper with the back of his heel!

Ten corners

It was all United but they couldn't add to that tally. They forced ten corners but some superb work by Arvidsson, centre-half Mild, and left-half Sandberg kept them out.

Their own over-intricacies didn't help, either.

They wilted — and then broke, and were finally swept aside like debris in a flood.

But if you hit a wall long enough with a hammer it has to give in sometime. And Stockholm's iron curtain finally caved in like steel that can stand strain no longer.

Charlton added to the lead when he crashed a shot into the roof netting after a magnificent feint, Law made it three with a searing half-volley, and completed his hat-trick, a minute later with an almost contemptuous penalty after Best had been pulled down.

Incredible

That goal gave Law the incredible figures of ten goals in his last four matches.

Charlton scored again after an electrifying 50-yard burst and shot, and then George Best netted with a calmly-placed 20-yarder to complete the destruction.

A minute from time inside-right Hans Karlsson scored for Stockholm from centre-forward Leif Eriksson's pass.

DAILY MAIL, November 11, 1964

| BORUSSIA DORTMUND | 1 |
| MAN. UTD. | 6 |

1964-65 INTER CITIES FAIR CUP, SECOND ROUND, FIRST LEG, MANCHESTER UNITED WIN 6-1

Charlton hits three but finishes second to best

From Ronald Crowther
DORTMUND, WEDNESDAY

With a bombshell burst of brilliance that they have never before achieved in their many raids on Europe, magical Manchester United blasted German rivals Borussia into overwhelming defeat here tonight.

And for five minutes after the finish of this Inter-Cities Fairs Cup second-round first-leg tie there were fantastic scenes.

Thousands of Borussia fans swarmed on to the pitch to pay tribute to a team that had dazzled and delighted them.

Spearheading the rush were RAF men from Cologne, with Union Jacks raised high on this fiesta night for English football.

In this triumph for superior skill over plodding endeavour, Bobby Charlton hammered out a three-goal rebuke to England team manager Alf Ramsey, for leaving him out of his side.

But, on this crystal-clear night, no star shone more brightly than the youngest player on the field.

He was 18-year-old Irishman George Best, who won the hearts of an 18,000 crowd by his complete mastery over Borussia's experienced captain, 30-year-old Gert Cyliax.

For Best, who flies on tomorrow to join the Irish side for their World Cup clash with Switzerland, in Lausanne, this was undoubtedly his greatest game yet.

CHARLTON HITS THREE
BUT FINISHES
SECOND TO BEST

From RONALD CROWTHER: Dortmund, Wednesday

BORUSSIA 1   MANCHESTER UNITED 6

WITH a bombshell burst of brilliance that they have never before achieved in their many raids on Europe, magical Manchester United blasted German rivals Borussia into overwhelming defeat here tonight.

And for five minutes after the finish of this Inter-Cities Fairs Cup second-round first-

Best not only scored one of the game's most exciting goals, but he played a big part in the build-up for three of the others, was unlucky once not to get a penalty award from the Italian referee, and also struck the post with another of his scoring efforts.

United made a jittery start and might have been a goal down after only 40 seconds but for the soundness of centre-half Bill Foulkes.

The breakthrough came after 12 minutes when David Herd breasted down a header from Law and lashed the ball home from the left.

Explosive

Then, after 30 minutes, Charlton made it a 2-0 interval lead after Herd had sent him striding on a stirring 40yd. burst that staggered four would-be tacklers, who he left in his wake.

Four minutes after the interval Best stole the ball from home centre-half Paul and won himself an astonishing ovation from the crowd as he went through to hit goal No. 3.

Ten minutes later Wolfgang Kurrat, Borussia's busy little right half, got his side's consolation goal from the penalty spot, but it was a dubious decision by the referee as Kurrat went down after a shoulder charge by Pat Crerand.

Best pin-pointed a centre for Law to nod home after 77 minutes. And Charlton — a midfield master as well as an explosive finisher in this game — hit the fifth and sixth goals in the 78th and 85th minutes.

And as Borussia — the team that thrashed Benfica by 5-0 last season — went wearily off the field a beaming Matt Busby told me:-

"This is our greatest show in Europe for many years. I am delighted with such a team performance against a side that went to the European Cup semi-final last season, and I am only sorry more of our fans couldn't have seen it."

ABOVE: *A rare moment for Borussia Dortmund as they get close to Dunne's goal in the form of Emmerich (left)*

LEFT: *Best (far left) scores his third, Cyliax (centre) can only hope for a save from Wessel which never comes*

THE GUARDIAN, December 2, 1964

MAN UTD 4

BORUSSIA DORTMUND 0

1964-65 INTER CITIES FAIRS CUP, SECOND ROUND, SECOND LEG, MANCHESTER UNITED WIN 10-1 ON AGGREGATE

Manchester United Merciful

Borussia sporting to the end

By Eric Todd

Manchester United beat Borussia Dortmund 4-0 in the second leg of their Inter-Cities Fairs Cup second round match at Old Trafford last night and they go into the third round with the highly convincing aggregate 10-1.

If the aggregate were convincing, United's display was rather less so than that in Dortmund judging by reports of those who made the journey. Of course only the sadists expected another rout; those who wanted only to see a sporting match certainly were not disappointed, and this more than compensated for the absence of sustained excitement. It was controlled admirably by the three Belgian officials and I must give full marks to the oft criticised spectators at the Stretford end. They behaved impeccably, there was not a toilet roll in sight, and Borussia were given a splendid ovation at the end. These things cannot be stressed too strongly at a time when football is struggling hard to regain its good name.

Charlton outstanding

The proceedings called for little detailed analysis. It was all too easy for United who played just as well as they needed to. I hope that this sort of outing does not make them lose their "killer instinct." Charlton however deserves special mention. He was easily the outstanding player and his display was almost a vote of censure on the England selectors who still seem to think he is best suited to the outside left position. If he has a bad game there against Holland he probably will be dropped. Such is his life!

Borussia tried hard all through and with United's permission they showed some neat touches in the second half without being able to finish off their moves. Cyliax excelled in a conscientious half back line and Busmuller in addition to defending well was as good a marksman as Borussia had. But they never offered a really serious challenge and they could have had few illusions about what was in store for them.

In spite of the dismal weather and the fact that the match promised to be little more than a formality, there was a fair sized and enthusiastic crowd. Of course, United in their present form would attract plenty of spectators to a training session.

Those people who wondered whether United would be in a charitable mood had their fears allayed in the first minute. Best cut inside and passed to Herd who, in turn, slipped the ball to Charlton and Charlton from 20 yards, drove it into the net off a post. Shortly afterwards Stiles delivered an accurate centre and Law beat Tilkowski with a good header but he was ruled offside. Law and United accepted the decision gracefully although they possibly had their private views of it.

In the driving rain mistakes became more numerous and neither side was quite able to control the ball as it skidded across the turf at varying speeds.

And when it was in the air, a capricious wind mocked most attempts at heading. At least it did until the eighteenth minute when, after a splendid pass by Best, Herd centred, and Charlton's header was far too much for Tilkowski. Then Crerand, 25 yards out, swung his left foot at the ball and Tilkowski did well to stop what developed into a powerful drive.

Borussia were given few chances to break loose from what was as near a stranglehold as made no difference, and when they did contrive to enter United's territory they were dismissed politely and firmly. Indeed, only twice was there any danger of P. Dunne having to touch the ball, and even then the danger did not materialise as Straschitz took a free kick from 20 yards but, hard as the ball was driven, Stiles headed it away nonchalantly. And when another free kick was awarded, Straschitz, seeing Stiles in the line of fire, was so upset he sent the ball yards wide.

After half an hour Beyer hooked the ball over the cross bar and was cheered sympathetically, although, the way things were going, Borussia needed a great deal more than sympathy. They nearly were rewarded when Busmuller delivered a capital shot on the run and P. Dunne made a smart save as the ball dipped awkwardly just before it reached him. Borussia improved towards the end of this half – or did United ease off? – and P. Dunne was thankful to concede a corner after a great effort by Cyliax.

Manchester United merciful

Borussia sporting to the end

By ERIC TODD : Manchester United 4; Borussia Dortmund 0

Manchester United beat Borussia Dortmund 4-0 in the second leg of their Inter-cities Fairs Cup second-round match at Old Trafford last night and into the third round

Those people who wondered whether United would be in a charitable mood had their fears allayed in the first minute. Best cut inside and passed to Herd who, in turn, slipped the ball to Charlton and Charlton, from 20 yards, drove it into

THE GUARDIAN, January 20, 1965

MAN. UTD   **1**

EVERTON   **1**

1964-65 INTER CITIES FAIRS CUP, THIRD ROUND,
FIRST LEG, DRAW 1-1

Manchester United are held

Everton owe great deal to West

By Eric Todd

Two bad mistakes resulted in two goals and led finally to a draw 1-1 in the first leg of the Inter-Cities Fairs Cup third round match between Manchester United and Everton at Old Trafford last night. The second leg at Goodison Park on February 9 will be well worth watching if it is as half as exciting as the first.

United. on the balance of play, should have won with quite a lot to spare. Seldom can Stiles and Crerand have supplied better ammunition to the men in front – they did equally well as defenders – and seldom can those men have shown less appreciation. Law understandably perhaps has not yet got into his full stride after his suspension and Herd, hard as he tried, sent too many passes astray. Charlton, Connelly and Best, however, worked tirelessly and were rewarded scandalously for their efforts and the fact that United enjoyed so much mastery is perhaps not much consolation. The attack, as I have suggested, was perhaps just a little lopsided but there was not much wrong with the defence and United, indeed, were the superior side.

Foulkes busy

Everton played a commendably open game without getting far with it, although Pickering gave Foulkes a busy time. In no department – except in goal, however – did Everton really match up to their opposites although what they lacked in comparable skill they undoubtedly made up in grim determination and that is something in this competition. No praise can be too high for West whose anticipation in various crises saved his side and earned him a generous ovation. Full marks also to the referee, one of the best I have seen in any class of football.

After the preliminary skirmishes which caused no embarrassment to either side and suggested that this would develop into a defensive battle, United confounded speculation in a

ABOVE: *Action from the matches against Everton*

Manchester United are held

Everton owe great deal to West

By ERIC TODD : Manchester United 1, Everton 1

Two bad mistakes resulted in two goals and led finally to a draw 1-1 in the first leg of the Inter-Cities Fairs Cup third and had the visitors' contingent apprehensive.

In the fourteenth minute, however, Everton not only raised the siege they took the lead with a series of impressive individual attacks. First Law, and then Charlton, by quite brilliant chicanery each left three defenders stranded and went desperately close to scoring. Then Herd, eschewing daintiness and deceit, drove the ball over West's upstretched arms and the crossbar from 25 yards. This was much to the liking of the home supporters and had the visitors' contingent apprehensive.

In the fourteenth minute, however, Everton not only raised the siege they took the lead with a fine goal, albeit they were aided and abetted by Foulkes, who miskicked when Wright drove the ball down the middle. Pickering was on it in an instant and as Foulkes raced after him in apologetic pursuit and A. Dunne came across with similiar optimism, Pickering shot the ball into the far corner of the net with P. Dunne still wondering whether to come out or stay at home.

United, nevertheless, were not beyond retaliation. A splendid centre by Crerand eluded West, Connelly, and Herd; West made a great save from an excellent shot with the left foot by Crerand; and thrice the Everton goalkeeper went down and saved worthy efforts by Charlton. Everton's only answers in quite a long time were a shot by Scott that P. Dunne saved, and one by Harvey which went wide.

United had to wait until the thirty-third minute for the equaliser, which was almost as much in the nature of gift as Everton's goal had been. Gabriel made a lazy pass back to West and Connelly, showing superb anticipation, nipped in and scored at leisure. Thereafter the tackling on both sides became exceedingly keen and the second half promised to be laden with excitement.

Shot blocked

United went straight into the attack after the restart. Wright, sticking out a leg, blocked a shot by Crerand with West at the other end of the goal, and a few seconds later Law put his head to an accurate centre by Crerand but West achieved a magnificent save. If it had not been for their goalkeeper Everton must have been a good way behind by now because his colleagues frequently were caught out of position by the persistency of Best and Charlton.

Everton were still defending desperately as the game entered its closing stages and Stevens, after committing one foul on Charlton, had his name taken for another one on Law. Just before the end Connelly ran in at full speed to meet a centre from Best but with his left foot drove the ball well wide.

THIS was football on a razor's edge, a match of tremendous tension and many splendours, a Fairs Cup tie worthy of a European Cup Final.

United, self-proclaimed apostles of the Soccer offensive, discovered what so many of their opponents have found—pressure can be so intense that survival decrees a ten-man defence.

For E... badly shaken by a dis...

I doubt if the Fairs Cup has ever seen football of this fury and fashion. And, of course, Everton paid for their glorious miscalculation.

No team in Europe can give United's attack this time and space and get away without conceding goals.

Despite all the Everton pressure, all United's desperate escapes, Everton couldn't crack this United defence more than once.

Vital

Each of United's forwards made one or more tackle or clearance inside his own area. But in the vital moments—in those seconds when Everton's defence was off-balance or too slow to clear—they struck ruthlessly. And this is what put them into the last six.

Take the opening goal. John Connelly cruised upfield Denis L...

dawdled on a clearance. David Herd intercepted and sent Law away. He passed to Connelly, whose cross hit Gordon West, bounced to Herd, coming into the middle, shot an easy goal.

It was moves like that, that Everton, for all their intense pressure, couldn't match.

Escape

But many Everton fans in the 54,000 crowd must have gone home near heartbroken.

One free-kick from Fred Pickering (34) was pushed along the goal-line by Pat Dunne. The ball rolled, to hit the inside of the post and then rolled out again.

Then there was another extraordinary escape. Nine minutes from time, when Roy Vernon hit a snap shot from 18 yards that had Pat Dunne beaten, it flicked a United defender and just passed outside the post

DAILY EXPRESS, February 9, 1965

EVERTON	1
MAN. UTD.	**2**

1964-65 INTER CITIES FAIRS CUP, THIRD ROUND, SECOND LEG, MANCHESTER UNITED WIN 3-2 ON AGGREGATE

Fairs Cup Furies

By Derek Hodgson

This was football on a razor's edge, a match of tremendous tension and many splendours, a Fairs Cup tie worthy of a European Cup Final.

United, self-proclaimed apostles of the Soccer offensive, discovered what so many of their opponents have found – pressure can be so intense that survival decrees a ten-man defence.

For Everton, badly shaken by a disputed six-minute goal, sent Jimmy Gabriel flying to attack in a magnificent death-or-glory bid for victory.

I doubt if the Fairs Cup has ever seen football of this fury and fashion. And, of course, Everton paid for their glorious miscalculation.

No team in Europe can give United's attack this time and space and get away without conceding goals.

Despite all the Everton pressure, all United's desperate escapes, Everton couldn't crack this United defence more than once.

Vital

Each of United's forwards made one or more tackle or clearance inside his own area. But in the vital moments – in those seconds when Everton's defence was off-balance or too slow to clear – they struck ruthlessly. And this is what put them into the last six.

Take the opening goal. John Connelly cruised upfield and passed to Denis Law out on the touchline. Everton stood off, waiting for the offside flag. Law passed deftly inside and with Everton arms upraised for a signal that never came, Connelly took the return and cracked a great goal.

Take United's winner in the 70th minute. Ray Wilson dawdled on a clearance. David Herd intercepted and sent Law away. He passed to Connelly, whose cross hit Gordon West, bounced to Herd, coming into the middle, who shot an easy goal.

It was moves like that, that Everton, for all their intense pressure, couldn't match.

Escape

But many Everton fans in the 54,000 crowd must have gone home near heartbroken.

One free-kick from Fred Pickering (34) was pushed along the goal-line by Pat Dunne. The ball rolled to hit the inside of the post and then rolled out again.

Then there was another extraordinary escape. Nine minutes from time, when Roy Vernon hit a snap shot from 18 yards that had Pat Dunne beaten, it flicked a United defender and just passed outside the post.

Add to these three or four last fraction saves by Dunne.

Everton's goal, 10 minutes after half-time, came after Vernon had been held 12 yards out. Alex Scott tapped the indirect free-kick to Pickering who cracked in the equaliser, hitting Tony Dunne on the way.

Manchester United make victory look easy

THE GUARDIAN, May 12, 1965

RACING STRASBOURG 0

MAN. UTD. 5

1964-65 INTER CITIES FAIRS CUP, QUARTER FINAL, FIRST LEG, MANCHESTER UNITED WIN 5-0

Manchester United make victory look easy

From Brian Crowther
STRASBOURG, MAY 12

From BRIAN CROWTHER : RC, Strasbourg 0, M/c Utd. 5

Strasbourg, May 12

Manchester United were so much superior to Racing Club, Strasbourg, here tonight that the crowd amused itself with a running beer can fight and a fireworks display. In the meantime matches, though he played a crucial part in four of the goals. Best was seldom at outside left, and Charlton was limping slightly during the first half, coming off for attention shortly after the interval. After standing in stockinged feet for a time on the touchline Charlton resumed in

ABOVE: *Connelly (centre) puts the ball past Schuth (on ground) in United's first leg tie against Racing Strasbourg*

Manchester United were so much superior to Racing Club Strasbourg here tonight that the crowd amused itself with a running beer can fight and a fireworks display. In the meantime United amused themselves with almost casual but classic football and a victory, 5-0, in the first leg of their Inter-Cities Fairs Cup quarter final match.

What will happen in the second leg at Old Trafford next week to this poor French side does not bear thinking about. United had no need to have any worries about this match once they had become accustomed to a rather bumpy and richly grassed pitch. It now seems certain that they will take a well earned place in the semi-finals against the winners of the quarter-final between Ferencvaros and Atletico Bilbao.

No matter what United's mood before the kick-off they could not have failed to be put on their mettle by the reception. And really the crowd at this small, compact ground expected much of them, knowing that Charlton was after all in a side which might not have been received more warmly at Old Trafford. United began, perhaps, too cautiously, and this resulted in a certain amount of attractive, if fragile football, interspersed with a great deal of bad passing, particularly by Crerand.

But Crerand soon threw off this affliction and became a leading figure in United's attack as the teams settled down to play a sort of exhibition football which lacked bite but was blessed with a minimum of hard tackling. This type of football was out of character for Stiles, of course, and he played hard throughout but managed generally to stay out of trouble.

United's style was unusual for them. Best was subdued and Charlton less active than in recent matches, though he played a crucial part in four of the goals. Best was seldom at outside left, and Charlton was limping slightly during the first half, coming off for attention shortly after the interval. After standing in stockinged feet for a time on the touchline Charlton resumed in much better form. In fact, it was not necessary for these two to be other than occasional contributors. Law, Herd, and Connelly were doing well enough almost on their own in the first half, with the assistance from time to time of A. Dunne and Crerand, on the left wing.

United went ahead in the nineteenth minute through Connelly, after some good work by Crerand, Charlton, and finally Herd, who centred accurately from the dead ball line to Connelly, standing by the far post, who formally tapped the ball home. They went further ahead five minutes before the interval, Herd scoring with a hard drive from an acute angle after Charlton and Best had opened the defence with diagonal passes.

In the meantime, as may have been gathered, little had been seen of Racing Club. Indeed, their two most promising shots throughout the match came from the backs, while most of their moves broke down at the penalty area. In the second half, United added goals through Law (sixty-first minute), a masterful downward header off Charlton's centre; through Charlton himself (seventy-second minute), he almost walked the ball into the net after receiving a long through pass from Crerand, and through Law, again almost at the end when he headed down a centre from the right. It was all too easy — as the small body of United supporters reminded the crowd.

DAILY EXPRESS, May 19, 1965

MAN. UTD 0

RACING STRASBOURG 0

1964-65 INTER CITIES FAIRS CUP, QUARTER FINAL, SECOND LEG, MANCHESTER UNITED WIN 5-0 ON AGGREGATE

French Pride Salvaged

Everybody knew it, including Strasbourg . . . United were through to the semi-final of the European Cup-winners' Cup before the first kick in this second leg. But that was poor consolation at Old Trafford last night.

United had nothing to fight for, Strasbourg nothing to hope. And that's how it seemed for most of this dreary show.

The 34,000 fans who had so gaily cheered their favourites before the game when they took their lap of honour as champions choked back their frustration as the gallant French salvaged some of their lost pride.

Strasbourg had shuffled their side, making seven changes – and they worked.

I did not believe that they could keep their word when they warned before the match: "We shall show you tonight that we have learned very quickly the lesson United taught us in Strasbourg."

Capable

But in fact they defended tremendously well with full backs Gonzales and Sbaiz backed up by that very capable goalkeeper Johnny Schuth, who completely shook off the sad memory that he had been beaten five times on his own home ground.

The first half made one wonder if these two-legged ties are really worthwhile.

For even the United players, though Bobby Charlton particularly tried hard to find a way through, could not shake off the feeling that they had only to go through the motions on this occasion.

And when they did decide it was time they showed the crowd how they walloped Strasbourg away from home the goals just would not come.

The second half belonged completely to United and even goalkeeper Schuth must have wondered how on earth they were kept out.

But the champions had failed to get into gear in time and Strasbourg had gained courage as every minute ticked by.

LEFT: *Dunne catches, Briat (right) is closely attended to by Foulkes in United's second leg tie against Racing Strasbourg*

BELOW: *Law beaten to the ball by Strasbourg 'keeper Schuth*

MANCHESTER EVENING NEWS, June 1, 1965

MAN. UTD.	3
FERENCVAROS	2

1964-65 INTER-CITIES FAIRS CUP, SEMI-FINAL, FIRST LEG, MANCHESTER UNITED WIN 3-2

Now Only Best Will Do, United

By Peter Gardner

If Manchester United can survive another blistering 90 minutes against fiery Ferencvaros in Budapest next Sunday it will rank as one of their best performances.

For, on the evidence of last night's first leg semi-final of the Inter Cities Fairs Cup at Old Trafford, the slick Hungarians must be odds on favourites to meet either Atletico Madrid or Juventus of Italy in the final later this month.

The slender one-goal lead the Reds will take behind the Iron Curtain is not likely to be sufficient to contain a side of the capabilities of Ferencvaros.

United deserved their 3-2 win if only because of their scintillating second-half display when, inspired by brilliant Bobby Charlton, they forced the Hungarians to throw up a wall of desperate defenders in front of goalkeeper Geczi.

But they have only themselves to blame that it was not a more clear-cut victory.

MISSED CHANCES

They had their chances — George Best had a couple in the first 10 minutes, and David Herd, while taking his goals splendidly, should have finished with at least a hat-trick.

Defensively, too, the Reds boobed, notably goalkeeper Pat Dunne, who should have quite easily gathered inside-left Rakosi's half-hit shot from the corner of the penalty area 14 minutes from the end.

It is a goal that could well cost United the tie for I cannot see them even holding Ferencvaros on Sunday.

Their defence, particularly the brilliant centre-half Sandor Matral, covered superbly and although the attack produced only two noteworthy shots — both of them resulting in goals — they stuck to their promise of not adopting a purely defensive policy.

That they were forced to defend so much was because of United's thrilling forward thrusts, all of which were inspired by the immaculate Charlton who stood head and shoulders above his front-line.

NIGGLING

Had the Reds set about their task in this manner during the first half they would surely have been going to Hungary merely for the formality of completing the tie.

Instead they lost their heads against the niggling Hungarians, and Belgian referee Hubert Burguet completely lost control.

So weak was he that I am certain that had an English referee been in charge of this game at least one player would have been sent off.

Fortunately, tempers cooled during the interval and United came out to take the game by the scruff of the neck.

Earlier full-back Novak had moved forward to shoot Ferencvaros ahead (23 minutes) and a subdued-looking Denis Law equalised with a penalty after his header had been handled on the line by Horvath (34 minutes).

Now for the battle of Budapest!

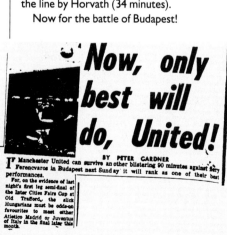

Recriminations amongst the United defence as Ferencvaros score their first goal in their first leg match

United players appeal (in vain!) for a penalty

THE GUARDIAN, June 6, 1965

TC FERENCVAROS 1

MAN Utd. 0

1964-65 INTER CITIES FAIRS CUP, SEMI-FINAL, SECOND LEG, 3-3 DRAW ON AGGREGATE

Manchester United get another chance

Crerand and Orosz sent off

From Albert Barham
BUDAPEST, JUNE 6

The semi-final of the Inter Cities Fairs Cup between Ferencvaros and Manchester United remains to be resolved here on June 16. The second leg here this evening, a hard, tough, and in flashes an evil tempered match, was won by Ferencvaros by one goal — scored from a penalty, so that the teams finished level 3-3 on aggregate.

How unfortunately appropriate it was that the penalty summed up the mood of the game. There were few honours, and the greatest misfortune of all was that two players, opposing wing half backs, Crerand and Orosz — who won a gold medal at the Olympics — were sent off for fighting.

The Hungarians pride themselves on their sport and their weather. Both seemed sadly amiss last night. A week's rain on the earth works caused by the relaying of the athletics tracks for the Universiad made the vast NEP stadium rather bedraggled. And the pitch, too, held an imp of treachery on its surface for foothold was precarious for the unwary. But with all the tension, which of course stemmed from the fact that only one goal separated them after the first leg at Old Trafford, and all the spoils that will come to the victors who meet Juventus in the final, there was no excuse for temperamental outbursts and even less for retaliation.

Great chance

The pattern was set within the first two minutes when the crowd whistled its annoyance. Ferencvaros could easily have been two goals up, yet they got neither. First Fenyvesi, the elder of the brotherly wing forwards, sent United the wrong way and tripped over the ball when Rakosi contrived to give Albert a great chance. He accepted it, but missed his kick. Seconds later there was uproar as A. Dunne swept away the feet of the younger Fenyvesi in clearing the ball. Ferencvaros appealed in vain for a penalty.

Certainly the decision to include both brothers added to the threat from Ferencvaros. But as I had seen before the great architect of this forward line was Varga. There seemed something almost predatory about this young tow-haired player as he stalked out to the wings or foraged in the centre, always trying to set up the chances for Albert. The match was a series of crises for United, who had difficulty in keeping their feet and difficulty indeed, in containing these eager and talented Hungarians. Twice within a minute in the first half as the steady pressure built to its point of crisis P. Dunne leapt across his goal to make

two graceful interceptions. One was to tip over the crossbar a shot from Rakosi, the other a great dive to hold a shot from Orosz which had been deflected to the foot of a post.

One of the greatest tests of all came in the twenty-ninth minute. Again this huge stadium echoed and re-echoed to the shrill whistling of the crowd and Stiles impeded Albert inside the penalty area. Somehow, this thin red line, pushed back on to the goal line by the referee, blocked the free kick. But perhaps in that attack, and the ones which succeeded it, came the answer to those who say that Manchester United are not a team with method. Here was defence organised as skilfully as any, and once again I saw the best of United in adversity. All they could offer as occasionally they prised apart the web the Hungarians wove around them in the first half was a headed flick from Herd as he bicycled up into the air to reach a ball lobbed high across the goal.

But, in spite of this siege, Ferencvaros had few shots inside the penalty area. Yet be that as it may, Rakosi issued a strong warning with a shot from 30 yards which scudded off United's crossbar and as the seconds ticked away towards half time Stiles, in another determined

LEFT: *Only goal of the second leg tie, scored from the spot by Novak (far right), flies past Dunne*

Hungarian raid, handled the ball as Fenyvesi (M.) swept past him and Novak scored from the penalty.

Little reward

On into the second half bubbled this cauldron of a match in which toils and troubles and fouls were equally mixed. Stiles was the player against whom the crowd screeched their annoyance at his tackling. P. Dunne earned their grudging admiration as he pounced and leaped and foiled once again this fine forward line. But at least United had eased themselves from the stranglehold which the Hungarians had had on the match. The reward was negligible. Matrai, Horwath, and Novak were as adroit at cutting out the few chances United created as they were at stifling any initiative that United showed.

ABOVE: *Herd (centre left) collides with Hungarian 'keeper Geczi during the match in Budapest*

In the first leg at Old Trafford tempers had threatened to rule that match. Once again tempers flared, Stiles had his name taken, players wrestled and squared up to one another, and Connelly had his nose bloodied by the referee who knocked him over as Takosi came in to effect vengeance. The culmination of this unhappy sequence of incidents came 15 minutes from the end when Crerand and Orosz flew at one another like a pair of alley cats and the referee stood over the bodies to prevent further violence before sending both from the field. It was a sad end to a match which did have its moments of enjoyment, and I hope that by the time of the playoff wise heads will have instilled some sense of responsibility and tranquility to these two explosive sides, both of whom can play most attractively when they so choose.

Manchester United get another chance

◼ LOOKING BACK WITH NOBBY STILES ◼

One of Manchester United's least remembered campaigns in Europe was the run to the semi-finals of the Inter Cities Fairs cup in season 1964-65.

Yet as far as their little cup battler Nobby Stiles is concerned, United played their best ever European football.

"Everyone remembers us for winning the European Cup in 1968 and for other highlights like the encounters with Real Madrid and Benfica," says Nobby.

"But in my book our team in the mid-Sixties was at its peak for the Fairs Cup in 1965. We played some cracking football and were scoring five or six goals in nearly every round, even away from home.

"We opened cautiously enough with a 1-1 draw against Djurgardens in Sweden but we demolished them 6-1 in the return with the help of a hat-trick from Denis Law.

"We went to Germany and won 6-1 in the first leg against Borussia Dortmund, this time with a hat-trick from Bobby Charlton. For good measure we saw them off 4-0 at Old Trafford.

"The next round pitted us against Everton, which was a shame and understandably the scores were tighter, 1-1 at Old Trafford but with a 2-1 win for us at Goodison.

"There seemed to be no stopping us when we went to France and beat Strasbourg 5-0. The home return was goalless, but we had certainly scored some goals overall and we were very confident about the semi-final against Ferencvaros.

"The only doubt in our minds was the fact that it had been an extremely long season.

"We didn't even play Strasbourg until a fortnight after the end of the League season, and it was June before we tackled Ferencvaros.

"It had been a busy season and I know I had played 66 games if you include England Under-23 appearances. We had reached the semi-finals of the F A Cup, losing 1-0 to Leeds United in a replay.

"We were also champions after a run of 10 wins in 11 matches, but the long, tiring season was perhaps beginning to have an effect, and we didn't play particularly well in the first leg against the Hungarians.

"Denis Law scored a penalty and though a fellow called Novak put Ferencvaros level, we seemed to be OK after two goals by David Herd to lead 3-1.

"Then we gave away a silly goal, Pat Dunne misjudging a long lob which bounced into our net. So the trip to Budapest was always going to be difficult with just a one-goal advantage.

"The journey was awful to say the least, delayed in London by a strike and with another hold-up in Brussels, but we were ready to give it a good go.

"Ferencvaros had a good player, Florian Albert, and he had a real tussle with Bill Foulkes. Just before the interval he got the ball to Vargo who let fly with a shot. I flung myself to block it and stopped it with my shoulder.

"The referee gave a penalty against me for hand-ball. I thought it was a harsh decision. Novak scored with the spot-kick, and though we tried hard in the second half, we lost 1-0 to finish on aggregate 3-3.

"They didn't have the system of away goals counting double in those days so it was a play-off – and we lost the toss.

"We had to go back to Budapest with me feeling terrible as the player responsible for the penalty which had forced the third game. The journey by road from Vienna to Budapest seemed never-ending and by now it was June 16 when most footballers were on holiday.

"But we played well. In fact we paralysed them only to lose 2-1 because we couldn't put the ball into the net.

"So success in Europe eluded us for yet another season, though I still look back proudly on that period. We had won the Championship at least and we certainly had a good team normally bursting with goals.

"We had five players in double figures with League goals alone. Denis Law scored 28 in the League, and had a grand total in all competitions of 39.

"David Herd scored 28 in the League and Cup while John Connelly had a tally of 20, Bobby Charlton had 18 and George Best in his first full season had bagged 14.

"It was an attack dripping with scoring power and I shall always remember that season for some great football. It was a very good team and great to be a part of it.

"People said we used to play off the cuff without any tactics or planning, but in reality we were well organised and we had good players, which at the end of the day is what it is all about."

Nobby Stiles

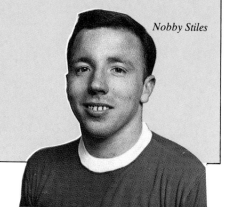

THE SUN, Thursday, June 17, 1965

TC FERENCVAROS	2
MAN. UTD.	1

1964-65 INTER CITIES FAIRS CUP, SEMI-FINAL REPLAY,
TC FERENCVAROS WIN 5-4 ON AGGREGATE

United out – Crerand is booked

Len Noad Reports
BUDAPEST, WEDNESDAY

Manchester United lined up in the centre circle to be cheered off Nep Stadium here tonight, after Ferencvaros had won the Inter-Cities Fairs' Cup semi-final play-off.

But in the closing minutes Pat Crerand, the fiery Scot who was ordered off on this ground last week, had his name taken, apparently for disputing a decision of the severe German referee.

Now Ferencvaros meet Juventus in a one-game final at Turin next Wednesday.

Referee Schulenburg kept the grip of a German vice on this Cup-tie that had got out of hand in the two previous games. He whistled for every semblance of an infringement.

By contrast to the feuding of the last games, this was ever-so-matey. When players collided, there was a helping hand, a handshake, an apology, a pat on the back.

That is, until those last five minutes, when, with United flat out in desperate attacks to save the game, Rakosi clashed with Crerand, and the name-taking followed.

Earned Place

Ferencvaros delighted a 75,000 crowd and earned their place in the final by a superb display of controlled, intelligent football.

Yet United, ironically, played much better than they had done in either of the earlier games.

In the first half-hour they mesmerised the Magyars with fast, incisive moves, only to run

ABOVE: *Action in the Hungarian goalmouth during the semi final play-off: Law (far left) and Horvath rise to the ball watched by Best (No 11), Geczi (hidden), Matrai and Connelly*

This was United at their best. Bobby Charlton snapped up a pass from Denis Law and flashed in a sizzling shot that Geczi gripped with superb confidence.

A minute or two later he was conceding a corner after Horvath had given away a free kick near the line.

George Best, his Beatle mop flopping, squirmed a way through the centre, but forgot the power in his shot.

Denis Law darted through to seize a pass from Crerand, but Geczi dived fearlessly and faultlessly at the Scot's feet to beat down the shot.

The masterly goalkeeper had luck to match his pluck, for when Denis Law sent David Herd racing through, the centre-forward's shot struck Geczi's knee and glanced off to safety.

A goal seemed bound to come, and it did – at the other end!

There was as little chance of a goal as a change of government in Hungary when right-winger Karaba got a pass 30 yards from goal.

Fearless dive

He surprised not only the crowd but United's goalkeeper by trying a first time shot, and it flew into the net behind the startled Pat Dunne.

Karaba was the killer. It was he who contrived the second Hungarian goal, ten minutes later.

FERENCVAROS .... 2 MANCHESTER UNITED 1

BUDAPEST, Wednesday.—Manchester United lined up in the centre circle to be cheered off Nep Stadium here tonight, after Ferencvaros had won the Inter-Cities Fairs' Cup semi-final play-of.

But in the closing minutes Pat Crerand, the fiery Scot who was ordered off on this ground last week, had his name taken, apparently for disputing a decision of the severe German referee.

Now Ferencvaros meet Juventus in a one-game final at Turin next Wednesday.

Referee Schulenburg kept the grip of a German vice on this Cup-tie that had got out of hand in the two previous games. He whistled for every infringement.

LEN NOAD REPORTS

Fenyvesi, who accepted the gift gleefully.

Now the stricken Manchester men had to forget defence and go flat out in attack. But you don't give a two goal start and a beating to Hungarian teams in this class.

Ten minutes from the end, after Geczi had defied Herd

against a goalkeeper, Geczi, whose saves were fantastic.

He carried the ball to the line, then cut back a pass to Rakosi. The inside-left's shot rebounded off Law, back helping his defence, and dropped at the foot of left-winger Fenyvesi, who accepted the gift gleefully.

Now the stricken Manchester men had to forget defence and go flat out in attack. But you don't give a two goal start and a beating to Hungarian teams in this class.

Ten minutes from the end, after Geczi had defied Herd with a flying save of breathless daring, the ball rebounded for John Connelly to score.

And in the last minute Denis Law burst through for a final despairing shot, only to see the effort nullified by the heart-breaking Hungarian goal.

The season, at last, was over for the English champions.

One final

But Ferencvaros play a one-match final in Turin next Wednesday.

They told the Fairs Cup Committee that because of League commitments and their trip to New York on June 28, they could not play a two-leg final.

At one stage it appeared that they would have to scratch and Manchester United would take their place against Juventus.

But yesterday the Fairs Cup Committee agreed to a one-game final.

Manchester United held to goal lead

Form slumps after the interval

From a Special Correspondent: HJK Helsinki 2, M/c Utd. 3

Helsinki, September 22. European match, flew magnifi-

THE GUARDIAN, September 22, 1965

HELSINKI HJK	2
MAN. UTD	**3**

1965-66 EUROPEAN CUP, PRELIMINARY ROUND,
FIRST LEG, MANCHESTER UNITED WIN 3-2

Manchester United held to goal lead
Form slumps after the interval

From a Special Correspondent
HELSINKI, SEPTEMBER 22

ABOVE: *Connelly goes past Laine and Kauppinen (left) of Helsinki during United's first leg tie in Finland*

BELOW: *Law (second from right) shoots on target, but Helsinki goalkeeper Heinonen (far left) is well in position to save*

M anchester United will probably win handsomely when they complete their preliminary round in the European Cup against HJK Helsinki in the second leg at Old Trafford on October 6. Indeed, they come home tomorrow having won the all important match here tonight 3-2.

Success, however, only came after an undignifled scramble. They failed to score in the second half, and the promising football of the early stages that produced a commanding lead of 3-1 was not maintained.

Quick score

Expectations that HJK, an all-amateur side, would tire in the second half were never realised. In fact, it was quite the contrary. Perhaps the United players placed too much reliance on the home players fading out because they contributed considerably themselves to the Finns' revival. United's efforts grew extremely ragged, and their shooting wretched with Herd being the most wasteful. Yet it was Herd who gave United a splendid

start by scoring in the first 30 seconds.

The approach play to this goal flowed with the smoothness worthy of the Football League champions playing abroad. Fitzpatrick, brought into the side because Crerand was still suffering from a thigh injury, started the move with a pass to Connelly. Then a familiar burst from Law in midfield ended with Herd shooting past Heinonen.

It was also Herd who sprinted out to the right wing and centred for Connelly to flick the ball into the net from short range for United's second goal in the fifteenth minute. At this stage one wondered how things could possibly go wrong. The United's professional class contrasted starkly with the amateur enthusiasm of HJK. This was apparent with players like Law and Charlton, of course, but even Aston, playing in his first competitive European match, flew magnificently past his opponents. He repeatedly outpaced Jalava and put across excellent centres, and in fact the nicest thing that looked likely to happen to the Helsinki captain and right back was the presentation to him before the match of a bouquet of flowers by Law. When Jalava at last managed to stop Aston there was ironical applause from the crowd.

Even in this period of United domination HJK gave a firm indication of things to come. Pahlman, their versatile band leader and television entertainer, pulled the score back to 2-1 with a swerving high free kick that Gaskell had in his hands only to drop behind him over the line. This was in the thirty-fourth minute and any Englishmen in the crowd probably thought this a fluke when it took United only three more minutes to score again. This time it was Law racing through on to Connelly's pass. Law was also on hand to kick off the line to keep the interval score line looking very healthy from United's point of view.

Hopes not fulfilled

High hopes, however, crumbled to bitter disappointment. Far from taking advantage of their lead, United relaxed to the extent of making HJK look a good side. It was from a casual backheel, typical of United's attitude now, from Law that gave HJK a corner. Then, as the ball was running loose, Peloniemi, a 17-year-old playing only his second first-team game, drove the ball past Gaskell.

United finished the match pressing strongly but as one watched their wild efforts to score it was difficult to feel any sympathy for them and the Finns were rightly delighted to have emerged with a highly creditable score line.

Manchester United stroll through

Finns are outclassed

By ERIC TODD: Manchester United 6, Helsinki HJK 0.

THE GUARDIAN, October 6, 1965

MAN. UTD.	6
HELSINKI HJK	0

1965-66 EUROPEAN CUP, PRELIMINARY ROUND, SECOND LEG, MANCHESTER UNITED WIN 9-2 ON AGGREGATE

Manchester United stroll through

Finns are outclassed

By Eric Todd

Manchester United, who won 3-2 in Finland, strolled at leisure through the second leg of their European Cup preliminary round match against Helsinki HJK last night at Old Trafford. They contented themselves with six goals and rarely looked like giving their opponents the satisfaction of even one in reply.

United spent most of the first half in formal assessment – rather a long time perhaps although in this competition caution is not necessarily a bad thing – but in the second half superior craft and stamina carried the day. It was all too easy and Helsinki had no effective answer to quick-thinking, quick-moving United forwards, among whom Best enjoyed himself thoroughly and Aston confirmed his usefulness. The United defenders had no real testing but A. Dunne distinguished himself with his clever positional play and immaculate appearances when Helsinki were enjoying brief moments of superiority.

Hard triers

These amateurs from Helsinki were splendid triers and Pahlman deserved better luck with his shooting while the limping Heinonen, though he failed to save some shots that he should have saved, stopped others that really he had no right to have done. When United got down to business, Kokko and Laine performed with considerable credit but in the final analysis things turned out very much as had been expected. Only very rarely are the Helsinkis of this world permitted to interfere with logic.

United did nearly all the early attacking without causing any undue embarrassment to Heinonen, but the first worth-while shot was delivered from 35 yards by Pahlman, whose jersey carried the number 17. The explanation was interesting. In the first leg in Helsinki Law and Pahlman, the respective number tens, exchanged jerseys, but while the wealthy United can afford unlimited outfits with that number, Pahlman's generosity apparently had temporarily exhausted his club's resources in that department. The significance of "17" was not apparent.

Pahlman, at least, was quite happy about it, and after testing P. Dunne with another good shot from far out, he was quick to notice that United's goalkeeper was some distance from his net, and was just too high with a long lob. At the other end Charlton was disappointingly wide with a shot with his left foot, but in the thirteenth minute Charlton centred from near the touchline and Connelly headed United into the lead, the ball entering the net off a post.

Deserved lead

United, who were not exerting themselves, deserved to be in front, although the cheerful Pahlman gave them something to think about with a tremendous shot after a corner. P. Dunne might have been in real trouble if the ball had not struck Lindahl amidships. Ten minutes before the interval Charlton shot from 10 yards, and the casual manner in which Heinonen punched the ball over the bar was quite astonishing. Almost on half time Best ran through unchallenged and scored a second goal for United.

Heinonen, still limping as the result of collision with Best in the first half, was beaten twice more in the first five minutes of the second half. Connelly scored easily when the ball rebounded to him off Heinonen's chest and then the Helsinki goalkeeper allowed a straight one from Best to go under his body. Heinonen made a wonderful save from a header by Law but in the sixtieth minute he was overwhelmed by a Charlton "special" from 25 yards.

Twenty minutes from the end Crerand received a shin injury and was carried away for a stitching operation, but shortly afterwards Connelly accepted a pass from Law and shot the ball into the far corner of the net, Heinonen for once making no attempt to save. Maybe, like his colleagues, he was overcome by the sheer impertinence of Connelly's effort.

Manchester United's unexpected triumph in East Berlin

Unfamiliar conditions prove no deterrent to goal scoring

By ALBERT BARHAM : ASK Vorwaerts 0, Manchester Utd. 2

East Berlin, November 17

Manchester United achieved more than just a win 2-0 in the first leg of their European Cup first-round match here today. They gave the 30,000 spectators, who braved the biting wind and bitter cold in the Walter Ulbricht Stadium here a magnificent display of

The ball went from Dunne to Best to Law and on to Herd. Seeming to climb an invisible ladder Law went high above the defence, heading the ball into goal. What a perfect piece of coordination that was with the final headed flick precisely placed over the head and arms of Weise who had been drawn and then left stranded three yards from goal. Is there another player in Britain who

THE GUARDIAN, November 17, 1965

| ASK VORWAERTS | 0 |
| MAN. UTD. | 2 |

1965-66 EUROPEAN CUP, FIRST ROUND, FIRST LEG,
MANCHESTER UNITED WIN 2-0

Manchester United's Unexpected Triumph in East Berlin

Unfamiliar Conditions Prove no Deterrent to Goal Scoring

By Albert Barham
EAST BERLIN, NOVEMBER 17

Manchester United achieved more than just a win 2-0 in the first leg of their European Cup first-round match here today. They gave the 30,000 spectators, who braved the biting wind and bitter cold in the Walter Ulbricht Stadium here a magnificent display of control and at times dedicated teamwork, though for an hour it made bleak watching indeed.

Under conditions quite alien to them – a bone hard pitch on which they had not even set foot before the game – United played to contain this strong East German Army side and to strike with individualism which is the great power of United. These are tactics widely employed in the away leg of any important European tie and in them United succeeded admirably. Yet this German side built up attack after attack assiduously but they did not, indeed they could not, create for themselves more than one real scoring chance.

Wayward Passes

But that does not mean there were no harrowing moments for United. One in particular came after only five minutes when Law carried

ABOVE: *Gregg punches clear from Vogt of ASK Vorwaerts in the first leg tie in Berlin*

Coluna (right) and Charlton (left) line up with the officials before the start of the 1968 European Cup Final at Wembley

The face says it all – a joyful Matt Busby surrounded by his victorious team

ABOVE: *Dunne (foreground), Gregg (in cap) and Vogt on ground watch the ball go into touch next to the Manchester goal*

THE TIMES, December 1, 1965

MAN. UTD.   3

ASK VORWAERTS   1

1965-66 EUROPEAN CUP, FIRST ROUND, SECOND LEG, MANCHESTER UNITED WIN 5-1 ON AGGREGATE

Germans Unable to Ruffle United's Defence

the ball back into his own penalty area and was robbed by Piepenburg and the shot was diverted only in the nick of time. There were other moments too when passes bounced astray on this pitch and went to opponents, and when the strength alone of Begerad, the cunning of Noeldner in particular, and the cleverness of Vogt and Nachtigall prised open one flank or the other of United's defence.

The covering was too fast, however, too relentlessly effective for the Germans to break through it. But in the three minutes just after half time United had their most disastrous moments. Three times United survived it seemed a little fortuitously. First Gregg beat a shot from Noeldner up into the air. Kiupel hammered a free kick wide of goal to the right and Gregg arched across his goal, clawing the ball down, and then Piepenburg hesitated fractionally too long as he prepared to shoot and United's covering once again foiled him.

The goals when they came were gems in themselves. But in this great open bowl, where only the band is under cover, the scattered few supporters hoping for a United victory had to wait 72 minutes for the crucial goal. The ball went from Dunne to Best to Law and on to Herd. Seeming to climb an invisible ladder Law went high above the defence, heading the ball into goal. What a perfect piece of co-ordination that was with the final headed flick precisely placed over the head and arms of Weiss who had been drawn and then left stranded three yards from goal. Is there another player in Britain who can time a leap quite like Law?

And the second goal in the eightieth minute came also from the initiation of Law, who though suffering from a head cold wanted very

much to play in this match. And what a great part he played in United's victory. He swept the ball past Krampe on the right wing and there was Connelly waiting to flick in the pass. It was a pity on this holiday in Berlin no servicemen were allowed across the check point to see this match, for the sector was declared out of bounds for the day.

This was no victory gained by any two men, however, or by the efforts of half a dozen. I cannot emphasise too strongly what a magnificent team effort it was in which each played his part – Gregg was always alert, Crerand prompted, and Best and Herd wandered tellingly, and there were seemingly magical moments for Law.

VERSATILE PLAYER

It was part of the scheme of things that Herd and Best were left upfield when all others were back defending stubbornly. In the German side none was more polished than Fraessdorf at right back. This great player can also play equally well at centre forward as Mr Busby, the manager of United, can testify, for he saw him play in that position against Magdeburg.

Mr Busby said afterwards he would have been quite happy to settle for a goalless draw and indeed the game seemed to be heading towards that. The victory obviously cheered him immensely. "We set out to hold them and come out and play when we could," he said, "and we did remarkably well." So well in fact that there should be little difficulty for Manchester United to reach the quarter-finals from the second leg of this tie at Old Trafford on December 1.

For there to have been more than desultory interest in last night's European Cup tie at Old Trafford, ASK Vorwaerts needed to cancel out quickly the two-goal advantage Manchester United established in East Berlin two weeks ago. In the event, they did not even hint that they might do so, and, as a result, United marched comfortably into the quarter-final round of the competition.

Not that the German side submitted easily. They scurried around busily in attack in the second half, but clearly lacked the resource to pierce a firm Manchester defence until it was too late to matter. They could have done with someone as deadly at rounding off moves as Herd proved for Manchester.

Foulkes was always a barrier to the Germans, and with Stiles seemingly always on hand to intercept, there was little reward for so much activity. All too frequently the Germans' shafts were aimed from too great a distance to have any telling effect, although Vogt's heavy artillery could not lightly be disregarded. Fraessdorf pointed the way to his colleagues in attack with at least four fine bursts up the wing from his full back position, each accompanied with a splendid shot, but his example, for the most part, was disregarded.

Once they had edged their way ahead early in the match, Manchester always seemed to suggest they were taking matters comparatively easily. Best's elusive shuffling and the

GERMANS UNABLE TO RUFFLE UNITED'S DEFENCE

Manchester United 3, A.S.K. Vorwarts 1

For there to have been more than desultory interest in last night's European Cup tie at Old Trafford, A.S.K. Vorwärts needed to cancel out quickly the two-goal advantage Manchester United established in east Berlin two weeks ago. In the event, they did not even hint that they might do so, and, as a result, United marched comfortably into the quarter-final round of the competition.

Not that the German side submitted easily. They scurried around busily in attack in the second half, but clearly lacked the resource to pierce a firm Manchester defence until it was too late to matter. They could have done with someone as deadly at rounding off moves as Herd proved for Manchester.

Foulkes was always a barrier to the Germans, and with Stiles seemingly always on hand to intercept, there was little reward for so much activity. All too frequently the Germans' shafts were aimed from too great a distance to have any telling effect, ... Vogt's he...... ...uld not

RIGHT: *Law's shot rebounds off the post into the path of Herd . . . who shoots . . . and scores!*

periodic penetrating darts of Law and Charlton gave ASK Vorwaerts their moments of discomfort, but Manchester's attacking power was kept in rein. In the second half they were largely content to rest on their defence.

The exploratory sparring lasted 10 patternless minutes; then both crossbars were struck and United went ahead to dowse the German side's hopes. Stiles intercepted, Law tapped on his pass, and Herd dutifully scored.

Spirits Revived

Fraessdorf revived flagging German spirits with a swerving shot which struck the crossbar while P. Dunne could only stand and admire its trajectory. But almost before the applause for this had died, Law did the same at the other end, with a header from Connelly's centre.

ASK Vorwaerts' replies were mere tokens, however, and Herd emphasized the fruitlessness of it all five minutes before half-time, when he prodded home Law's headed pass.

In spite of all their second half endeavour, spiced with long-range shots by Vogt, Fraessdorf and Grossheim, ASK Vorwaerts could achieve nothing until eight minutes from the end, when Begerad passed inside A. Dunne for Piepenburg to score. But the stroke of time found Manchester in attacking mood again, for Herd to round off a Connelly-Law move.

THE TIMES, February 2, 1966

MAN. UTD.	3
BENFICA	**2**

1965-66 EUROPEAN CUP, QUARTER FINAL, FIRST LEG, MANCHESTER UNITED WIN 3-2

Manchester Foxed by the Great Eusebio

Precarious Lead Plucked from Magnificent Match

From our Association Football Correspondent

"**Y**ou are old Father William . . ." some may say, but it is a long time since I have enjoyed anything more. Last night Old Trafford was an international occasion; the field was decorated by some fine players and a 64,000 crowd enjoyed every moment of it – so much indeed that they applauded both sides on to the field at half time and off it at the finish. It was a great match.

Whatever happens in Lisbon in the second leg of this quarter-final tie in the European Cup, Manchester United at least have this victory under their belts. One goal may not be enough to take them into the last four, since Benfica, the champions of Portugal, who have reached the final of this senior European competition four times in the past five years, winning twice, remain unbeaten on their own soil. But tomorrow is tomorrow and who is to know but that Manchester United may yet be the first to succeed where many have failed.

To try to describe everything that happened within the 90 minutes of last night would be like trying to remember an evening with an Oscar Wilde, so many were the shafts of wit and poetry.

RIGHT: *Foulkes (left) heads United's third goal in their first leg victory over Benfica*

"Knew the Business"

We were presented with a necklace of events by two sides who "knew the business" as a visiting Frenchman said. And the night was made in a sense by the fact that Benfica, having taken the lead at the half hour allowed themselves the luxury of coming out of any defence to keep the night alive. But having been put behind, Manchester United themselves redoubled their earlier efforts and burst into a 3-1 lead, only to be foxed for the second time on the night by the great Eusebio who had made the first goal and now the second.

But that is anticipating each pearl of the necklace. Here was a match played at a sizzling speed, full of creation and movement. For Manchester, Charlton was in World Class, the equal on this occasion of Eusebio, who needs no space in which to move, a dark flash who shoots like a thunderbolt from all angles and at any range. For United, too, Herd was a bombardier, pressed on by the fluid movement of the darting Law and a delicate Best.

Casual Style

For Benfica there was, of course, Eusebio, lazy, almost casual, in movement, but eating up the ground as he changed direction, sending the defence one way and moving the other; little Simoes also jinking down one flank; and the long-striding giant Torres, at centre forward, another player with lazy strides, but seven league boots and a head that can almost reach a ball from the overhanging clouds.

Here, in fact, was a reiteration for those who believe in attacking football, and one can only hope that there will be some matches – at least one, we pray – like this, when the World Cup comes to be played in England next July.

One goal perhaps in the bank, as we have said before, may not be enough for Manchester United. But at least this night cannot be taken away. It was something to remember.

It was a night, too, when Manchester for all their attack and counter-attack did not quite take the last edges of their chances. Twice they hit the woodwork of Costa Pereira's goal. After only five minutes Herd, like a bird, rose to head Best's free kick against a post. Then 10 minutes from the end, Law headed a centre from Connelly at point-blank range; the Portuguese goalkeeper by instinctive reflex turned the ball upwards; and Law, rising again off springheels, headed once more only to see his effort strike the top of the crossbar.

Failed to Cover

All this is part of any 90 minutes of a game, but the first hard and positive fact came at the half

■■■■■■■LOOKING BACK WITH GEORGE BEST■■■■■■■

George Best quit serious football at the tender age of 26, Slack Alice, his aptly named night club in Manchester, got her man young.

But like many a genius, the talented boy from Belfast did his great work early, and no footballer has packed more artistry into a career. Best remains for many the greatest player ever to wear the red shirt of Manchester United and certainly he did more than anyone to attract people to football in general, and to Old Trafford in particular. In the mid-Sixties he took football into the pop world – a cult figure immensely attractive to girls.

His dexterous feet made of him an idol and hero, but they eventually turned to clay, and towards the end he was undoubtedly a destructive influence on the mangement careers of Wilf McGuinness and Frank O'Farrell. His increasing clashes with referees, combined with a tendency to run away at critical times, made him a difficult man to manage in a game where the team is all important.

All that was at the end, though, and it is a mistake to assume that, because he retired at a frustratingly early age, he had a short career. George Best had 11 seasons of first-team football for Manchester United and played well over 500 games for them. Hardly the record of a fly-by-night!

In the League he made 361 appearances, scoring 137 goals. In the FA Cup and League Cup competitions he scored 30 goals in 71 ties. In Europe he played 34 games and scored 11 goals, and of course he appeared in many friendly games.

It was in European competition that he made the break-through from home star to world status. Playing in the European Cup of season 1965-66 he turned the second leg of United's quarter-final with Benfica into a virtuoso performance.

United had won the first leg by the narrow margin of 3-2 at Old Trafford and the plan for Lisbon was to open with caution in an effort to protect their slender one-goal advantage. But as Matt Busby was to say later: "George Best must have had cotton wool in his ears during our team talk."

For the Irish imp went straight out to take the match by the scruff of the neck and score twice in the first 12 minutes to inspire a runaway 5-1 victory.

Best vividly remembers the game he lit up in the Stadium of Light: "We went out in front of the noisiest crowd I ever experienced. I felt superb. The atmosphere sent the blood coursing through my veins. It seemed to add power to my muscles, imagination to my brain.

"The Lisbon fans had never seen their team so humiliated. I remember counting our players during the match. Every time I looked up there seemed to be nothing but a United man to pass to. I couldn't go wrong."

After the game a man rushed up to him brandishing a knife. It was an alarming moment – until the stranger explained that all he wanted was a lock of the Irishman's hair in memory of a fantastic performance.

The Portuguese newspapers christened him El Beatle . . . symbol of the Swinging Sixties.

ABOVE LEFT: *Gregg (on ground) shows his disappointment at conceding a goal to Benfica.*

MANCHESTER FOXED BY THE GREAT EUSEBIO

◆

PRECARIOUS LEAD PLUCKED FROM MAGNIFICENT MATCH

From Our Association Football Correspondent

Manchester United 3, Benfica 2

"You are old Father William . . ." some may say, but it is a long time since I have enjoyed anything more. Last night Old Trafford was an international occasion: the field was decorated by

not quite take the last edges of their chances. Twice they hit the woodwork of Costa Pereira's goal. After only five minutes Herd, like a bird, rose to head Best's free kick against a post. Then 10 minutes from the end Law had a centre f-

hour after much Manchester attacking set on fire by the flame of Charlton. Suddenly, in riposte, Benfica forced a corner on the left; the lithe, free-moving Eusebio bent an inswinger from the flag bang onto the tall head of Augusto and there was the ball in the back of Gregg's net past a United defence which had suddenly failed to cover.

Yet, within 10 minutes of half time United scored twice to go in with a lead. The equalizer came from a flowing movement between Stiles, Law, and Best, and it was Best's through pass, as incisive as the knife of any surgeon, which put Herd clean through to hit Pereira's net.

With only seconds to go to the interval Best took a bad corner from the right; it was blocked, but Charlton, moving like the wind, recovered the ball far out on the right, turned like a ballet dancer and, with his back to the goal, swivelled a left foot cross into a crowded goalmouth for Law, sharp as a needle, to flash it home. United led 2-1.

Came that applause at the interval for both sides and with half an hour left Cantwell took a free kick on the left into a crowded goalmouth and Foulkes rose above the company to head Manchester 3-1 into the lead. But it was now that Benfica showed their experience and their quality as a side who have their pedigree in this hard competition. Their back section of the 4-2-4 now played it strong and hard with Germano particularly tough.

Gregg Confused

The crowd roared and chanted its songs. But the Portuguese did not give ground. They counter-attacked. This was a battle in depth and three times Eusebio, floating free with deceptive footwork, lashed rocketing shots just beyond Gregg's post. Then, with 20 minutes to go little Simoes crossed from right to left and Eusebio, turning on the smallest coin at the far byline, bent the centre back which completely confused Gregg and left Torres to do something which even I could have done, on the goal-line.

That was 3-2 and it was almost 3-3 before the finish when some tremendous play by Eusebio and a shot over the bar by him followed by a free kick from some 40 yards which went past Gregg – fortunately for him on the right side of a post – left Manchester still in the lead. Whether they will still be in the lead on the night of March 6 in the second leg in the presence of 90,000 Portuguese we must await. But last night we shall remember.

DAILY HERALD, Wednesday, March 9, 1966

BENFICA   **I**

MAN. UTD   **5**

1965-66 EUROPEAN CUP, QUARTER FINAL, SECOND
LEG, MANCHESTER UNITED WIN 8-3 ON AGGREGATE

BEST SMASHES OUT BENFICA

W EDNESDAY.— With the most magnificent and devastating football I have ever seen produced on a foreign field by any British side —club or international —Manchester United tonight swept into their third European Cup semi-final.

Benfica 1
Manchester Utd 5
aggregate 3-8

into this spectacular Estadio de Lus came to celebrate a seemingly inevitable Benfica triumph. After all, the Eagles, twice champions of the Continent, had won 18 and drawn one of their 19 European contests, scoring 78 goals against 14.

Never had any foreign side scored more than two goals in a

the sinewy Best, who streaked away for goal. He spurted past two white-shirted Benfiva defenders as if they were statues before slamming a swift right foot shot low to the corner.

Two minutes later Denis Law masterminded a superb third goal. The 1964 European Footballer of the Year worked the ball in from a deep position, cleverly drew two defenders before slipping the ball to Best, who played it on for Connelly to crack in a third.

This was United in incredible command. Matt Busby's men, so eager to regain the prestige they lost with a crashing 5—0 defeat by Sporting in this city

---

Wednesday. – With the most magnificent and devastating football I have ever seen produced on a foreign field by any British side – club or international – Manchester United tonight swept into their third European Cup semi-final.

Benfica, the Eagles of Lisbon, who previously had never been beaten in 19 European games on their own ground, were more than just beaten tonight . . . they were pulverised.

Shimmering

United, who came here with a 3-2 lead and in the words of Matt Busby "to prove themselves," were three up after just 14 minutes.

George Best, the 19-year-old Belfast genius touching new heights in his already meteoric career, scored the first two in the 6th and 12th minutes.

John Connelly, producing the form he has never shown in an England shirt, notched the

third two minutes later – from a Best pass.

The 80,000 crowd jammed into this spectacular Estadio de Lus came to celebrate a seemingly inevitable Benfica triumph. After all, the Eagles, twice champions of the Continent, had won 18 and drawn one of their 19 European contests, scoring 78 goals against 14.

Never had any foreign side scored more than two goals in a competitive match on this ground.

ABOVE: *Best's shot flies past Benfica 'keeper Costa Pereira – one of United's five goals in their second leg win*

Before the 10pm. kick-off, to a tumultuous cheer and with rockets lighting up the Lisbon night sky, Eusebio was presented with a statuette to mark his selection as European Footballer of the Year.

Inside 12 minutes he should have handed his award over to brilliant boy Best. The lad with the Beatle haircut tonight produced the shimmering skills and spectacular craft of a vintage Matthews, Finney, Garrincha – think of who you will.

Mastermind

Best headed the first from a pinpoint free kick by Tony Dunne. Goalkeeper Costa Pereira was stranded in no man's land as the ball soared into the top corner.

Then in the 12th minute came a goal that was almost a replica of his magnificent solo against Wolves in the FA Cup last Saturday. Charlton played the ball back to Gregg, who booted a mighty clearance two-thirds the length of the field.

Herd nodded the ball back to the sinewy Best, who streaked away for goal. He spurted past two white-shirted Benfica defenders as if they were statues before slamming a swift right foot shot low to the corner.

Two minutes later Denis Law masterminded a superb third goal. The 1964 European Footballer of the Year worked the ball in from a deep position, cleverly drew two defenders before slipping the ball to Best, who played it on for Connelly to crack in a third.

This was United in incredible command. Matt Busby's men, so eager to regain the prestige they lost with a crashing 5-0 defeat by Sporting in this city two years ago, also had two other first-half goals disallowed and saw goalkeeper Costa Pereira produce two incredible saves from Herd and Charlton.

ABOVE: *Law*

Shaken

At half-time the conquering Manchester men walked off to a polite applause ... the capacity crowd were too stunned to give them the royal reception they so thoroughly deserved.

In the second half it seemed as if United would again dominate all, with Best again threading his way through the middle. But then after only seven minutes, from one of the first concerted Benfica raids of the match, right-back Shay Brennan sliced through his own goal – a woeful mistake when there was neither danger nor pressure on him.

Gregg had to speed swiftly and bravely to the edge of the penalty area to clear from Torres.

But with the aggregate score at 6-3 in United's favour, there was never the alarm or

ABOVE: *Crerand on his way to score United's fourth goal*

desperation that Benfica so wanted to see in the opposing ranks.

All around me in a crowded Press box journalists from all over Europe were saying: "Congratulations, tonight we are seeing the first British champions of Europe."

Antonia Valencia, the leading journalist of Spain, told me: "They are worthy of Real Madrid at their greatest."

With twelve minutes to go to set the seal on a memorable victory, Pat Crerand shot United's fourth goal – and as if on cue thousands got up and started to stream away from the stadium.

They did not want to bother with the final minutes of the first-ever European defeat of their beloved Eagles.

Law made the fourth goal, making a superb pass on to the penalty spot for the unmarked Crerand to smack into the net.

Law neatly threaded his way through them just to prove that nothing Benfica or their crowd could do tonight would stop the march of the most thrilling and deserved British club achievement on the Continent.

Charlton waltzed through for a dazzling fifth goal . . . the revenge was complete. And fittingly by the same total – FIVE.

LEFT: *Charlton (with ball left) about to put home United's fifth goal, Cavem (centre) chases in vain*

. . . but they can still do it

BELGRADE, Wednesday.—If Manchester United are to become Britain's first European champions they will have to play considerably more 'ike it in the return leg of th... final at C... next Wed...

Th...

DAILY HERALD, Wednesday, April 13, 1966

PARTIZAN BELGRADE 2

1965-66 EUROPEAN CUP, SEMI-FINAL, FIRST LEG, PARTIZAN WIN 2-0

By Peter Lorenzo
BELGRADE, APRIL 13

If Manchester United are to become Britain's first European champions they will have to play considerably more like it in the return leg of this semi-final at Old Trafford next Wednesday.

The same team whipped Benfica 5-1 in the last round. But tonight they had no punch, sparkle or rhythm.

The aristocrats of British soccer had one excuse . . . they played for the last 12 minutes with George Best little more than a passenger. He again wrenched his injured right knee going

▬ LOOKING BACK WITH DENIS LAW ▬

Denis Law describes it as his most joyful match in Europe . . . the night Manchester United beat Benfica in Lisbon 5-1 in the quarter-final of the European Cup.

United had gone to Portugal for the second leg with only a bare one-goal lead.

They had beaten Benfica 3-2 at Old Trafford, but the Portuguese players left the pitch smiling. Few people thought one goal would be sufficient to account for probably the most powerful team in Europe.

"Benfica in 1966 were the cream. They had been in three European Cup finals and had taken over from the legendary Real Madrid as top dogs," explained Denis Law.

"Two years previously we had been beaten 5-0 in Lisbon in the Cup Winners Cup, and when we went out all the Portuguese fans were holding their hands with all five fingers giving us the salute.

"Sir Matt Busby had made tactical plans for a careful start because we could ill afford to give away an early goal that would wipe out our slender advantage.

"To say we were keyed up would be an understatement. There was an 80,000 crowd packing the famous Stadium of Light, and I wasn't exactly pleased when Pat Crerand, kicking a ball about in the dressing room, banged it against the mirror.

"The glass shattered, and though no-one said anything, I imagine everyone was thinking about seven years bad luck. It certainly didn't help the mood, yet we went out and were three goals up on the night in the first quarter of an hour.

"It was incredible and the best performance in my view from a United team in Europe. It was a beautiful experience and a joy to share in that splendid team effort.

"George Best, only 19 at the time, grabbed the headlines and no-one begrudged him that; after all it was cheeky George who scored the first two goals and helped lay on the third for John Connelly.

"In the last quarter of an hour I put Pat Crerand in for a goal and Bobby Charlton waltzed through for the fifth.

"My name was missing from the scoresheet, but it was of no consequence because I knew I had played well, just like everyone else in the team.

"It was unusual for the three so-called stars, Charlton, Law and Best, all to turn it on in the same match, but they did that night. So did Nobby Stiles, Pat Crerand, John Connelly and the rest of them.

"Everything came off for us. By rights we should have gone on to win the European Cup that year, but we played badly in the semi-final against Partizan Belgrade, losing 2-0 in Yugoslavia and winning only 1-0 back at Old Trafford.

"So we missed out on final glory. But Sir Matt Busby called our performance in Lisbon 'our finest hour' and I think he summed it up well."

up for a high ball but even before had never been at ease with his leg, or the opposition.

Yet for all their sluggish laboured ineptitude United should still have had the game sewn up inside 20 minutes. By then Law and Best had squandered easy chances and Herd had landed a centre on the top netting instead of to the far post for the unmarked Law.

Close Call

Then, in the 38th minute, from United's best move of the match, Law hammered a cross from Best against the bar.

United were made to pay for their careless marksmanship in the second half. Partizan scored twice in the first 14 minutes, the first following hesitancy by Gregg, the second a beauty worthy of any European contest.

In the lead against a side they considered played "the most modern football in the world," Partizan had United on the run.

Cheered on by a capacity 50,000 crowd they dominated play for a brief spell and came desperately close to adding a third. Right-half Becejac, scorer of the magnificent second goal, completely miskicked when the ball was whipped back to him 10 yards from United's goal.

Right-winger Bajic headed wide from an excellent position and then Gregg, guilty with the first goal, atoned completely with a superb, courageous clearance when centre-forward

ABOVE: *Team members at lunch before their first leg tie against Partizan Belgrade. From the left: Stiles, Gregg, Best, Sadler, Fitzpatrick*

Hasanagic bore down upon him from the penalty spot. The United keeper threw himself to his right to save a situation that would have made it perilously difficult for the return leg.

As it is, a two-goal deficit should not be beyond United.

The Yuogoslavs, extremely respectful of United's reputation and ability, made it public they wanted a 4-0 lead – at least – to win through.

I side with my Yugoslav friends. I still think United will become the first British side to

---

They called Denis Law the Demon King because in his 11 years at Old Trafford he was a master marksman with a tremendous scoring rate which saw him notch 28 goals in 33 European games.

He was voted European Player of the Year in 1964. He was electric near goal. When he jumped he seemed to have a personal sky hook which kept him suspended head and shoulders above the rest.

He was as sharp as a tack with razor reflexes, and he went in where it hurt which is probably why you don't see him turning out in testimonial and friendly matches these days.

He has a legacy of injuries to knees and neck which have exacted a price. Not that he complains; quite the contrary, he is a bundle of chatter and cheerfulness, quite different from the rather intense character of his youth.

Denis Law had to fight hard for his success. As a youngster he was small and no-one would have asked him to model for Mr Atlas.

Perhaps that's what gave him a natural aggression and determination which at times had him in the sin bin.

But his fire and fury endeared him to the fans and served him well in a career which started with Bill Shankly at Huddersfield and took in Manchester City, Torino, Manchester United and City again.

Denis no doubt has warm memories of every club he played for, including Scotland, but he looks back on his time at Old Trafford with particular affection.

"It was the swinging sixties in soccer as well as with the Beatles and all that, and I think we saw football at its best.

"I was privileged to play in a great side. Sir Matt Busby had recovered after Munich and I came home from Italy to join the team he had rebuilt.

"It was a splendid team to play in with players like Pat Crerand, Bobby Charlton, Nobby Stiles and George Best. Over a period of five years United were outstanding for entertainment and goals.

"We always felt that if the opposition scored one, we could score two, if they scored two we could get three. It didn't always work out, but that was the feeling, and it was all very special

for me."

Manchester is still home to Denis and his wife Diane, with four of their five children still with them in Bowdon, Cheshire – Gary 22, Robert 18, Ian 16 and Diana 13.

The fifth, 20-yr-old Andrew is at sea with BP Shipping.

Denis is with the Manchester company, Speedlith Litho Graphics, a print repro house, but is a familiar voice on radio as perceptive and sharp with his comments on football as he was in opposition goalmouths as a player.

Denis Law, 1966

ABOVE: *Connelly (diving centre) tries a spectacular header watched by Law (right)*

RIGHT: *Goalmouth action as Partizan (white strip) clear*

contest the final of Europe's No. 1 competition – if they play with something approaching their normal form and flair.

Great Player

United have lost their first European Cup match this season. They have played worse in the competition – in the first game in Helsinki last September – but then the opposition wasn't skilled enough to take advantage.

Partizan who are through to the semi-finals for the first time in their history, are not in the class of Inter-Milan, Real Madrid or Benfica.

But Velibor Vasovic, a 26-year-old left-half in the Duncan Edwards mould, both in build and commanding talent, is one of the finest players in Europe if not in the world. He is the strong-man focal point of a team of honest endeavour but lacking the inventiveness and flexibility of most European Cup semi-finalists.

Before the game Vasovic, the Partizan skipper, was presented with a statuette to commemorate his selection as Yugoslav "Foot-baller of the Year." It's ironic to remember that before the Lisbon game, Benfica's Eusebio was presented with a statuette to mark his selection as European "Footballer of the Year" ... for in comparison Vasovic is twice the

player that Eusebio is.

Swift Goal

Apart from comfortably containing all that Law and the others had to offer, the hulking Vasovic had the enterprise and energy to be the forceful originator of most Partizan attacks.

It was his pinpoint accuracy that led to the second goal in the 59th minute. Following a foul by Crerand, a free-kick was swung right across field to the unmarked Vasovic loitering some 15 yards inside United's half.

Swiftly he slotted a long pass through to right-half Becejac, who skilfully breasted the ball down and turned to hit a fast low shot into the corner of the net.

Fierce Header

Partizan's first, two minutes after the restart, followed a long cross from right-back Jusifi. Gregg started to come out, changed his mind and stayed on the line – to be beaten by a fierce header from Hasanajic.

With the Partizan goals, United's faults became even more marked – and an unhappy afternoon for them was climaxed when Nobby Stiles had his name taken.

Yugoslav inside-left Miladinovic was also booked in the second half for arguing.

THE SUN, April 20, 1966

MAN. UTD.   **1**

PARTIZAN BELGRADE   **0**

1965-66 EUROPEAN CUP, SEMI-FINAL, SECOND LEG, PARTIZAN BELGRADE WIN 2-1 ON AGGREGATE

End of a Busby Dream

Crerand and Slav get Marching Orders

By Len Noad

Manager Matt Busby's dreams of European Cup triumph for Manchester United were dashed by the powerful Partizan defence at Old Trafford last night.

United scored the only goal of this match after 73 minutes — but were unable to grab a second — needed to force a play-off in this semi-final tie.

United's goal was the result of an amazing error by Partizan's brilliant goalkeeper, Soskic. An error which blazed this otherwise frustrating game into a finale of nerve-shattering excitement.

Nobby Stiles made a weak cross from a short corner in the 73rd minute. Soskic for once was caught unawares and though he flung himself desperately across his goal he was only able to palm the ball into the net.

Although Manchester did almost all the attacking in the first half they failed to break down the calm, methodical Partizan defence.

Shorn of the jinking genius of George Best their sole idea appeared to be to find Denis Law with a long ball through the middle.

But Partizan kept their left half-back to cover the centre-half and there looked little prospect of a breakthrough.

United appeared to be overawed by the

SUN SPORT Manc.

END OF A BU
Crerand and Slav get marching orders

PAT CRERAND ... fateful

MANAGER MATT BUSBY'S dreams of European Cup triumph for Manchester United were dashed by the powerful Partizan defence at Old Trafford last night.

United scored the only goal of this match after 73 minutes—but were unable to grab a second— needed to force a play-off in this semi-final tie.

United's goal was the result of an amazing error by Partizan's brilliant goalkeeper, Soskic. An error which blazed this otherwise frustrating game into a finale of nerve-shattering excitement.

Stiles

ABOVE: *The ball in the Yugoslav net as United score the only goal of the match* LEFT: *Goal-mouth action from the same match*

two-goal deficit facing them and tenseness affected their normal flowing attacks.

Fisted Out

They had their first shot at goal after eight minutes but David Herd's solo effort only just had enough pace to reach the goalkeeper.

Three minutes later Herd headed the ball through a defensive chink to Law, but he just failed to reach it.

After 20 minutes Law, now playing in an advanced striking position, was put through by Connelly. He rounded the goalkeeper, but his speed took him away to the left of the goal and he could only hit Soskic with his final effort.

Just before half-time the goalkeeper came out intelligently to fist away from Herd as Law came crashing in. And almost on the whistle Connelly was too slow to accept a first-rate chance near the penalty spot.

United were desperately pressing,

but the safe hands of Soskic were equal to everything they could throw at him.

In the 70th minute, after Stiles had been pulled up for a foul, Crerand and inside-left Mihaslovic exchanged blows and were immediately sent off.

As they crossed the touchline two policemen intercepted them as they appeared likely to continue their dispute and United club skipper Noel Cantwell raced across to escort Crerand to the dressing-room.

This incident followed a spate of fouls which the referee had dealt with leniently.

Denis Law and David Herd had become a double spearhead after the interval when Partizan's tactics were obviously to hang on to the lead they built up in Belgrade last week.

But in the odd breakaway Miladinovic shot just over the bar after Stiles had been lectured for tripping right-winger Bajic.

Although Manchester United finished fourth in season 1965-66, it wasn't good enough in those days for a place in Europe. However, they turned their absence from the glamour scene to good advantage.

They became the 1967 champions with Alex Stepney signed to take over in goal and become, in Sir Matt Busby's view, the biggest single factor behind winning the championship again.

It was Busby's fifth League title with a team which also now included players like Nobby Stiles, David Sadler and John Aston.

They clinched the title with a tremendous scoring flourish, winning 6-1 at West Ham with goals from Denis Law (2), George Best, Bobby Charlton, Pat Crerand and Bill Foulkes.

The stage was set for United to become the first English club to win the European Cup with their historic 4-1 final victory over Benfica in extra time at Wembley in 1968.

Their success gave them a crack at the World Club championship and of course gave them entry into the European Cup the following season before bowing out of Europe for a lean and troubled eight years.

Demon Denis finds —goal touch again

By DEREK HODGSON

Manchester United 4

Hibernian Malta 0

★★

DENIS LAW, United's Demon King, has been resting between engagements this

DAILY EXPRESS, September 20, 1967

MAN. UTD. 4

HIBERNIANS VALLETTA 0

1967-68 EUROPEAN CUP, FIRST ROUND, FIRST LEG, MANCHESTER UNITED WIN 4-0

Demon Denis Finds Goal Touch Again

By Derek Hodgson

Denis Law, United's Demon King, has been resting between engagements this season. Last night (with his Christmas bookings in danger) Law proved quite conclusively that there is little wrong with the old thunderflash, in head or feet.

He chose this European Cup first leg against part-time Maltese champions to score his first goal this season — and if the opposition was barely footballing standard, his was the goal that demonstrated there would be no Maltese miracle.

For Hibernians turned out to be far from as naive and innocent as they sounded on arrival.

They know all about defensive wingers, sweepers, and funnelling defences. So that United, leading by only the 11th-minute goal from David Sadler, were looking distinctly embarrassed when Law struck.

In the 43rd minute, psychologically the worst possible time to concede a goal, he let fly right-footed from 30 yards with a low shot that Alfred Mizzi dived to but couldn't possibly stop — the ball bounced high from his body to curve into the net behind him. It was a shot Bobby Charlton would have claimed with pride.

In the second half Law then demonstrated a few jack-knife headers as the Maltese, gradually being worn down, resigned themselves to a 90-minute siege of the penalty area.

They got in one shot only at Alex Stepney in the 87th minute — he had previously fielded the ball five times.

IT'S THIS PATHETIC LACK OF FIRE-POWER FROM HIBERNIAN THAT MAKES ME THINK UNITED SHOULD WIN THE SECOND LEG NEXT WEEK BY A GREATER MARGIN UNLESS THE HEAT AND SAND-ED PITCH SLOW THEM DOWN.

Hibs were without their international captain Louis Theobald, but his brother Eddie, captain for the night, revealed himself as the most accomplished player from left half.

Released

As for little Francis Mifsud, the boy winger who got lost on his way from London, he was so occupied with his defensive duties marking Brian Kidd, Manchester will never know his capabilities.

United's second-half goals were scored by Sadler (58), Law (61), and Sadler released from his chains for once might have had four or five goals.

Hibernians' coach Father Hilary Tagliaferro said afterwards: "We got the result we set out for and but for the goal just before half time, which was a bad time psychologically, the score might have been even closer.

"The heat will affect Manchester United more than they realise in Malta and this score means we shall certainly draw a record crowd of about 20,000."

BELOW: Sadler (right) sees United's third goal in

RIGHT: United's second goal flies past Mizzi, the Hibs' 'keeper

ABOVE: *United go all the way in Europe at last!*

RIGHT: *Sadler (centre mid-air) heads United into the lead in the first leg match against Hibernians Malta*

The Maltese constabulary stands by as the referee has words with, among others, United's Denis Law

The end of the affair

From DEREK HODGSON

Hibernians 0, Manchester U. 0 ★★
(United win 4—0 on aggregate)

27 SEP Malta, Wednesday

MANCHESTER UNITED, caked with dust, sweat and sand, sprinted off the Gzira Stadium oven at the end of this European Cup-tie knowing that their torrid love affair with Malta had dropped several degrees in temperature.

If they felt like the cast of the Desert Song they also played like them. And not even leading man Matt Busby, extremely vocal on the trainer's bench, could save the show.

They had these excuses: A 4—0 first leg lead; they were [...] in more than 80 degrees [...]

DAILY EXPRESS, September 27, 1967

HIBERNIANS VALLETTA 0

1967-68 EUROPEAN CUP, FIRST ROUND, SECOND LEG, MANCHESTER UNITED WIN 4-0 ON AGGREGATE

By Derek Hodgson
MALTA, WEDNESDAY

Manchester United, caked with dust, sweat and sand, sprinted off the Gzira Stadium oven at the end of this European Cup-tie knowing that their torrid love affair with Malta had dropped several degrees in temperature.

If they felt like the cast of the Desert Song they also played like them. And not even leading man Matt Busby, extremely vocal on the trainer's bench, could save the show.

They had these excuses: a 4-0 first leg lead; they were playing in more than 80 degrees temperature and the pitch was like nothing met before, with an incalculable bounce and an even more disconcerting acceleration of the ball.

In addition, they could claim they twice hit the Hibs' bar; that 'keeper Freddie Mizzi made four great saves, and that this Hibernian team, as I observed at Old Trafford, needs no advice in modern defensive tactics.

They played a sweeper behind the back four in the first leg. This time they turned out another defender at outside left and made it plain that any goals scored would have to be earned.

Lack

So United much as they may have wished to demonstrate their skill and scoring power preferred particularly in the second half to think about another day . . . probably Saturday.

But they cannot altogether excuse a woeful lack of penetration.

Naturally Malta's best-ever crowd of 25,000 was bitterly disappointed as United got as many jeers as cheers when they ran off. Hibs the sacrificial lambs, are Malta's heroes tonight and it would be churlish to deny them an hour of glory which I suspect will not be their last.

United were even less popular in the 52nd minute, when Nobby Stiles brought down John Priviterri. There was a scuffle among players, the crowd began screaming insults, and mounted police cantered down the sidelines.

In the next five minutes, both George Best and Francis Burns were sent crashing on to the dusty limestone. Fortunately this was the last incident. The match resumed in almost monotonous pattern of nonstop but ineffective attacking by United.

THE DAILY TELEGRAPH, November 15, 1967

PK SARAJEVO 0

1967-68 EUROPEAN CUP, SECOND ROUND, FIRST LEG, DRAW 0-0

By R. H. Williams
Sarajevo, Wednesday

Manchester United finished their European Cup-tie at Kosevo Stadium here tonight proudly stroking the ball about among themselves and, I hope, grateful for the good luck that helped them to do exactly what they came to do.

Their opponents were reduced to 10 men from the 35th minute, when one of their three front men, Prodanovic, was taken off with a leg injury, and Sarajevo had looked even more unlucky before that when the referee disallowed an apparent goal by the young local hero, centre-forward Musemic.

Sarajevo, especially with this sort of luck, were not quite good enough to make their prospects at Old Trafford on November 29 particularly rosy.

They will presumably have 11 men there and there is certainly enough skill in the side to make United respectful.

They are not likely to ingratiate themselves with the Old Trafford crowd by their tackling. Although crunches were not audible from my distance they were distinctly visible and Best and Kidd particularly came in for some hard treatment.

No Incidents
Stepney Superb

But United took their knocks like gentlemen,

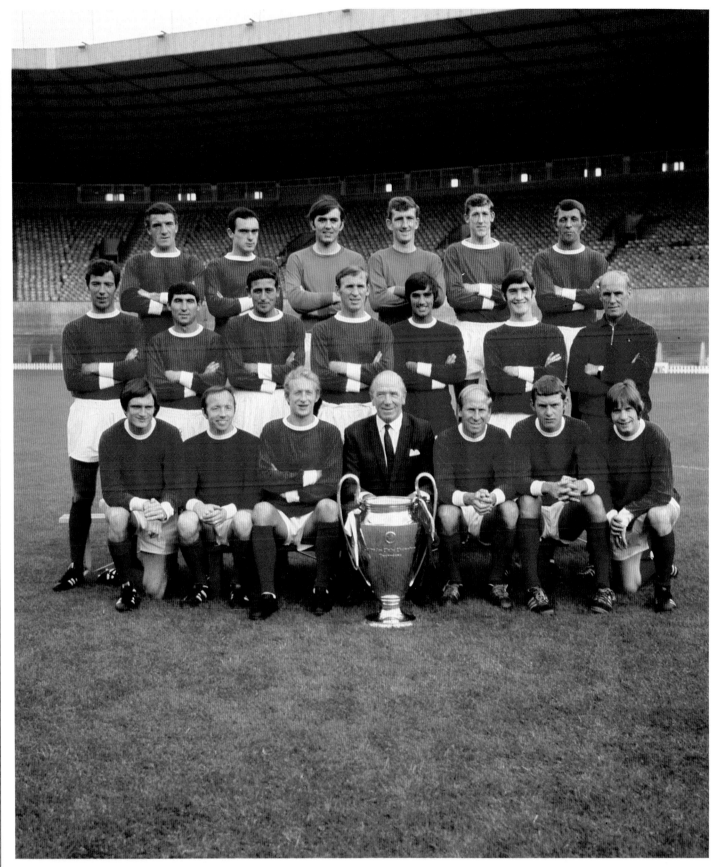

The triumphant team at home at Old Trafford with the European Cup

Action from the World Club Championship 1968: United play Estudiantes of Argentina

which proves that it is possible, and no incidents occurred that might have inflamed soccer sociologists.

United's defence naturally took the greatest credit. Stepney was superb and Dunne, Crerand and Foulkes were outstandingly firm and positive defenders.

Kidd, after taking on the Sarajevo defence almost single handed, did a brave job and when United in the final stages decided they could afford to attack he revelled in the sudden freedom and might even have scored with a flamboyant, Law-like overhead kick, but it was not quite accurate enough.

Wonderful Save
Desperate Times

The first 22 minutes contained the real contest and at the end of that period United were a shade lucky not to be a goal down. In fact, from my position high above the half-way line, they were.

United had been playing well back, with only Kidd lying upfield, and naturally Sarajevo had done their best to take advantage.

In the seventh minute Stepney made a wonderful reflexive dive to save from Antic and tipped a strong 30-yard shot from Prlyaca over the bar, but generally United, sometimes in some desperation, had kept their opponents at arm's length until the 22nd minute.

Prlyaca then slipped the ball through to Musemic, who swayed to his right and rounded Foulkes before shooting. Stepney could not move fast enough this time but he partially stopped the ball, which trickled beyond him towards, and I thought over, the line.

Stepney recovered and dived on the ball as Dunne tried to rescue him. But although the ball still looked comfortably over the line from my viewpoint, it did not from the linesman's and, to the horror and disgust of the crowd, a goal was not awarded.

In the first half United did not make a single chance for themselves. The nearest approach to one was when Aston intercepted a goalkeeper's clearance and flicked the ball to Kidd, whose off-balanced shot was blocked.

Just before half-time Fitzpatrick had his name taken after an ordinary-looking foul, possibly for showing dissent.

Strain Tells
Kidd Denied

Immediately after the break United looked almost certain to take the lead when a cross from the left-wing by Best eluded Muftic, but as Fitzpatrick arrived on the spot like a second Denis Law he tried to scramble the fast-moving ball into the net but failed to connect.

It was in the second half that the strain of trying to play an attacking game with only 10 men drained the sap from Sarajevo. Prlyaca, a most useful forward, who can work the ball well and has a devastating shot, faded and without his prompting the attack died on its feet.

With 15 minutes to go and United moving more readily into the attack, Kidd put in a worthy shot from 25 yards which Muftic thankfully fingertipped over the bar. It was a sign that United forwards were now in business, and the crowd seemed to sense that their team's brave effort had failed.

United finished the game playing proud football, passing the ball about at last in lordly style, leisurely but recognisable as that of a team who, luck or no luck, had everything under control.

THE TIMES, November 29, 1967

| MAN. UTD. | 2 |
| PK SARAJEVO | 1 |

1967-68 EUROPEAN CUP, FIRST ROUND, SECOND LEG, MANCHESTER UNITED WIN 2-1 ON AGGREGATE

United Can Look Ahead with Rising Hopes

Sarajevo Offer Fine Resistance

**By Geoffrey Green,
Football Correspondent**

Manchester United are in the last stage of the European Cup. Having drawn 0-0 away and last night at Old Trafford beaten Sarajevo – the champions and losing cup finalists of Yugoslavia last year – they can now look forward to the future with rising hope.

In the next round they will have Denis Law back from suspension and with him, possibly, Stiles, now the lighter by a cartilage. By then their sails should be trimmed.

On winning the Football League Championship, Matt Busby, the manager of United, said: "We have the team to win the European title". Without a couple of his key men, the fact that they have survived this test speaks a volume. Indeed, one of their important figures last night, in an undramatic way in a traumatic match, was Burns, normally a full back but now wearing the number seven shirt and playing an intelligent midfield role. At Old Trafford anyone plays anywhere and the well of skill is deep.

Here was a splendid match – movement, deep technical content and excitement. The fact that Prljaca was sent off for a violent tackle on the elusive Best, half an hour from the end, should not be allowed to cloud the issue.

This was a man's match in every way – full of swift artistry, point, counter-point in defence

European Cup

MANCHESTER UNITED FAVOURED BY FORTUNE

INJURY-HIT SARAJEVO ALMOST CAUSE UPSET

By R. H. WILLIAMS

Sarajevo 0   Manchester United 0

SARAJEVO, Wednesday.

United can look ahead with rising hopes

Sarajevo offer fine resistance

By GEOFFREY GREEN, Football Correspondent

Manchester United 2, Sarajevo 1

Manchester United are in the | United tackling was too forthright. | cross by Kidd, a header by Best which
last

and attack and hard physical challenge. If the Slavs now think that much of the United tackling was too forthright, Manchester themselves could point out a deal of body checking and other irregularities. This is what happens when the two ideologies of how to play football come face to face.

That is perhaps a worn out plot, but on this night there was an exciting velvety charm about it all. There were figures, who with their brushwork filled in the picture. One, of course, was Best – a player full of fantasy; a player who lent magic to what might have been whimsy. He may have been provocative as he goaded some of the Yugoslav players with gesture. But Best now lives the life of a marked man, and these days has to suffer much.

Talented Team

A beautiful performance depends on a balance of all its elements and for much of this night there was some beautiful playing. Sarajevo were talented, with men like the hard, little Siljkut, Bajic and Antic, progressive in attack, and Fazlagic, from the rear.

Manchester withstood it all and from the opening set up a barrage that led to their first goal after only 11 minutes. There was a header, just wide, by Best after a move between Crerand – in great form – and Brennan; then, from 25 yards, Kidd almost uprooted Mustic's left hand goal post.

Then came the strike – a clever move again between Brennan and Crerand which opened the way; a cross by Kidd, header by Best which Mustic parried at full stretch, only for Aston to storm in and squeeze the rebound home inside the near post.

Earlier Antic had three corner chances to have put Sarajevo in a strong position, but by half-time all the action had taken place in front of Mustic as efforts by Best (three times), Burns and Kidd nearly found their mark.

The 62,000 crowd was in a hum at the interval. That is always a sign. And within minutes of the re-start there was a tip over the crossbar by Stepney from Antic. Yet always Best remained the centrepiece of the chess-board. He was the knight and the bishop as he slanted on varying angles, once hitting a post,

ABOVE: *Referee Machin of France is in no doubt – Prljaca is sent off in the second leg tie between United and PK Sarajevo*

then drawing a great save from Mustic until finally Prljaca was sent off for that tackle.

Perhaps by subtle suggestion he had been goaded into it. Maybe it was a case of half a dozen of one and six of the other. At any rate, from the free-kick Aston pulled back Crerand's pass from the left by-line (some fair minded Mancunian even thought it was over the line), Foulkes headed on to the crossbar and there was the irrepressible Best to volley home United's second goal.

To their great credit, Sarajevo, with clever footwork and positional play, sought out every avenue until the end. After Stepney had made a terrific save from Antic in the fading minutes, there was Delalic to head in a cross by Blazevic to narrow the margin. But it was too late.

THE GUARDIAN, February 28, 1968

MAN. UTD.	2
GORNIK ZABRZE	0

1967-68 EUROPEAN CUP, QUARTER FINAL, FIRST LEG,
MANCHESTER UNITED WIN 2-0

Now it's up to Manchester United's Defence

By Albert Barham

Manchester United came through the first battle of their quarter final of the European Cup with a sense of frustration and foreboding which lasted until the last minute.

Until then one goal against Gornik, the Polish champions, at Old Trafford, seemed too slim ever to win this tie. Then as the final seconds of this thrilling match ticked away Kidd made United's chance a fortnight hence in Chorzow a real one of getting through to the semifinals.

We shall know then, though, whether United's defence has any flaws. There were too few chances for Gornik to exploit any last night. They were forced back and seemed content to be so on defence for almost all the game. One can understand it for this was a remarkable performance of defensive football. United threw everything at them – and that is considerable when measured in the skill, speed, and understanding that United had. Yet this was a triumph in a way for Gornik until those last few moments. It was a triumph particularly

ABOVE: *Kidd (second from left) watches as his back-heel goes in for United's second goal against Gornik Zabrze*

for Kostka, the goalkeeper. Surely he can never have had a greater game than he did last night. But this was not his night alone.

Oslizlo marshalled the defence most competently. There were few gaps for United to prise apart for a shot. They did have their chances but perhaps a little overeagerness may have been apparent. One can understand the feeling that this Polish side, conquerors of Dynamo Kiev, is among the best of the last eight left in this, Europe's major competition. But the battle in Chorzow will prove if United's defence is equal to its attack.

Many clubs have gone to Old Trafford de-

Now it is up to Manchester United's defence

By ALBERT BARHAM : Manchester United 2, Gornik Zabrze 0

Manchester United came through the first battle of their quarterfinal of the European

have had a greater game than he did last night. But this was not his night alone.

Oslizlo marshalled the defenc~

And how strongly the side tried for goals. But there was no way round or over this Polish defence that United could discover.

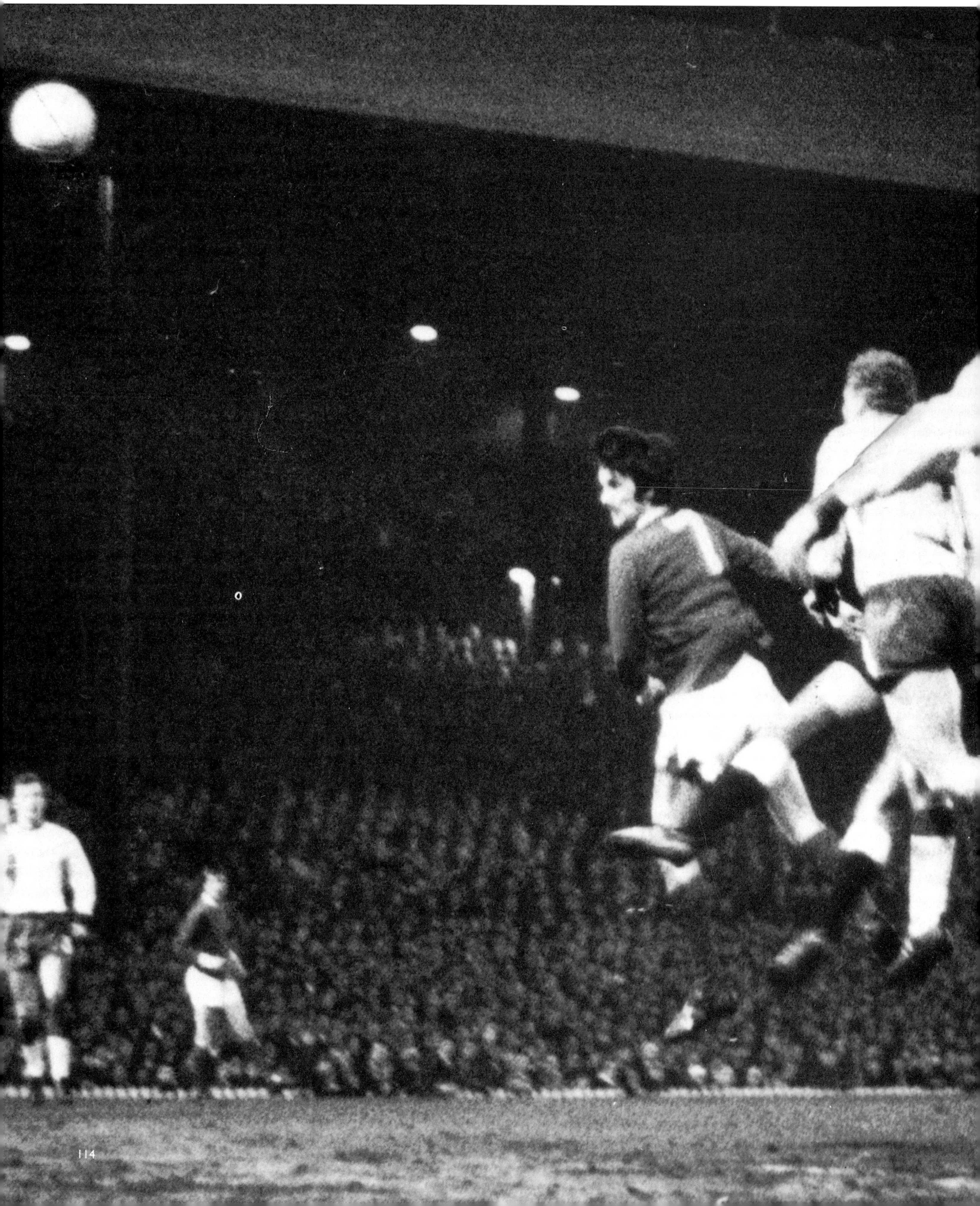

termined to play tightly in defence. Few, however, have faced such tremendous pressure and power from United as did the Poles even as the game opened. Within the first minute United took complete command and the ball was whipped off Best's toe as he was about to shoot, and after the corner which was conceded, Kostka made the first of a remarkable series of saves.

Tremendous Drive

Crerand had a tremendous drive from outside the penalty area tipped over the crossbar. Young Ryan, brought in because Law was unfit, was fed astutely by Crerand and from his curling centre Best was the next to give Gornik an anxious moment. This was the kind of scintillating play to send the capacity crowd into raptures, but the goal United sought just would not come.

Gornik's magnificent defence, marshalled by the old international, Oslizlo, with Kuchta and Latocha alongside him, and with as many men as they required, only too eager to retreat to hold United, was remarkably calm and clever. But it was Kostka who caught the eye. He was the last man, of course, in this fine rearguard, and in the first half he was their saviour so many times, leaping to punch the ball clear, and every United forward was foiled by him. How long, one wondered, could this last. Yet by half time United were no further forward.

The obvious threat which these Poles can produce when given a chance was shown only twice in the first half. One knew the speed of Musialek and he showed it with one fine run down the wing, and Lubanski, the most forceful and indeed the only permanent forward, gave Stepney a most difficult shot to save. The other occasion came when Stiles made a bad pass, and the move ended with Stepney just winning a race for the ball with Lubanski. This was the full Polish side which defeated Dynamo Kiev in Russia, and one can well understand how the Russians were confounded by this hard, strong, and extremely clever side.

How hard Charlton worked in midfield. So too did Crerand. And how strongly the side

tried for goals. But there was no way round or over this Polish defence that United could discover. Corner followed corner and all were cleverly played away or saved by Kostka, leaping high to punch away from United's forwards. Best perhaps, inevitably with his sleight of foot, received some hard treatment, particularly from his constant shadow Latocha. But this was no rough and tumble match. It was full of skill.

Once again, however, the latent power of Gornik's attack was shown. Again it was Lubanski who caused the danger. United, of course, were committed as they had to be at that time to all-out attack and time was running short. But this threat from the Poles came primarily from a long run by Szoltysik, and Stiles was unable to contain Lubanski, so once again Stepney had a difficult shot to save.

But on the hour at last United gained reward for almost constant attack. The scorer was Best, who for once shook off the close attention of Latocha. The move was made by Dunne, who sent the ball on to Crerand. In his turn Best was sent along the edge of the penalty area and he cut in and scored from the most acute of angles. Small wonder that the crowd cascaded down the terraces at the back of the goal. The reward had been delayed for so long.

Less Apprehension

There was a suspicion that the ball struck Florenski before it eluded Kostka for United's goal. Certainly the goal took just a little apprehension from United, but one goal, I felt would not be sufficient to win this tie. Perhaps, too, there was a little over-eagerness in United's play and their shooting might have been more accurate.

Certainly there was little chance in the air, for Kostka commanded that so capably. This was a night of triumph for Kostka, for in the seventy-fifth minute he saved from Aston a shot which few goalkeepers would have managed to have even got to.

The bombardment continued. And still Gornik's defence would not give an inch. Corner kicks were lobbed like howitzers but all failed to explode into another goal until the last minute. Header followed header, shot followed shot, and always there was Kostka there at the last. But in the final minute he was beaten again, Ryan shot and through a forest of legs Kidd managed to backheel the ball into the net. So United go to Poland with a lead which may well prove decisive.

LEFT: *Best (No 7) in full flight*

Magnificent defence put United in semi-final

THE TIMES, March 13, 1968

GORNIK ZABRZE	1

MAN. UTD.	0

1967-68 EUROPEAN CUP, QUARTER FINAL, SECOND LEG, MANCHESTER UNITED WIN 2-1 ON AGGREGATE

Magnificent Defence put United in Semi-Final

From Geoffrey Green, Football Correspondent
KATOWICE, MARCH 13

A fter a round trip of some 14,000 miles, embracing Malta, Yugoslavia and now Poland, Manchester United have reached the semi-final round of the European Cup for the fourth time since 1957.

True, they lost here tonight in the vast Silesian Stadium before the 100,000 demanding, noisy concourse by a single goal, scored by Lubanski, Gornik's vaunted bombardier, 19 minutes from the end. But that was not enough to save the Poles. On aggregate United were through by 2-1, which now makes that second strike of theirs by Kidd in the final 60 seconds at Old Trafford a fortnight ago, worth its weight in gold.

So United overstepped the sinister date of the 13th of the month and took care also to beware the approaching Ides of March. They did so by biting on the nail, defending magnificently in the deepest, hardest conditions of winter to be imagined, and by keeping their heads and feet on a snow covered pitch, icy below, which made the setting more fit for ice hockey than football.

Bitter Night

Up to half-time, indeed, they fought on in a semi-blizzard of snow which almost obliterated the red line markings within 10 minutes. Later, the driving snowflakes, swirling

From GEOFFREY GREEN, Football Correspondent—Katowice, March 13

Gornik Zabrze 1, Manchester United 0

like a necklace in the lights, fled to leave us in the grip of a dark, bitter night. It was so cold that even these hardy Poles, the miners of Gornik, turned to lighting bonfires on the open terraces.

So Matt Busby and his team have fought a step nearer their dream of the past 10 years to conquer their last football Everest, the European Cup. Real Madrid, Benfica, of Portugal, or perhaps Juventus, the Italians, are the ones who now probably stand across their path. But should at last these talented and experienced Lancastrians, so well blooded in this fierce competition, survive the coming semi-final round in the spring time – and we hope in sunnier climes – then surely they would take Wembley's stage as the favourites on May 29. What a day that could be, should they get there.

Lubanski's late goal tonight was the first United have conceded after nearly three and a half hours play on the Continent in this season's competition. That speaks volumes for their tactical planning and defensive ability when the chips are down.

Hard Match

The Poles, for all their sporting, correct behaviour in a hard match, were at the end deeply sad, and their manager, with a face as long as a pessimistic horse, was disappointed at United's defensive covering in depth. But, as Busby said: "This is European football. We had only a slender lead. We came here to contain the foe and we did the job we set out to perform. The Poles themselves defended deeply at Old Trafford".

That is true, and comparing the two matches one can say without fear of contradiction that the pressure on the Gornik goalkeeper, Kostka, was far more severe in Manchester than anything Stepney had to endure here tonight. In fact, had it not been for Kostka's great performance a fortnight ago, it would have been all over bar the shouting even before coming to Poland.

As it was, tonight the Manchester rearguard played magnificently. The heroes were Stiles, Sadler, who read every move intelligently, the two full backs, Dunne (playing the whole of the second half with his left ankle heavily strapped following an injury just before half-time) and Burns. In front of them there was that little

terrier, the long haired Fitzpatrick, who gained strength from those locks as he operated as a fiery shield in front of, and sometimes behind, that rear wall of four.

Manchester's tactical alignment was supposed to be 4-4-2, with Herd brought into the firing line to add physical strength and the hopes of a long range shot. In the event, as Gornik built up their attacks, United's tactical formation became more like 5-3-2, and here in midfield, especially after half-time, we saw the great control of Bobby Charlton directing operations, playing a fine captain's part and slowing down and changing the tempo.

At Charlton's side Crerand also had a good second half, while up front there was always Best threatening with his little ballet steps in the snow. Gornik could never ignore him as they bent to attack. Best at times appeared to have the ubiquitous power of being in two places at once while suggesting a nerve racking influence in another.

The near things matter little now. Lubanski, Musialek and Lentner were always a threat as Gornik tried to turn the screw. But they were cleverly shielded round the edges of the penalty area and the slower the minutes unwound for Manchester, the faster they must have felt as they drained away from the Poles.

Their attacks reached a frenzy once they had scored with just enough time left to save themselves in a play-off. But Manchester United, with Stiles and Fitzpatrick, I repeat, quite outstanding, shadow boxed them splendidly. The goal itself was preceded a few seconds earlier by an indirect free kick on the Manchester United penalty spot following an infringement by Stepney.

The whole United team massed themselves along their goal-line. Kuchta's shot was blocked, but before United could come off their line properly to realign themselves, Kuchta found Lubanski with a pass from right to left and the dangerous Gornik striker hit home a great shot on the run from the left, the ball flashing home off the underside of the crossbar.

That as the one chink; the one positive strike; and the one shot that mattered in a hard, passionate but sporting match. By the end a grey sadness for the Poles had surged over the white setting; the sky took on a more leaden hue and a chill wind blew through the eastern world.

ABOVE: *Aston (far right) tries a header, but Betancourt in the Real Madrid goal has it well covered*

BELOW: *The same attempt seen from another angle – Law second from left*

THE TIMES, April 24, 1968

MAN. UTD.	1
REAL MADRID	0

1967-68 EUROPEAN CUP, SEMI-FINAL, FIRST LEG,
MANCHESTER UNITED WIN 1-0

Manchester United Toil for Meagre Reward

By Geoffrey Green, Football Correspondent

This was the match Manchester United had for so long dreamt about – the first leg of their fourth appearance in the semi-final round of the European Cup, and their great chance at home to build up a working lead against their old friends and foes, Real Madrid, whom they first met and lost to at this stage of the competition 11 years ago.

It was a golden evening; the merest whisper of a breeze touched the flags on the rim of Old Trafford and there was a lovely glow in a cloudless sky as the evening sun went down. And it was in this setting, when it was all over and Manchester United had gained no more than an advantage of a single goal, that one wondered whether the sun had also gone down once more on their effort to scale the Everest of European club football.

It was in this atmosphere of a 63,000 full house, totally committed to the occasion, and another unseen audience of several million television viewers, that United played their hearts out against a deep and experienced defence to gain so meagre a reward in a sporting match worthy of two great clubs. But it is not over yet, however unpropitious the signs.

Three weeks hence we shall perhaps know the answer when these two play in the second leg at Bernabeu Stadium, Madrid, during the festival of San Isidro, the patron saint of the Spanish capital.

Meanwhile, at Old Trafford last night there

Manchester United toil for meagre reward

By GEOFFREY GREEN, Football Correspondent

Manchester United 1, Real Madrid 0

This was the match Manchester United had for so long dreamt about—the first leg of their fourth appearance in the semi-final round of the European Cup, and their great chance at home to build up

the festival of San Isidro, the patron saint of the Spanish capital.

Meanwhile, at Old Trafford last night there were two teams of high reputation and regard. For four-fifths of the night it was Manchester United moving forward against a deeply laid defensive formation

shot to the roof of the Real net.

This might have been Walter Hammond driving a half volley gloriously past extra cover off the full meat of the bat. In that moment Old Trafford exploded, a frightened cat ran the length of the pitch from one end to the other, and one felt that

were two teams of high reputation and regard. For four-fifths of the night it was Manchester United moving forward against a deeply laid defensive formation which saw Gonzalez, Zunsunegui, Zoco, Sanchis and the deeply withdrawn Jose Luis drawn out in an iron ring across the horizon of Betancourt, under the Madrid crossbar.

In the opening minutes Betancourt made a great diving save to Aston's header from a cross by Best at the foot of the post, and from the ensuing corner there was Crerand up to

hit the Spanish woodwork as his shot beat Betancourt's dive. There were more near things, too, as the minutes unwound, and near the end there was a blinding miss by the hard-working Kidd, who blasted high over the bar after yet another opening engineered by Crerand, Best, and Charlton.

In the end all Manchester United had to show for their driving work was a glorious goal by Best, 10 minutes from the interval. Aston broke on the left from Kidd's long pass, and as he pulled the ball back diagonally from the bye-

ABOVE: *Zocco (jumping centre) clears from Best (centre dark shirt)*

line, in came Best to thunder a left foot shot to the roof of the Real net.

This might have been Walter Hammond driving a half volley gloriously past extra cover off the full meat of the bat. In that moment Old Trafford exploded, a frightened cat ran the length of the pitch from one end to the other, and one felt that here at last in another sense the cat had really been set amongst the Spanish pigeons.

But that was the end as far as Manchester United's positive efforts were concerned. Real, relaxed and aristocratic, played with a certain simplicity and sophistication, playing for space and position with all their experienced timing coming to their aid – all this in spite of the raging pressure that continued to explode around their penalty area.

Pirri was superb, an artist in midfield: Perez looked dangerous with his speed at outside right, and there, too, was Grosso, working the midfield with the tireless Pirri. And if anybody needs a special accolade, it is Sanchis, for the masterly way he followed the gyrations of the elusive Best.

In all respects it was a fine, sporting match, finely controlled with the minimum of fuss by a Russian referee who later said: "The No. 1 footballer and gentleman on the field for me was Bobby Charlton, and I have never had more pleasure in taking such a match."

Exposed nerves

So we lived through a night of exposed nerves. It was like biting on a sensitive tooth as the roar rose and fell like a solid wall across the stadium. The action was compelling enough to dispense with the lighting of a slow fuse. The promise of an explosion was implicit from the start, and its effect was hardly helped by being forecast. But this, in effect, was but a preamble to the tightrope that must be walked between victory and defeat some three weeks hence.

When the scene moves to Madrid, Real, of course, will turn on their attacking tap. Then, too, they will have the dangerous Amancio back in their attack, with perhaps another change also in the presence of a certain De Diego. At least then we shall see whether Manchester United can stand up to the pressure as they did so well in the snow of Poland in the last round.

If they do, then they will be worthy, at last, to take their place in a European final at Wembley. A lot may happen before we know the final answer, but at least there will be the chance to see whether Charlton, Best, Crerand, and even Law – not the man of old, but searching and eager for the ball – can liberate their creative abilities.

Those who think Manchester United's chance has gone, should be reminded of two years ago when they led Benfica only by 3-2 from Old Trafford and then destroyed the Portuguese on a magical night by 5-1.

THERE AT LAST
United v Benfica in Busby's final

THE goals that kept United in the game . . . Real defender Zoco slices the ball into his own net to make it 1—1 (left). Then David Sadler beats Betancort with a flick from a Crerand free-kick for United's second.

—THE WAY TO THE FINAL

By RONALD CROWTHER

REAL MADRID . . . 3   MANCHESTER UNITED . . . 3

Manchester United win 4—3 on aggregate

Madrid, Wednesday

WITH a great and glorious fighting comeback that will rank among the all-time epics of football, Manchester United stormed their way through here tonight to the European Cup Final before an angry and astonished crowd in the vast Bernabeu Stadium.

DAILY MAIL, May 16, 1968

REAL MADRID	3
MAN. UTD.	

1967-68 EUROPEAN CUP, SEMI-FINAL, SECOND LEG, MANCHESTER UNITED WIN 4-3 ON AGGREGATE

There at last
United v Benfica in Busby's final

BELOW: *Team group before the second leg match in Madrid, back row left to right: Stiles, Crerand, A Dunne, Stepney, Charlton, Foulkes; front row: Brennan, Kidd, Sadler, Best, Aston*

With a great and glorious fighting comeback that will rank among the all-time epics of football, Manchester United stormed their way through here tonight to the European Cup Final before an angry and astonished crowd in the vast Bernabeu Stadium.

No transformation I have ever seen could rival this breath-taking drama, for 45 minutes before United marched off the field in triumph they had appeared to be on the brink of certain defeat.

But for Matt Busby, the man who has striven so long and so hard for success in Europe and who has never lost faith in his club's ability to achieve it, this was the night on which a dream came true.

Now he will proudly lead his men out at Wembley on May 29 as the first English team to play in the final.

For veteran centre-half Bill Foulkes this was also a wonderful, wonderful night of rich fulfilment.

TOP: *Zocco (third from right) unfortunately puts the ball past his own 'keeper in the second leg match against Manchester United*

ABOVE: *Jubilant United fans mob Charlton after the 3-3 draw with Real Madrid, Kidd (behind) helps him to his feet*

Menacing

Eleven years ago he played in this same stadium in United's first-ever European Cup semi-final. Tonight as the only survivor of that side, he scored the final, clinching goal.

And even though much of the goodwill that has so long existed between United and Real was destroyed by ugly incidents out there on the Spanish pitch, the team from Old Trafford became only the fifth in 13 years to prevent the famous Madrid club from breaking through to the final.

Everything had seemed set fair for United after the first half-hour in which they put up such a stubborn and highly disciplined defensive fight.

But the storm suddenly broke about their heads.

Real, swift, resourceful, and menacing in every move, had spared them nothing.

Then came a highly controversial free-kick that yielded the first success for Real in the 31st minute when link-man Pirri nodded the ball home after meeting Amancio's cross.

Seconds earlier the ball had gone over United's line and the Italian referee had given a goal-kick. But then he consulted a flagging linesman and awarded the free-kick for a foul by Aston on Pirri.

Tottering

Ten minutes later things looked gloomy for the English side when Real captain Gento suddenly broke loose at a breakneck pace on the left and made it 2-0. As full-back Sanchis slipped the ball through to him, Brennan stuck out a foot and missed it, and then turned to see his lapse drastically punished.

For veteran Gento, without halting in his gallop, turned the ball into the net from what had seemed an impossible angle.

This was to be the first of three goals in three minutes as the game swung back and forth in a dramatic manner just before the interval.

Zoco, under great pressure from persistent Kidd – the young man who will celebrate his 19th birthday on European Cup Final day – turned the ball into his own net. United were right back in the fight again, but one minute before the interval they were tottering once more on the verge of defeat.

This time, Amancio, who had fought his way clear of the obstinate Stiles, was the scorer. Time seemed to be running out for United.

In the electric atmosphere of this great stadium it had been a first half in which emotions had spilled over. Stiles, the man detailed by Busby to shadow Amancio was in trouble with the referee after only two minutes for a rash tackle.

Later a clash between Stiles and Amancio halted the game for three minutes while the Spaniard lay on the pitch ringed by photographers and demonstrative Real officials.

Spanish supporters howled abuse at United from all sides of the stadium. But this time Amancio was the aggressor for Stiles had passed the ball when he suddenly came from behind and punched the United half-back.

Booked

Stiles struck back and there appeared to me to be some play-acting about the manner in which Amancio slumped on to the pitch.

Three minutes before the interval Stiles was booked for his latest foul on Amancio and in the second half Sadler also had his name taken for tripping Velasquez.

But the rough treatment did not all come from United, for Charlton, Kidd, and Crerand, among others were all flagrantly fouled.

If anyone had told me as the dejected looking United side walked off at half-time that they would be the winners I would not have believed them.

But, with new-found zest, they hurled themselves on to the attack on the resumption.

With 19 minutes left Sadler, who had previously been playing alongside Foulkes in defence, scored a goal that put an entirely different slant on things.

As Charlton pushed through a free-kick from midfield and Best headed the ball up and over a defensive screen, Sadler slipped round it to turn the ball just inside a post. Now, only a goal behind in the game and on level terms on aggregate, United seemed set at least for a play-off in Lisbon.

But six minutes later Footballer of the Year, Best, beat Sanchis down the flank and pulled the ball back for Foulkes, of all people, whose appearance in the penalty area staggered the now ragged Real rearguard.

Foulkes, who coolly side-footed the ball home, made sure of this moment of triumph like a man who had waited so long.

DAVID MEEK SAYS

The fighting comeback of all time

Madrid, Thursday.

IN Yugoslavia it was a trial of temperament, Poland a trial of tactics, and now here

Manchester Evening News, May 16, 1968

REAL MADRID	3
MAN UTD.	3

1967-68 EUROPEAN CUP, SEMI-FINAL, SECOND LEG, MANCHESTER UNITED WIN 4-3 ON AGGREGATE

Real Reds Reign in Spain

The fighting comeback of all time

David Meek says
MADRID, THURSDAY

In Yugoslavia it was a trial of temperament, in Poland a trial of tactics, and now here in Spain it was the fighting comeback of all time.

Manchester United are in the final of the European Cup after trailing 3-1 at half time to mighty Real Madrid in this pulsating semi-final.

Not many in the 120,000 crowd would have given a peseta for their chances of pulling back into the match at that time.

But Matt Busby, with the 11-year ambition of winning this competition at stake, put it boldly to his players in the dressing-room during the interval.

"Although we were 3-1 down I reminded the players that the aggregate score was 3-2 and that we were in effect only one goal behind.

"I told them to go out and play. After all, if you are 3-2 down at half-time in an FA Cup-tie you don't consider you are finished."

Flair and force

And this is what United did with such flair and

PAT CRE

Better our B perfo

THIS was Manche
Our 3-3 draw

force that the Spanish champions crumbled and lost their grip for the Reds to force a 3-3 result and take the tie on an aggregate of 4-3.

United defended well for the first half-hour. Although it was a rearguard action in which they had five men back in defence and only two – George Best and Brian Kidd – up front, they stayed cool and calm.

Then the Real pressure told its tale with a goal from Pirri after a free kick and then a breakaway burst by Gento.

Zoco raised United hopes by putting through his own goal, but Amancio put the Spaniards ahead again to establish a 3-1 lead at half-time.

In the last 20 minutes David Sadler sidefooted a smart goal and then Bill Foulkes equalised.

United in this half were magnificent. They shattered Real and one felt that if the game had gone on any longer the Reds would have had a winning result in Madrid.

United were obviously at their happiest when they were attacking. So should they have steered clear of this defensive approach to the match which rebounded on them in that fatal first half? United manager Matt Busby is quite clear about the answer:

"It was the right thing to do, even if it looked as if the tactics had gone wrong. I would play it exactly the same way if we turned back the clock.

"You just cannot come here and leave yourself wide open. We had to play it tight while we were in front.

Bill Foulkes, a stalwart with Nobby Stiles in defence, managed to get the winning goal, and Britain's most experienced player in European football more than justified the manager's faith in his recall.

To inside-left David Sadler went the testing versatile role of helping in defence in the first half and then moving fluently into attack in the hour of need, while Stiles had the most difficult task of marking Amancio, Real's leading scorer.

Best and Kidd largely had to struggle on their own in the first half, but after the interval they came powerfully into the game.

Bill Foulkes

MEEK SAYS

ighting back I time

Madrid, Thursday.
is a trial of temperament,

PAT CRERAND SAYS

Better than our Benfica performance

Madrid, Thursday.

THIS was Manchester United's finest hour

Manchester Evening News, May 16, 1968

REAL MADRID	3
MAN UTD	3

1967-68 EUROPEAN CUP, SEMI-FINAL, SECOND LEG, MANCHESTER UNITED WIN 4-3 ON AGGREGATE

Real Reds reign in Spain

Better than our Benfica performance

Pat Crerand says
MADRID, THURSDAY

This was Manchester United's finest hour. Our 3-3 draw with Real Madrid after being 3-1 down replaces our 5-1 win at Benfica two years ago as United's greatest performance.

And what a fantastic scene it was when we returned to our dressing-room.

Manager Matt Busby, unashamedly and understandably crying, hugged us all one by one.

Some of us – myself included – went straight into the showers without even taking off our kit.

I don't think anyone knew what they were doing. It just wouldn't sink in. We had dazed looks in our eyes.

Minutes afterwards the boss was still completely speechless and when later I couldn't see

him, I thought we would find him lying somewhere.

When, in fact, he did return to the dressing room we all broke into a spontaneous round of clapping.

Denis Law, self-confessed as one of the game's worst spectators, said he was applying for the next heart transplant.

Now let's switch back to the dressing-room at half-time. Everyone else thought we were dead. Real certainly thought so.

But here comes the crux of the game – Busby's interval talk. He rounded off by saying: "We must go out and attack. If we are going to lose it might as well be by six goals."

That did the trick. We are a footballing side and a defensive game is alien to us. We had never lost heart and we knew we could still do it.

From the start of the second half we were always in control and I thought every one of our team was magnificent.

I would just like to single out one player, left winger John Aston. He had had a tough time from the crowd at Old Trafford and I wish even more of them had been at the Bernabeu Stadium to see him.

He had the toughest job of all, being expected to be on the left wing when we attacked, but dropping back to stop the dangerous Pirri when Real had the ball.

He did the job superbly and I just don't know where he got the energy and strength from.

As to the final against Benfica at Wembley a week on Wednesday – WE MUST HAVE A GREAT CHANCE.

Finally, I would like to thank on behalf of the entire club all the fans who came so far to support us. We appreciated it greatly and your reward was, I'm sure everyone will agree, a match never to be forgotten.

LOOKING BACK
■ WITH BILL FOULKES ■

Bill Foulkes was the rock of Manchester United for 18 years. He was an archetype centre half, all solid muscle, durable, single-minded and effective.

Sir Matt Busby will be remembered for the creative artistry he encouraged in his teams, but he knew all about strength as well.

He chose Bill Foulkes 679 times to play for him in League and Cup. Other players came and went. Bill Foulkes seemed to roll on for ever.

He linked the Johnny Carey era of the early fifties with the famous Busby Babes, survived Munich, shared in the European Cup triumph and played until 1970.

Bill Foulkes was in at the start of Busby's pursuit of success in Europe and it was as if fate had taken a hand in singling him out to score the goal which put United into the final of the 1968 European Cup.

Of course other goals were scored as well in two titanic tussles with Real Madrid, but the coup de grace fell fittingly to Bill Foulkes who only scored twice in a total of 52 European ties.

"I still don't really know what possessed me to go forward and score the goal that won the tie for us," he confesses.

"After so many games with no thought of scoring, it seems almost unbelievable as I look back.

"I was even lucky to be playing. I was rarely injured but that season I was out from about January. I missed the first leg of the semi-final against Real Madrid at Old Trafford and had played just two League games when the manager picked me for the return in Madrid.

"I think Matt went for the experience. I wasn't really fit. My knee had blown up in the final League game against Sunderland and the Madrid match was just four days later.

"My knee was strapped up and I was hobbling. I only got by thanks to some brilliant covering and defending by Nobby Stiles and Tony Dunne.

"We had gone to Spain with just a goal from George Best as our advantage from the home leg and at half-time it seemed as if it was not going to be enough.

"We were 3-1 down on the night. Tony Dunne had scored with a long lob as Brian Kidd

Champions of Europe at last!

By ALBERT BARHAM: Manchester United 4, Benfica 1

rushed in to unsettle their goalkeeper, but we were struggling.

"George Best was double marked and had been heavily tackled. Bobby Charlton and Pat Crerand, who normally ran the games for us, hadn't shown, and we were all a bit depressed at the interval.

"But Matt with his typical simple logic pointed out that on aggregate we were only one goal behind and at least a replay wasn't beyond us.

"His reasoning made an impression and we went out again thinking 'we can do this'. Perhaps Real Madrid sat back a little as well and gave us more room to play.

"For suddenly George began to figure and Brian Kidd. We got a corner which hit David Sadler and went in. So it was 3-3 on aggregate and it seemed to me as if both sides then stopped playing, perhaps too frightened of losing.

"Nothing happened until we got a throw-in. Paddy Crerand was taking it and no-one seemed to want the ball. I shouldn't have done but I called for it. Paddy looked and then decided against.

"He threw it to George who promptly shot off down the wing and eluded three or four tackles. Perhaps it was with moving slightly forward to call for the throw-in that prompted me to keep running.

"Anyway I reached the corner of the box and again I found myself calling for the ball. George saw me and I thought I was going to be ignored again. You must appreciate that I was never famous for attacking skills!

"I thought George was going to shoot, but instead he cut back the most beautiful ball to me. It was perfect and I just had to side-foot it in at the far side.

"There wasn't a sound from 120,000 Spaniards and my first thought was that it couldn't be a goal. My next recollection was trying to get bodies off me as the lads piled in. I was really worried about my knee.

"There was still 10 minutes to play but we hung on and scoring that goal remains as probably my most precious moment in football. It opened the door to the final for us, and of course Wembley against Benfica proved the end of the rainbow, the moment of triumph for Sir Matt Busby.

"I had come the whole way with the Boss trying to become champions of Europe. I thought the destruction of our team at Munich would have been the end of it, but he patiently put together another team.

"I'm proud to have been a part of it and for those of us who had lost our friends coming home from a European tie in 1958 it seemed the right tribute to their memory."

At last the European Cup comes to England from Manchester United's night of triumph at Wembley last night. They won just as they promised they would, not so much for themselves as for their manager, Matt Busby. Thus 11 years of trial and tragedy, effort and frustration fulminated in this great victory when it seemed, as in the semifinal Madrid, that the deck was

and Best so often cruelly hacked down in full flight.

This indeed was a match to remember, though it started slowly, for tension was so acute and the reward so great. But once the first nervous tension had been relieved the match blossomed. The fuse was lit by Charlton's first goal. And it could so easily have been lost by United between the eightieth and the ninetieth minutes. For then one saw the greatness of Eusebio and

"They all go forward, and they all come back," he said, "and the speed could upset my team." So it seemed. Crerand fed the attack astutely, and Aston, in particular, capitalised on it, for Adolfo did not seem to know quite how to take him.

One thing Benfica knew was that they had to stop Best. Cruz was detailed as the chief hatchet man. At least half a dozen times in the first half Best was hurled to the turf. It was crude, perhaps; it certainly was effective.

meant, of course that Benfica had to attack with all the power at their command, and that is considerable. Every member of this forward line played against England in the World Cup semifinal at Wembley two years ago. But, in concentrating on attack, they left a defence thinly stretched, and once Best was right through only for Henrique to race from his goal and slide the ball away, yards outside his penalty area.

Now it was Eusebio's turn, and

THE GUARDIAN, May, 29, 1968

MAN. UTD.	4
BENFICA	1

1967-68 EUROPEAN CUP, FINAL (PLAYED AT WEMBLEY), MANCHESTER UNITED WIN 4-1

Champions of Europe at last!

By Albert Barham

At last the European Cup comes to England from Manchester United's night of triumph at Wembley last night. They won just as they promised they would, not so much for themselves as for their manager, Matt Busby. Thus 11 years of trial and tragedy, effort and frustration culminated in this great victory when it seemed, as in the semi-final in Madrid, that the deck was stacked against them.

They won 4-1. And what a victory it was.

They were taken to extra time by Benfica but in seven minutes of it the Portuguese were crushed by three goals. Those three goals came at a time when all the power and grace of Benfica's forwards — each one an international — had put them back in the game with a goal ten minutes from time by Graca that nullified Bobby Charlton's scored 27 minutes earlier.

Appropriate

What finer player could there be to score United's first goal than Bobby Charlton. This was his first goal in European Cup football since the previous, and up to now greatest, triumph of United — against Benfica in the Stadium of Light two years ago. It also fell to him to score the last. And in between was a goal taken as coolly as on the practice pitch by Best and one from Kidd to celebrate fittingly this his nineteenth birthday.

But goals apart this again was a great triumph of team work and team spirit. Every player gave his all from Stepney, who three times was United's saviour against the powerful shooting of Eusebio, to Foulkes, who has missed only three of United's matches in their 11 years of waiting for this supreme moment. And there was too the covering of the backs, the prompting of Crerand, and the sight of Aston enjoying himself on the wing, and Best so often cruelly hacked down in full flight.

This indeed was a match to remember,

ABOVE: *Exchange of pennants before the European Cup Final between Manchester United and Benfica (left to right) Charlton, Referee Lo Bollo, Coluna*

ABOVE: *One against three – Charlton takes on Benfica's defence*

BELOW: *Eusebio celebrates after scoring Benfica's only goal*

though it started slowly, for tension was so acute and the reward so great. But once the first nervous tension had been relieved the match blossomed. The fuse was lit by Charlton's first goal. And it could so easily have been lost by United between the eightieth and the ninetieth minutes. For then one saw the greatness of Eusebio and the rest of this national Portuguese forward line. It was then United's defence creaked and Eusebio was able to exploit it. But three goals between the third and tenth minutes of extra time put out the spark. In ten minutes Benfica went from a team in command to a team in defeat – and they knew it.

Following Celtic

Do United carry on where Celtic left off last season after bringing the Cup to Britain for the first time. One further honour can come United's way. They will meet Estudiantes of La Plata, a side from Argentina, who are the South American champions, for the World Club Championship. One can only hope that it will not be as ill fated as Celtic's escapades in Argentina and Montevideo last year.

Stakes were so high, and the tension so great, that the first half was one of attack in every sense of the word. Some of the tackles were harsh in the extreme. The worst to suffer was Best, as was to be expected, Coluna, who was brought down by Sadler, and Crerand, who was felled by, of all people, Eusebio, who went into him with all the power of his body after 36 minutes.

United in the first half certainly took the attack to Benfica. It is there that the United have their flair. And it was, as Otto Gloria, Benfica's manager, said, it would be – the speed of United which could upset his side. "They all go forward, and they all come back," he said, "and the speed could upset my team." So it seemed. Crerand fed the attack astutely, and Aston, in particular, capitalised on it, for Adolfo did not seem to know quite how to take him.

One thing Benfica knew was that they had to stop Best. Cruz was detailed as the chief hatchet man. At least half a dozen times in the first half Best was hurled to the turf. It was crude, perhaps; it certainly was effective. And

TOP: *Best (centre), scorer of United's second goal*

LEFT: *Kidd (second from right) celebrates his 18th birthday with a header for United's third*

125

for another foul on Best, Humberto had his name taken. But, for all the free kicks which were conceded by Benfica just outside the penalty area from these infringements, United could not capitalise. The rear four men of Benfica combine so well, and their power is shown by the fact that until the final, they had conceded only two goals.

United went close on several occasions. As early as the third minute Crerand's free kick floated over, but Sadler could only claw down the ball with his boot and push it straight to Henrique. Aston and Charlton combined again, and for a second time Sadler was the culprit. The move developed with return passes with Kidd, but Sadler, in a good position, shot wide.

Slow build-up

Benfica like to build up their moves slowly, with care and precision. And, as Benfica had to watch Best, so United had to watch Torres, the tall centre forward with a great gift not only of scoring goals but making them with his head. And, of course, there was Eusebio, policed, as is now customary, by Stiles. United knew full well the power of Eusebio's shooting. And in the eleventh minute he demonstrated it admirably. One of the best of Benfica's moves developed between Graca and Torres, and the ball was swept out to Eusebio, lurking on the right wing. Eusebio took the ball in his stride and hammered in a shot which made Stepney's cross bar twang like a bow string.

Foulkes was detailed to watch Torres, and in

TOP: *Dispute flares as Crerand lies injured*

ABOVE: *Charlton (in dark strip) makes it four for United, Benfica's 'keeper Henrique can only watch it into goal*

Action from the World Club Championship 1968: United play Estudiantes of Argentina

Law leaps in United's 2nd leg tie against AC Milan, May 1969

ABOVE: *Stepney collects, Eusebio (right) and Sadler battle it out behind him*   BELOW: *Sadler (left) with a scorching shot (saved!)*

129

ABOVE: *Matt Busby (stooping right) encourages his tired team before the start of extra time*

ABOVE: *Sadler celebrates with Crerand and Best close behind*

his handling of him he was penalised several times. From one free kick, just outside the penalty area, one of Eusebio's especially fierce shots was deflected off the wall of United's defenders, and Stepney did well to gather it.

For so long it had seemed that this match would be stalemate. Each side knew so much about the other from previous encounters. United had, last night, six of the side who plucked the feathers from the tail of the Eagles of Lisbon in that 5-1 triumph two years ago. But the second half blossomed into an exciting encounter. And who could be neutral on a night like this?

Aston was enjoying himself on the left wing. As the second half opened he sent in one shot which Henrique failed to hold with his hands, but smothered with his body. Moments later, Aston crashed in another shot. But the real drama was reserved for Bobby Charlton. His goal in the 53rd minute set the game aflame, and the crowd almost hysterical with delight.

A move developed down the left. Over came Sadler's crossfield pass: up went Bobby Charlton to glide the ball with his head, into the far corner of the net. It was the first goal Bobby Charlton had scored in a European Cup tie since that memorable night in Lisbon two years ago. Last night's goal was just as brilliantly taken, but this time it was more crucial.

Having conceded this goal, meant, of course

ABOVE: *Aston and Charlton parade the Cup*

OXFAM'S BUSINESS
PROJECT 7101
Pursuing integration equipment in Oxfam's business for a technical training institute in India. New centres will train integration mechanics urgently needed by hospitals, schools, and commercial concerns to prevent wastage of food.

OXFAM HOUSE No.
c/o BARCLAYS BANK LTD., OXFORD.

THE GUARDIAN

37,910   Manchester Thursday May 30 1968   Price 6d

Busby dream comes true at long last

BY ERIC TODD

THE football might of Benfica, indeed of Portugal itself, was brought low by Manchester United at Wembley last night. In the presence of 100,000 frenzied spectators who had paid heaven knows what prices for admission, United won 4–1 after extra time and, for the first time in the 13 years of the competition, the European Champions' Cup has come to England. Better still to Lancashire. And, perhaps best of all, to Manchester United.

As a corollary rather than as a relevant postscript, Manchester City at present are spreading the gospel in the Americas as recently crowned champions of the Football League. If only West Bromwich had been situated in Lancashire instead of in Staffordshire the County Palatine would have had a memorable hat trick.

It was written that more things are wrought by prayer than this world dreams on and Manchester United and their countless admirers will testify to the efficacy of that belief. Ever since United removed Real Madrid from the semifinals, football enthusiasts in this country and in remote lands—beyond the seas have entreated the gods to look favourably on Old Trafford with particular reference to the team and to Matt Busby, its manager.

No matter that those gods chose to ignore similar supplications on behalf of Tottenham Hotspur, Wolverhampton Wanderers, Ipswich Town, Burnley, Liverpool, and Everton in seasons past. Nor for that matter those on behalf of Manchester United, who had fought losing battles in three previous semifinals, on the road to one of which in 1966 they thrashed Benfica on aggregate 8–3.

This time surely United would not be denied in spite of the menace of the incomparable Eusebio, of whom nearly as much has been written these past few days as has been allocated to the other 21 players put together. Which is saying a lot. Nor in spite of the fact that Benfica's forward line was that which played for Portugal in the World

Cup two years ago. Speculation was rife as the crowds closed in from every side.

If the scenes after the match defied adequate description, those before, challenged it seriously. With several hours to go, United's followers captured the heights around the stadium and slept a perspiring sleep through the hot afternoon.

Touts, who would flog tickets for the next world, given the opportunity, reaped another rich harvest, as did purveyors of unofficial programmes, all unmindful of the terrible warnings of retribution and eternal damnation carried on sandwich boards. The Stretfordenders of Old Trafford, present in their legions, were concerned only with the damnation of Benfica. And so it proved, although their heroes made rather harder work of it than they need have done.

Best flattened

United had most of the play in the first half, but many of their attacks ended abruptly with the flattening of Best, three times by Cruz—who once trod on Best's face for an encore—and three times by Humberto, who finally had his name taken. Sadler went very close to scoring on two occasions, although he blundered in the twenty-eighth minute, when, after receiving a perfect pass from Kidd, he shot wide from ten yards.

When they were not attending to Best, Benfica attacked fitfully, without causing Stepney any anxiety until he made a smart save after the deflection by one of six United players when Eusebio took a free kick. In taking another free kick, Eusebio failed narrowly to be the first man so far as I know who has

dispatched the ball over the stands. All eyes of course were on Eusebio, who produced the best shot of the first half. Stepney was given no time to move. He could only stand and hope as the ball rattled against his crossbar.

Early in the second half, Aston, playing the game of his young life, tested Henrique with two long shots. Then, in the fifty-third minute, it happened—Dunne to Sadler, Sadler a lob of geometrical precision into the Benfica goalmouth, where Charlton, leaping up, flicked the ball into the net with his balding head. "We shall not be moved," roared the United followers, and it certainly seemed that Benfica—Eusebio excepted—would not move anyone. If United had taken all their chances, Benfica would have been beyond redemption by half time.

Ten minutes from the end, however, United faltered and Stiles thumped the ground in anguish after Augusto and Torres had paved the way for a goal by Graca. It was unbelievable after United's domination. Almost as unbelievable were two saves in the last five minutes by Stepney from tremendous shots by Eusebio, who was gracious enough to congratulate United's goalkeeper.

In seven minutes of the first period of extra time, however, United destroyed Benfica with further goals from Best, Kidd (19 yesterday), and Charlton. Apart from a few thunderbolts hurled by Eusebio and treated almost with contempt by Stepney, Benfica were out of the hunt.

Inevitably, it was a night for tears, rejoicing, memories, and may be pathos as well. Yet I suspect that the emotion transcending all others was that of

unqualified universal pleasure for one man—Matt Busby, manager of Manchester United, Busby, who once might have joined them as a player for a transfer fee of £150 and who in 1945 visited the then chairman of the club and inquired almost nonchalantly : " I believe you are seeking a team manager ? Well, I am interested." There is no need here to recount his exploits as a player and as a manager. They are known by heart anyway. Now the European Cup has been added to Old Trafford's bulging cupboards. What next? The world club championship? An eventual seat on the board for Matt Busby? Sufficient unto the day are the honours thereof.

Wonderful support

And when we are " old and grey and full of sleep and nodding by the fire," what, I wonder, will be the most clearly defined memory of Wembley, May 29, 1968 ? That of the bemused spectator who, seeing United in all-blue strip, demanded to know: " How's Chelsea got into this act ? " Of the wonderful vocal encouragement of the oft-maligned supporters of United ? United's missed chances? Eusebio's lethal shooting? Foulkes, tho'wd chain ' horse, playing Torres out of the game? Or of Matt Busby marching on to the pitch at the final whistle and shaking hands with the Benfica players and officials before turning to his own men ?

Or will it be the memory of Matt Busby, the man who "learned to labour and to wait," embracing his magnificent backroom boys, and then watching his men do a lap of honour ? And did he look up briefly at the heavens as if seeking—and getting, no doubt—the approval of the spirits of Munich ? And did he look, too, with pride on his bright young men, his hopes for years to come, and maybe more so on Charlton and Foulkes, who have been with him almost since they learned to kick a football ? Home are the hunters, home from the hill. At last.

Albert Barham, page 19 ; today's homecoming, page 20

VICTORY HUG for jubilant Matt Busby and Bill Foulkes, watched by Brian F

By JOHN JACKSON

MATT BUSBY, the man who rebuilt Manchester United after the
Munich air disaster in 1958, said

his team become the first English
club to win the European Cup,
beating Benfica of Portugal 4-1 in
extra time

THE I
HUND
YEAI

Busby's
men

BELOW: *The happy manager – Foulkes ot the
left, Crerand behind*

250,000 welcome United

**Church bans
dance
for Oxfam**

**RAF flying
school's last
parade**

that Benfica had to attack with all the power at
their command, and that is considerable. Every
member of this forward line played against
England in the World Cup semi-final at Wembley two years ago. But, in concentrating on
attack, they left a defence thinly stretched, and
once Best was right through only for Henrique
to race from his goal and slide the ball away,
yards outside his penalty area.

Now it was Eusebio's turn, and back came
Aston to thwart him. Benfica seemed just a
little jaded as their attempts to neutralise the
United's goal were swept away. It was under-
standable, perhaps, for the best they had
produced was not good enough. United had
one anxious moment midway through the
second half when the wily Simoes turned on all
his grace to send over a looping centre to
Torres, but the ball again was prodded away
from him by Dunne, who was having a splendid
match in United's defence.

But this was United's night. They would not
be denied. Back they stormed, and Kidd, on
this his 19th birthday, might well have had a
chance to celebrate it with a goal but he was
brought down heavily by Humberto.

Best, with a shrug of the hips and a twinkle
of toes, made a mockery of any preconceived
plans to mark him. In the last ten minutes he
burst through and shot. Henrique blocked that
shot, which went to Sadler, and this time
Henrique's body was in the way.

Vast experience

But this Benfica side are vastly experienced in
European Cup football. And in finals, too. This
was their fifth final, and, nine minutes from the
end all their experience showed. They drew

12 SUN Thursday May 30 1968

European Cup-Win Special

Soccer in the SUN

THE DREAM is glorious reality . . the man and the team have achieved the target they have chased for 12 long, patient years. The European Cup belongs to Matt Busby and his beloved Manchester United.

It was like the World Cup Final all over again at Wembley last night, when, as with England, character and skill triumphed in the demanding minutes of extra time.

Three goals inside eight minutes in the first period of extra time, scored by George Best, 19th birthday boy Brian Kidd and that prince of footballers Bobby Charlton, wrecked Benfica as United swept to victory and the distinction they so richly deserved—the first English club to win Europe's premier soccer prize.

As tear-soaked Matt Busby, the man who stands for all that is noble and wholesome in this wonderful game, said "I am the proudest man in the world tonight.

"We have chased this trophy for a long, long time and now it is ours."

GOOD HANDS

As Otto Gloria, manager of the also-proud Eagles of Benfica said sincerely and quietly: "The title is in good hands."

Eusebio and ashamed joy overflowed at the end of this wonderful match that began so victory and disappointing. Instead of the Eusebio fiesta we had all anticipated, the first half was a foul-ridden, tough, tense session.

At [...]

United 4

Benfica 1

By PETER LORENZO

Murphy and Busby talk new life into tired limbs . . before the extra-time transformation.

BUSBY'S MARVELS WIN LIKE A DREAM

HITS ON HEAD

LIONS HIT BACK TO SET A RECORD

From IAN TODD

BELOW: *What a welcome! The European Cup comes to Manchester*

level with a goal by Graca. Augusto sent over the ball, Torres nodded it down and Eusebio, full of guile, deceived the defence by going away and taking the defence with him. It opened up the gap for Graca, who, with only a narrow angle of the goal to aim at, shot and scored.

United's defence, which had held the twin threat of Eusebio and Torres so well, began to creak. And Eusebio, one of the finest forwards in Europe, was just the man to exploit it. Twice he burst through in the closing minutes

and twice Stepney saved his shots, the last a fierce one from close range. And, though Best once again wriggled through, the match was destined for extra time.

No more dramatic opening to extra time could be imagined. United swept forward and twice in two minutes they scored. In the third minute, Stepney's clearance was headed on by Kidd to Best. And here was Best seen at his most brilliant. He took the ball round the defenders, and round the goalkeeper too, before popping it into the net.

Then it was Kidd's turn. This came in the fifth minute. Sadler had a part in that goal. The first attempt at a header was beaten out by Henrique, but back it came for Kidd to head in. And United were not finished. One shot bounced on the bar before, in the tenth minute, Bobby Charlton scored again, and the creator of this goal was Kidd. It was Kidd's pass which Charlton turned into the net to complete the discomfiture of Benfica, who surely did not know quite what had hit them in this sudden burst of attacking play.

LOOKING BACK WITH BRIAN KIDD

The year 1968 saw Manchester United achieve their destiny.

Sir Matt Busby saw his beloved club win the European Cup just 10 years after the nightmare of the Munich tragedy.

He had taken his shattered self back to the beginning again after the destruction of an air crash that killed eight players and wounded several others, two of whom would never play again.

As Brian Kidd, the babe of the rebuilt United, says: "I honestly felt it was something that was meant to be. We arrived at this old hotel at Egham just outside London for the final of the European Cup with everyone convinced that we just had to win.

"We knew we had to do it, if only for Sir Matt Busby who had patiently created another great side after seeing what was possibly an even finer one wiped out on the way home from a European Cup game in Belgrade."

Brian joined United straight from school at St Patricks in Collyhurst, the same establishment which had produced Nobby Stiles. His father was a Manchester bus driver who spent a lot of his life working the No. 47 route past Old Trafford. Perhaps this is what had made him a Manchester City fan after being held up by huge crowds on Saturday afternoons.

Brian made the break-through just turned 18 on a tour of America and Australia. He finished with 10 goals, just one behind George Best and level with Bobby Charlton, certainly enough to earn him a place in the FA Charity Shield of 1967.

He stayed in the side all the way to the big Wembley date in May for the final against Benfica, the champions of Portugal with their stars like Eusebio, Torres, Simoes and Coluna.

"I first tasted the real electric thrill of European football in the semi-final against Real Madrid. When I walked out at the Bernabeu Stadium in Madrid I felt drained with nervousness," said Kidd.

"But for the final we were playing in England and so were certain that we had to do it for the Boss.

"I think the early part of the game was a slight disappointment. It didn't come alive until extra time. We had taken the lead early in the second half with a header from Bobby Charlton. He said it must have skidded off his bald patch. He certainly didn't score very many with his head!

"It seemed for a while as if that would be it . . . a one-goal win, because Eusebio had hit the bar early on, and as I say, it looked as if we were fated to win.

"But 10 minutes from the end, Jaime Graca equalised after the towering Torres had nodded the ball across the goal. Suddenly we were hanging on for grim death and we had Alex Stepney to thank for a couple of super saves against Eusebio.

"You could sense the game slipping away from us and at half-time we were exhausted. Nobby Stiles said it was just like the 1966 World Cup final all over again when Germany equalised at the death.

"But Sir Matt talked to us and urged us to start playing our football again. Sure enough we had a great five-minute spell in the opening minutes of extra time.

"I flicked on Stepney's long clearance for George Best who wriggled past two defenders before taking the ball round their goalkeeper, clipping it home cool as you like.

"Then before the cheers had died down came my moment of glory, the treasured moment I will never forget . . . a goal to celebrate my birthday. I was 19 on May 29, 1968, and what a present!

"Bobby Charlton's corner was only half cleared and I got in a header at goal. A lot of people talk about it coming back off the bar, but in fact Henrique, the goalkeeper, scooped it out.

"In doing so he had come forward off his line and I was able to lob him with a second header. It was the clincher. Bobby Charlton zoomed one into the roof of the net from my cross and we had broken them, winning 4-1 to become the first English European champions."

It was the end of a long, arduous trail through tragedy and triumph with Brian Kidd, the new boy in the side, emerging a hero who knew victory was meant to be.

Always popular with the Stretford Enders, he went on to make 255 League and Cup appearances for United. Then he played for Arsenal, Manchester City, Everton and Bolton before trying his hand in America.

He returned to play for Preston where he was in turn assistant manager, and finally manager. He also organised Manchester United's contribution to the Football in the Community project.

He is back working where he started . . . at the grass roots of life and loving every minute of it.

He has gratefully accepted the opportunities football has brought him with a good education for this three children and a comfortable home, but at heart he is still very much a Collyhurst boy.

"I have been very lucky and have never really looked on football as work. Now I am more than happy to go back to where I started. I can still relate to the lads and perhaps they think of me as a local boy who made good.

"I am one of their own and they respond when I go about my new job visiting schools, coaching boys' clubs and organising games for the unemployed. I do anything to promote football among young people. I love the game and it is important that we get the interest back in soccer after some terrible set-backs."

Brian Kidd – only 18 and playing to good effect in his first season, 1967-8

LOOKING BACK WITH BOBBY CHARLTON

"My thoughts on the day of the European Cup final were that we just wouldn't lose.

"I can remember thinking that we had come too far and had been through too much for us to fail in that final match.

"The European championship had become like a holy grail for Manchester United, and I think the older players felt as if we had been pursuing a sort of football golden fleece."

Bobby Charlton had been in on the great European adventure with Sir Matt Busby almost from the start and he felt keenly that their destiny on that warm May evening was about to be fulfilled.

"We stayed in an old Elizabethan hotel at Egham before the match. It was a big sporting day with the Derby in the afternoon and with David Coleman running a Grandstand on television from the gardens of our hotel," he explained.

"We had everything going for us. We were on our own patch at Wembley. We had a good record against teams from Portugal, and after coming from 3-1 down in Madrid to win the semi-final I thought it would be impossible for us to get beaten.

"It was very humid during the day and I knew it would be hard work, but I also knew that we would find something extra. That's something British teams have always had, this resilience, especially in extra time; England had produced it to win the World Cup two years previously.

"We should have been dead and buried against Real Madrid when we were 3-1 down, and the fact that we had come back and beaten them gave us all an invincible feeling.

"I thought there was no point in my worrying because Benfica had a lot more to worry about.

"I had been very disappointed in some of our semi-final performances, especially the one against Partizan. We had a good team in 1966 and losing 2-0 over there had been bad news.

"I knew it would come one day, yet it was in the nick of time. Without being disrespectful to the players involved, the 1968 team was not our best.

"Manchester City won the League and we had faded. A lot of us were past our peak. I knew I wasn't going to get another chance and about half the team were in the same boat.

"But as I say, defeat was never in our minds. Our first goal confirmed the thought because I scored it with a header – and that never happened very often.

"We felt some despair when they equalised to force us into extra time. But even then I thought that our background of stamina training would stand us in good stead. We knew

they must be tired as well.

"Then came that sparkling 10 minutes in which we scored three goals . . . George Best, Brian Kidd and I turned in the final one.

"Benfica were a formidable side going forward but I thought their defence might creak, and that's how it worked out. Our defence rose to the occasion with some key saves from Alex Stepney against Eusebio, and steady displays from Bill Foulkes, Shay Brennan and Tony Dunne.

"Nobby Stiles was an important cog in that team. He used to tidy up for us. He seemed able to sense trouble and where danger was going to come from. So he was always there, a great reader of the game.

"He was a bit like a sheepdog keeping everything under control. If one of the sheep tried to break away he would dart into action and put them back in the pen.

"Johnny Aston had a particularly good game in the final, running the legs off their full back to produce some great crosses. He pulled their defence wide which gave the rest of us more room.

"When the final whistle had gone I remember thinking that it was the ultimate achievement, not just for the individual players but for the club and Matt Busby.

"I suppose I can't speak for everyone, but at the same time I think I probably do, when I say

Bobby Charlton

that we felt that it had been a duty to the club.

"For some of us it had become a family thing. We had been together so long, and while people recognised that we had had some great teams, there was nothing in the European record book until 1968 to show for it.

"Sir Matt had made us pioneers in Europe and winning the European Cup was not just a Manchester occasion, it was for the whole country.

"I missed most of the celebrating that night. I was absolutely drained and kept fainting. I couldn't make the reception. Norma told me that Matt had got up late in the evening to sing 'What a wonderful world' and I guess that just about summed it up for all of us."

Bobby Charlton is probably the most enduring and popular among Manchester United's famous players.

Mention of Manchester in the most far-away places is quite likely to prompt a smile of recognition followed by: 'Ah, Manchester United . . . Bobby Charlton!'

Even the guards at Checkpoint Charlie in Berlin smiled when Bobby Charlton appeared on the scene as United crossed into East Germany on a European mission.

He joined the club as a schoolboy from Ashington in the North East, a product of the Milburn and Charlton families rich in football talent.

He became a first-team regular a couple of months before the Munich crash of 1958 and went on to make a club record 604 League appearances spread over 17 seasons of First Division football.

As well as scoring many memorable goals in Cup football, he notched 198 in the League. For England he scored 49 goals in 106 internationals.

But it was the manner of his game which made him so appealing, always so graceful with his football spiced by those thundering shots. He represented a Corinthian spirit, perhaps its last significant representative, always sporting, durable and dedicated.

He has been a Footballer of the Year for both England and Europe. He is the holder of the OBE and CBE.

His qualities have enabled him to move successfully into professional life with a travel business and very fittingly he has launched his soccer schools for youngsters which are thriving. Here is a football idol without feet of clay, an admirable mentor for youth. Just as appropriately he is now a director of Manchester United, the club he served so brilliantly as a player.

MANCHESTER EVENING NEWS, September 26, 1968

ESTUDIANTES	I
MAN. UTD.	**0**

1968 WORLD CLUB CHAMPIONSHIP, FIRST LEG,
ESTUDIANTES WIN I-0

"Savagery": United Poise Saved a Riot!

Stiles out of return

By David Meek
BUENOS AIRES, THURSDAY

Sir Alf Ramsey was right . . . too many of the Argentinian footballers play like animals.

The England manager was publicly rapped for his remarks about Argentina during the World Cup, but one-goal-down Manchester United leave South America today convinced that Sir Alf's controversial summing up hit the nail bang on the head. For it was only United's poise that saved the match erupting into a riot.

As United manager Sir Matt Busby put it: "Holding the ball put a player in danger of his life. It was disgraceful."

As they fly home tonight they count the cost of their first leg against Estudiantes for the World Club Championship:

BOBBY CHARLTON has a deep stud puncture on his lower shin that needed two stitches and prompted this comment from the club doctor: "He was lucky to escape a broken leg."

NOBBY STILES has a cut over his eyebrow and a swollen eye, the result of being first butted and then punched.

He must also count the personal cost of being sent off for a trivial gesture, despite the punishment he received.

This means he will miss the return leg at Old Trafford on October 16.

Skipper Bobby Charlton describes the ruthless Estudiantes tackling: "Their ideas and interpretation of football are just different from ours. We didn't really get a chance to play."

And Denis Law told me: "In the first minute someone ran by and pinched me. Next they were pulling my hair. It was all so childish."

FALSE

Stiles, nursing a cut and swollen left eye, voiced his dissatisfaction about his sending off: "I can't understand it," he said. "When Bilardo butted me my only reaction was to claim a foul."

This opinion was backed up by Sir Matt Busby. "Bilardo behaved worse than Nobby has ever done in his life."

"I object to Stiles' sending off because it was based on his false reputation of being a tough player. What do you expect of a man who was butted in the eye five minutes after the game started."

"They are crucifying Nobby Stiles because of a reputation he has been given which is quite unfair," said the United manager. "He was sent off in this match because of a reputation and build-up around him in the Argentine which is quite disgraceful."

And team-mate David Sadler had this to say: "Nobby was great. He turned his back and walked away from everything. He was butted, punched, pushed and kicked and then got sent off for getting offside."

The United manager said he felt pleased with the result. "Only conceding one goal means we have a better chance of winning in Manchester."

Nobby was great. He turned his back and walked away from everything. He was butted, punched, pushed, kicked, and then sent off for getting offside.—David Sadler

Disallowed

United hopes soar as David Sadler's shot beats Estudiantes goalkeeper

ESTUDIAN
WORLD CLUB CHAMPIONS
MAN. UNIT

'Savagery': United poise saved a riot

Stiles out of return

From DAVID MEEK
Buenos Aires, Thursday.

SIR ALF RAMSEY was right . . . too many of the Argentinian footballers play like animals.

The England manager was publicly rapped for his remarks about Argentina during the World Cup, but one-goal-down Manchester United leave South America today convinced that Sir Alf's controversial summing up hit
For it was only

Sir Matt would not comment on the referee but of linesman Esteban Marino he said: "He does not know his job."

While the game was not a repeat of the Celtic-Racing Club fiasco of last season, it was a match played against a background of violence.

PROUD

It was a tribute to the United players' temperament that they restrained themselves so well under such fierce provocation.

Of United behaviour Sir Matt said: "I was extremely proud of the way the boys accepted every provocation with hardly a murmur."

"This was the most trying game I have been involved in. Under the circumstances it was a very good result for us. The lads defended magnificently."

It was, of course, the defence who bore the brunt of the game, and though this department have had their shaky moments at times this season, they pulled together in great style against the South American champions.

They were beaten only once, in the 28th minute, when Conigliaro headed in a Veron corner.

David Sadler and Bill Foulkes, were outstandingly effective in the middle, while Tony Dunne gave danger man Veron hardly a kick at the ball, and Francis Burns operated with the flair of his best form of last season.

Pat Crerand was forced into defensive positions at times, but rarely failed to come out of them working the ball creatively.

And Nobby Stiles was the hero, popping up in all the tight spots to harass Estudiantes into mistakes. It is perhaps significant that the Estudiantes goal came shortly after his injuries while he had double vision in one eye.

Sadler even found time to join in the attack in the 38th minute for Bobby Charlton's free kick which he flicked through a crowd of players into the goal.

The referee, Senor Sosa Miranda, of Paraguay, at first awarded a goal, but then noticed the linesman's flag was up.

He changed his mind after speaking to the linesman, who tells me that there was a United player standing near the far post. I am afraid I did not see him.

"That was a bad decision," Charlton told me. "I had to hit the ball round a wall of three players for David to run on to. How could he be offside? It's ridiculous."

United had few other chances because the ruthless tackling in midfield effectively broke up any really sustained or considered attack.

THE TIMES, October 17, 1968

MAN. UTD.	1
ESTUDIANTES	1

1968 WORLD CLUB CHAMPIONSHIP, SECOND LEG,
ESTUDIANTES WIN 2-1 ON AGGREGATE

Hungry Manchester Kept At Arm's Length

By Geoffrey Green, Football Correspondent

Manchester United for the moment may be the champions of Europe. But they are not the world club champions. That title, for what it is worth in this frenetic world, now belongs to Estudiantes of Buenos Aires, who by this draw at Old Trafford last night, have claimed the inter-Continental Cup, which goes with this event by an overall aggregate of two goals to one.

What am I to say on such an explosive occasion like this, explosive, that is, over the last 10 dramatic minutes which saw George Best of Manchester United and Medina sent off the field with only minutes to go; two more Argentines, Bilardo and the substitute Echicopa both booked to have their names added to the Yugoslavian referee's list to those earlier of Medina and Veron, which brought the sort of ending to the night which I had feared from the very beginning.

Yet, truth to tell, for 80 of these 90 minutes of biting of nails and expenditure of one cigarette packet after another, this had been a calm match in such circumstances. To be honest I have seen much worse from the Yugoslavs and even once, I remember, in a semi-final between United and Leeds.

Yet it was the climax that was left in one's gullet rather like the last words said at a party where the drinks had been flowing fast and free. It was not a nice taste and I am sure that most of the 64,000 people, who streamed out of Old Trafford last night and who, may I say, behaved themselves impeccably in the circumstances, left as disappointed as I.

There was little football in the highest terms

BELOW: *Morgan (right) scores United's late equaliser past Poletti (left) of Estudiantes in Buenos Aires*

but rather too much fear which hung over from the last meeting and perhaps if Charlton, for one, could sit quietly at this moment I am sure he would repeat these lines: "The fly I envy sitting in the sun, on the green leaf, and wish my goal was won".

The trouble with United this night was, although they had talent it was without character; nor did we see much of their talent because there was no character on this occasion to set it free. They found themselves facing hustlers, highly intelligent, markedly skilled, men who knew every wrinkle in the book, men who could look after themselves in the darkest corners.

The thing was to watch some of their antics after the ball had gone away from the player when the eyes of the referee and most of the crowd had moved on. Those were the moments that mattered and it was one of these moments that led finally to the departure of Best, who all night had been cabin'd, cribb'd and confin'd. It was after he had crossed a centre from the right that he was caught unfairly by Medina. In a flash his Irish temper flared. There followed, sadly, a right hook. Down went Medina and if Sir Henry Irving had learnt nothing from his years on the stage he should have been present at that moment to see the exaggerated writhings.

But no excuse, two wrongs do not make a right and Best, who had earlier been spat in the face and had retaliated then only with a gentle pat to his opponent's cheek, now paid the full price. It was following this incident and the immediate booking of those last two Argentines that Morgan moved in with little more than three minutes left, to hit home Crerand's free-kick from the right to make it one-all.

In the dying minutes United made their last great challenge, and as the whistle blew there was Kidd to hit in Morgan's cross for what everybody thought was the winning goal which, had it counted, would have taken both these teams to Amsterdam on Saturday for a play-off. But the whistle had gone and Estudiantes, I am sure, had relaxed and not covered themselves. They knew they were home.

They were home because of their magnificent defence, who kept the hungry Manchester team at arm's length for most of the night.

The first 80 minutes were calm by comparison for one reason only. Perhaps I am being cynical when I say this, but they were calm because the Argentine players were clever enough to sneak a goal within the first five

minutes, when Veron, sneaking in behind a static United defence, headed home a free-kick from Madoro. This put them two up and, knowing themselves and their defensive capabilities, which is the basis of Argentine play, they must have known then that they were home.

There was no need for anything except to shadow box and cover quietly with the occasional drifting touch which the referee failed to see. At least Manchester refused to fall into the old trap of reprisal and revenge until near the end. Although the night gnawed at the crowd and a situation that had become threadbare, Manchester United refused to diminish themselves in their attitude.

There may have been bad blood left over from the past, but it was not apparent. There may have been knives somewhere but now they were sheathed and out of sight as Manchester pounded back for the equaliser before the interval with near efforts from Best, Charlton, Sadler, and a half-chance for Law, a taste which gave the Scotsman the hunger to go for an outside ball, crash into the goalkeeper and be taken away from the field to have four stitches inserted in a gashed knee: an honest accident which brought on Sartori.

Later all through the second half Sartori, for all his inexperience seemed to offer a new hope while Best and even Charlton were caged.

Just before half time Stepney was called upon to make his one real save of the night when he turned a shot from Conigliaro over his crossbar. Apart from that he virtually was unemployed, save for that early moment of picking the ball out of his net. All through the second half Manchester drove on but with no real imagination. A goal seemed as far away as ever, for all the efforts of Sartori, Charlton, young Kidd and the rest.

The Argentine defence was quite masterly in the way it covered and recovered, each man falling into place as I said before in a zonal scheme. They were tongued and grooved and there seemed no way through until at last in those frantic closing moments Morgan shot home. But by then, as the climax approached the knives at last were out and the game had changed its character.

For most of the night at least we were reprieved, but I now come away from Old Trafford more than ever doubtful whether these sort of occasions are necessary. The prizes have become too big; the passion too great.

Daily Herald, September 18, 1968

| WATERFORD | 1 |
| MAN UTD. | 3 |

1968-69 EUROPEAN CUP, FIRST ROUND, FIRST LEG, MANCHESTER UNITED WIN 3-1

Three-goal jig by Law

By Peter Lorenzo

LOOKING BACK ■ WITH NOBBY STILES ■

It's not everyone who can claim to have been "nutted" by the manager of a World Cup winning team!

But Nobby Stiles, at one time El Bandido of world football, can claim that distinction.

You have to go back a few years, but the fact is that Carlos Bilardo, the man who guided Argentina to their World Cup triumph in Mexico in 1986, is well remembered by Manchester United . . . especially by Nobby Stiles.

For Bilardo was an aggressive young man as a player and he was a member of the team which lined up against the Reds to contest the World Club championship in 1969.

The first leg in Buenos Aires was a bloody affair with Bilardo in the thick of the action and at one point smashing Stiles in the face with a head butt.

"That was bad enough, but Bilardo then threw himself down as if it was me who had hit him. I think the referee was going to send me off, but I was able to point to the blood running from my cut eye and it made him change his mind," explained Nobby.

"In actual fact I was sent off later in the match and I was pig sick. Paddy Crerand and I had talked at half-time about how we should try and beat the offside trap they were working. We agreed that if our forwards came out with their defence then I should make some deep runs through and catch them off guard.

"I thought we had worked it but the linesman signalled I was offside. I didn't think I was and I just threw my hand in the air. The referee sent me off for dissent.

Three-goal jig by Law

In their long and varied history of European competition, Manchester United have never had a victory or an experience quite like this one at Dublin's Lansdowne Road ground.

For a start, it was the first time they had ever played on a rugby pitch, and Scottish referee Bill Mullan had to wait until George Best had signed autographs for a couple of adoring girl fans before he could start the second half.

Then after Denis Law, already a hat-trick marksman, miscued his fourth early in the second half by hitting a penalty low against a post, the referee refused to restart the match until a wild-haired character who had raced on to the pitch threatening to punch his head off, had been removed from the crowded ground.

Invasions

Before the game so many ticketless fans scaled the 10ft. boundary walls that they hopelessly outnumbered police.

Thousands of gatecrashers spilled to within two feet of the touchlines and after two mass invasions of the pitch in the second half, the 50,000-plus crowd — 48,000 tickets were sold!

"It was a bit silly and I was very upset because I thought I had let the side down. There was a lot going on in that game and it seemed ridiculous that I should be sent off for waving my arm.

"Mind you, the referee was a funny chap. He was smoking a cigarette when we all came down the tunnel to go out on the pitch. A lot of people smoke but you don't expect to see the ref having a puff like that!

"It was a different world in South America. Before the kick-off there were gaily dressed folk dancers performing watched by steel-helmeted riot police armed with tear gas guns. It was quite incongruous, and certainly a highly charged atmosphere when we walked out with clouds of red smoke billowing out from a bomb someone had let off.

"I suppose even before the game had started I was regarded as the villain of the piece. I knew I always had a reputation as a fairly aggressive player, but the South American press had really gone to town.

"They called me an assassin, and even in the match programme I was described as 'brutal, badly intentioned and a bad sportsman.'

"I could hardly expect the home fans to be on my side after that – and they weren't. Bilardo was clearly out to get me and I think the referee must have read the programme as well. I certainly didn't get much sympathy from him.

"The situation had its lighter moments. I remember coming out of the stadium after the match. It was dark and shadowy when I suddenly felt something thrust into my back and a voice whispering into my ear: 'Now then El Bandido.'

"I thought my end had come – until I realised it was Brian Kidd!

"I missed the return leg in Manchester, suspended because of the sending-off. Estudiantes weren't as bad at Old Trafford, though there were two players sent off, George Best and Hugo Medina, after George had retaliated.

"But we weren't at our best. We conceded a goal after five minutes and it killed us. Willie Morgan scored near the end to make it 1-1 on the night, but of course we lost on aggregate with the 1-0 defeat in Buenos Aires.

"It was certainly an education."

Sir Matt Busby always felt that Stiles had had a raw deal in South America.

"They crucified Nobby because of an unfair reputation. He was sent off because of the reputation and a build-up in the Argentine press which was quite disgraceful," he said.

Now Nobby is better remembered by the fans at home for his famous victory jig round Wembley after helping England win the World Cup in 1966.

The sight of his toothless grin as he danced round the pitch, socks round his ankles, was a

Nobby Stiles

heart-warming spectacle which captured the hearts of old ladies as well as soccer supporters!

He played through all the international teams from schoolboy level to World Cup, and with United won two championship medals and a European Cup winners medal.

He was always a hundred per cent committed. Bobby Charlton reckons that some of his awkward looking tackles were simply the result of him not wearing his spectacles because he was always short-sighted. Certainly his timing improved when he started to wear contact lenses!

United missed him when he left after 11 years of first-team football in 1971 to join Middlesbrough. After two seasons at Ayrsome Park he spent eight years with Preston, the first as a player, then three as coach and four as manager.

He spent a period in Canada with Vancouver Whitecaps coaching for his brother-in-law, Johnny Giles, who was the manager. He followed John to West Bromwich where his most recent appointment has been as youth coach.

He says: "I enjoy working with youngsters. I have run the full gamut in football from player to manager and this is what I like doing best. I have mellowed a lot now of course.

"My son John is with Leeds United and plays like his Uncle, John Giles. He got sent off once and people said he must be a chip off the old block, but he isn't really, quite a different kind of player. My other sons, Peter and Robert, don't play professionally.

"We still live in Sale, not far from Old Trafford, and the first thing I look for outside my job is Manchester United's result. My association with the club will always be there."

– were warned over the loudspeakers: "The referee says he will call off the game the next time."

It has been more than 40 years since a soccer match was last played here on this hallowed rugby ground. I think it will be at least another 40 years before they allow another one.

Manchester United, in this their first defence of the European prize they won so gloriously last May, were never in trouble, or under pressure and they might have doubled their score.

But a sense of showmanship and flamboyance, particularly by Best and Brian Kidd, denied them the extra goals.

The match was virtually decided after just eight minutes. Two brilliant reverse passes, the first from Pat Crerand, recalled to the side at right half, and Best, teed it up for Law to slot in the first of his hat-trick.

After 22 minutes a brilliant Best "goal", following another magnificent move by Charlton and Sadler, was mysteriously disallowed.

Jack-knife

After Law had hit a short-range jab against a post in the 29th minute, the Scottish international headed No. 2 four minutes from the interval with a jack-knife leap to convert a left-wing cross from Kidd.

Nine minutes after the restart, Law stroked in his third following a bewildering run and pass by Best. A minute later Best was pulled down by right-back Bryan. It seemed a harsh decision, and maybe it was justice for Law to clip a post with his penalty.

Another minute and Jimmy Rimmer came on to replace Alex Stepney in goal. Stepney had injured a foot in the first half and with the vital match against Estudiantes in mind next week he wisely finished the match watching from the touchline.

Coventry-born John Matthews cracked a loose ball firmly past Rimmer in the 63rd minute to make it 3-1.

Twelve minutes from time Alfie Hale, Waterford's best forward, headed against the bar.

But if United could have forced themselves to take the match seriously there would have been a repeat of the 6-0 hammering they gave Shamrock Rovers on their last European Cup trip to Dublin 11 years ago.

But how can you be serious about a football match played on a rugby pitch in front of a gay Irish crowd!

DAILY EXPRESS, October 2, 1968

MAN. UTD.	7
WATERFORD	**1**

1968-69 EUROPEAN CUP, FIRST ROUND, SECOND LEG, MANCHESTER UNITED WIN 10-2 ON AGGREGATE

Gallant Irish find way into United hearts

By Alan Thompson

In the context of all the Waterloos and Agincourts being fought all over the Continent last night, this win by the European Cup holders did not have much significance. It was a foregone conclusion.

But as entertainment it was excellent, no less – and for that, much of the credit must go to Waterford.

Outclassed

Never once did the League of Ireland champions foul intentionally, never once did they turn game with dour defence. Always they tried to play open, attacking football, and though, inevitably, they were outclassed, they still made it a pleasant evening. For that I heartily thank them.

And the players of United thanked them, too. In a most especial and heart-warming way.

After the massacre was over, the United team lined up on either side of the tunnel and made the men of Waterford go in first to the cheer ringing in their ears and the sound of applause from 11 of England's champion footballers.

The crowd really warmed to them. The Irishmen and I will forever cherish the memory of the Stretford Enders, not I think always the most generous of crowds, chanting "Waterford, Waterford". In the second half to help them along.

RIGHT: *Burns (right) beaten by a sliding tackle from Griffin of Waterford*

FAR RIGHT: *United applaud their opponents from the field*

BELOW: *Worm's eye view of Law's second goal in United's second leg match against Waterford*

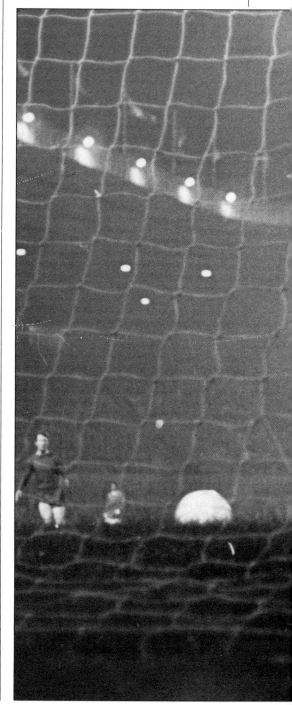

And yet it needed a slow handclap from those same Stretford Enders to set the game alight. It seemed as if the cutting edge of United had been blunted on the hard steel of Estudiantes last week.

They had made their chances early on but had been unable to profit from them and the crowd got a little restless after 35 minutes. But that gentle slow handclap was enough to set United alight and in the 37th minute Nobby Stiles set the goal chart moving with a blast from the corner of the penalty box.

Five minutes later, Waterford goalkeeper Peter Thomas looked to have a 35-yard shot from Bobby Charlton well covered, but Denis Law deflected the ball into the bottom corner of the net.

The avalanche was saved for the second half ... and it was not long coming. Charlton beat Paul Morrissey in the 47th minute, drew Thomas out of his goal and squared for the unmarked Denis Law to complete the necessary formalities.

The ever-alert Law completed his second hat-trick against Waterford on the hour, when he headed in from Crerand's cross ... but still there was more to come.

Full-back Francis Burns went up for a corner in the 67th minute and lobbed in over Thomas's head after Best lost the ball.

Willing

But probably the biggest cheer of the whole evening came in the 70th minute – when Waterford at last scored through right-winger Al Casey.

I doubt if there was a man among the crowd who was not willing Waterford on to at least one goal, and when it came, there were great gasps of pleasure and as loud a cheer as United's folk ever gave their own goals.

Thankfully, though, United never subjected the Irishmen to the indignity of making this an exhibition. Law was on hand again in the 72nd minute to stab in after Thomas had tipped away a shot from David Sadler ... and then five minutes from time Charlton lashed home the seventh.

THE GUARDIAN, November 13, 1968

MAN. UTD.	3
RSC ANDERLECHT	**0**

1968-69 EUROPEAN CUP, SECOND ROUND, FIRST LEG, MANCHESTER UNITED WIN 3-0

Kidd scores – and old confidence returns

By Albert Barham

T hree goals to take to Brussels in a fortnight's time – that's a bonanza for Manchester United, if you like. And all achieved with that power United have, to surprise, shock and finally delight their supporters. They did it all last night at Old Trafford. To every one of the 51,000 present.

Here was a tie in the European Cup in which United genuinely were apprehensive. They were without Best and Morgan, the twin striking forces on the wing. There was the gamble on Law and his knee. There was the fear that United's defence might creak once too often and let these nippy Belgian forwards through. For they were skilled. They were fast. They were intelligent. But United held them – albeit after a couple of very nasty shocks – and went on to score three and missed a penalty for good measure.

Kialunda rules

After all the dull, drab games one has seen recently, here was a pleasant breeze of real football. It was fast, flowing exciting and clean – apart from a few heavy tackles by the large Congolese gentleman, Kialunda, who ruled the Anderlecht defence. And at the end, United, who had started badly, and whose passing was dreadful, finally found all their old form.

At first they had no bite. They survived a couple of very dodgy situations. Then the

passing improved. Dunne bolstered the defence and Crerand and Charlton drove them forward. And they scored. With the coming of the first goal came all the old confidence. Finally, they applauded this fast, clever Belgian side off the field.

The wheel has turned full cycle for United. A half century of matches in European competition have gone by since they first met Anderlecht 12 years ago in United's opening match in this competition. Anderlecht have prided themselves for years on having an all-Belgian side. Now winners of the Belgian championship five years in succession, they are rebuilding. And in have come the foreigners. They look to France for Herbet, a most competent player, to Germany, and to the Swede, Nordahl, son of the famous Gunnar Nordahl of Milan, who is loaned from Juventus.

Competent defence

For the first half of this match, United looked as though all their fangs had been drawn. They were held by this most competent defence in which Peteers played a prominent part. But he was injured late in the game and replaced by Mulder, a Dutchman with a fair turn of speed but who came on when United were in their most aggressive mood. He could do little.

United were held for quite a while. Twice, in fact, the Belgians almost scored, each time through Devrindt. In the twenty-second minute, he went round Sadler and was off like a flash. Stepney stuck out a foot like a tentacle – he could do nothing else – and the ball struck his boot and ricocheted high into the crowd.

Then, after Law, with his springheeled leaps had twice been within inches of scoring, United's great chance came – and went. Charlton, out on the left wing, sent over a high pass towards Ryan. Cornelis, a most experienced defender, surreptitiously stuck out a hand and a

penalty was justly awarded. Up strolled Law, took a couple of steps forward, and stroked the ball towards the post. But Trappeniers with a flash of intuition anticipated him and smothered the shot.

It looked for all the world as though United had had it. But it was not to be. Puis, who seems to specialise in taking curling free kicks, took his second of the evening and the ball hit the post. Whether this latest escape brought United back to reality no one will know. But from that moment on there was no stopping them. They found all their old power, all their old form, and swept forward relentlessly.

The first goal came after 51 minutes. The move was begun by Crerand and Charlton and taken on by Ryan. From his cross, Kidd leapt high above the defence to head in. After 70 minutes United gained the lead of two goals for which they hoped. It was the first from Law. The pass came from Charlton and Law, with one of those graceful headed flicks of which he is the past master, beat the Belgian defence. There might have been another when Sartori, an eager beaver of a lad, shot but the ball struck Nordahl on its path towards goal.

Law again

But it mattered not in the end, for in the seventy-eighth minute Law scored his second and United's third. It came after Sartori had had a shot blocked, Kidd tried but saw his shot smothered as well. Law gathered the ball in the crowded goal-mouth and banged it into the net.

So United go to Brussels far more happily than they could have anticipated in their hearts. Anderlecht are a most useful Belgian side, but fortune eventually was with United. Perhaps the knowledge that United are nothing if they are not in Europe came to them in their moment of need.

Kidd scores—and old confidence returns

By ALBERT BARHAM : Manchester U. 3, R.S.C. Anderlecht 0

Three goals to take to Brussels in a fortnight's time —that's a bonanza for Manchester United, if you like. And all achieved with that power United have, to surprise, shock and finally delight their supporters. They did it all last night at Old Trafford. To every one of the 51,000 present.

tie in the European

tion have gone by since they first met Anderlecht 12 years ago in United's opening match in this competition. Anderlecht have prided themselves for years on having an all-Belgian side. Now winners of the Belgian championship five years in succession, they are rebuilding. And in have come the foreigners. They look to France for Herbet, a most competent player, to Germany, and to the Swede, Nordahl, son of the famous Gunnar Nordahl

though United had had it. But it was not to be. Puis, who seems to specialise in taking curling free kicks, took his second of the evening and the ball hit the post. Whether this latest escape brought United back to reality no one will know. But from that moment on there was no stopping them. They found all their old power, all their old form, and swept forward relentlessly.

The first goal came after 51 minutes. The move was begun

LEFT: *Law (second from right) scores United's second goal in their first leg tie against Anderlecht*

BELOW: *Anderlecht frustration personified!*

THE DAILY TELEGRAPH, November 27, 1968

RSC ANDERLECHT	3
MAN. UTD.	1

1968-69 EUROPEAN CUP, SECOND ROUND, SECOND LEG, MANCHESTER UNITED WIN 4-3 ON AGGREGATE

Sartori's goal decisive for Manchester United

By R. H. Williams

BRUSSELS, Wednesday

Anderlecht retrieved most of the glory they had conceded in their 3-0 defeat at Old Trafford but the margin was too great for them to pull back and the holders reached the European Cup quarter-finals with a final flicker of excitement here tonight.

The Belgians deserved all the warm applause that their fans gave them, but United had been given the priceless fillip of a goal after only seven minutes which not only made their victory virtually assured but naturally imposed the pattern on the rest of the game.

It happens ironically in these contests that the winners are often on the receiving end rather than not, but this hardly detracts from a victory that was achieved, for all that, in reasonable comfort.

Anderlecht are a skilful side who would be welcome any time in England because they have the rare capacity to impose their skill without provoking undesirable counter measures.

ABOVE: *Stiles (left) and Hanon compete for the ball*

RIGHT: *United's only goal of the second leg against Anderlecht*

Sartori's goal decisive for Manchester United

By R. H. WILLIAMS

Anderlecht 3   Manchester United ... 1
(Manchester United win on aggregate 4—3)

BRUSSELS, Wednesday.

ANDERLECHT retrieved most of the glory they had conceded in their 3—0 defeat at Old Trafford but the margin was too great for them to pull back and the holders reached the European Cup quarter-finals with a final flicker of excitement here tonight.

The Belgians deserved all the warm applause that their fans

anxious moments in defence and when Mulder scored with a venomous shot after 18 minutes they knew they were in for a pounding.

Stepney made a good save from another shot by Mulder

Action from the semi-final 2nd leg tie between Manchester United and AC Milan, May 1969

Davies celebrates his goal

Sporting game

It was a sporting game, and if Sartori had not scored that precious goal in the seventh minute it might have turned the other way. But once they had the lead United set out to hold it, and even though they conceded three goals to the Belgians they had, of course, an extra one in hand because a goal scored away from home counts double in the event of a tie.

Sartori's goal came after United had exposed the Belgians' offside trap promisingly two or three times, and as Charlton took a throw-in on the right, Crerand slipped a perfect pass inside for Sartori, who took his chance like veteran.

United for a time still looked more dangerous in attack but they had packed their side with defenders and committed themselves to a passive game. They must have felt safe, with a four-goal lead, but there were still anxious moments in defence and when Mulder scored with a venemous shot after 18 minutes they knew they were in for a pounding.

Stepney made a good save from another shot by Mulder and Fitzpatrick failed to quell United's remaining fears when he fired over the Anderlecht crossbar when a chip over the advancing goalkeeper might have turned Crerand's pass into a goal and an unassailable lead.

The task still looked too much for the Belgians, but they had shown their attacking skill at Old Trafford and they produced it again now. After 58 minutes Bergholtz headed their second goal from a corner and after 70 minutes he scored again, leaving Anderlecht only one goal short of an overall draw.

Unexpected bonus

They pierced the United defence once more, but Stepney was there to fist a shot from Nordhal over the bar, a save that represented possibly the Belgians' last chance.

United have had more anxious Cup-ties in Europe, but not much more. Their injury position was genuinely serious and they were deprived of Best by suspension and Morgan by ineligibility. Sir Matt Busby brought in Foulkes to replace Kidd, and with only three forwards in the side there could not be much doubt about their tactics.

Sartori's goal was an unexpected bonus, and if they embraced him more than the rest at the end it was no more than he deserved. What might have been a difficult struggle despite the 3-0 victory at Old Trafford was still a comfortable win in the end, even if it did not look it.

DAILY EXPRESS, February 26, 1969

MAN. UTD. 3

RAPID VIENNA 0

1968-69 EUROPEAN CUP, QUARTER FINAL, FIRST LEG, MANCHESTER UNITED WIN 3-0

By Alan Thompson

The magical, twinkling devilry that makes every man who wears the red shirt of Manchester United a supreme champion came bubbling through again last night.

And once again they march proudly into the semi-final of the European Cup.

Next week's second leg in Vienna is a formality and in this week that is for them a fabulous fiesta of Cup ties they can cockily say: "Two down with one to go." The other is Everton on Saturday.

I said that United would win this one 3-1, but frankly, after less than half an hour Rapid had not a chance of scoring, not even a hope, as United monopolised the night.

They won in the end via those wonders of the wing, George Best, who scored two goals, and Willie Morgan, who scored the other.

But it took them almost until half-time to find their way onto the score sheet. Then they had a chunk of luck ... but if ever a side deserved it it was the European champions.

If they had not won – and won handsomely – I would have labelled it the biggest robbery with violence since Jessie James last saddled his "hoss".

For they had three goals disallowed for offside and the referee turned a blind eye to what I thought were two blatant penalties in the first half.

Just in case you are under any doubt let me say that they were not, emphatically not, lucky. It's just that they should have had, and moreover deserved, a bagful of goals against this all-international Austrian side.

Bounced

United went in front in the 43rd minute. A George Best-Denis Law duet ended with full-back Gebhardt taking the ball off Law's toes and crashing against his own post as he tried to clear for a corner.

Fortunately for United the ball bounced to Morgan who evaded one scything tackle and centred. Now the ball was partially cleared to Best, standing on the edge of the penalty area and he despatched it low into the corner of the net.

The second half was oneway traffic as United's forwards ploughed furrows towards the Rapid goal. They took charge after an hour and overworked goalkeeper Fuchsichler saved with his feet from Kidd before tipping a centre by Charlton off Law's head.

Charlton showed his midfield brilliance in the 66th minute when he picked up a loose ball midway in his own half, skipped over the outstretched legs of Grausam and sent Morgan streaking through the middle before passing to Kidd and meeting the return centre to score a superb goal.

Four minutes later this match – and the one in Austria – became a foregone conclusion. Stiles chipped through to Best who should have lost the ball five yards from goal to Gebhardt.

But he got a second chance when the full-back failed to clear and shot into the roof of the net on the turn with his foot.

Rapid should have gone in front in 18 minutes when Floegel put Kaltenbrunner through with only Stepney to beat. But instead of taking his time, and he was not short of that commodity, he put the ball gently into the grateful hands of Stepney from about three yards.

I thought that United should have had a penalty in the 22nd minute. Charlton went through Vienna like a dose of salts, but was nudged by Fak just as he was about to shoot, lost his balance, and finished up on the running track.

They had legitimate claims for another penalty in the 28th minute. Charlton sent Best away on one of his zany runs with Floegel in pursuit. Eventually Floegel tripped him and Best fell well inside the penalty area. But the referee let play go on.

What they said . . .

SIR MATT BUSBY: I thought the boys were a bit on edge in the first-half but once we got a goal it eased the pressure, and they came through very well and made many chances.

I'm very confident that we shall get through in Vienna and obviously this result, coming after the Birmingham Cup-tie, is just what we need as we prepare for the sixth round match with Everton.

RUDOLPH VYTLACIL (Rapid coach): I was very pleased with our fighting spirit but United are a well-drilled English team and I am afraid they got right on top in the second half. It was a silly goal that we gave away just before half-time when we had played to a plan and done so well.

I think we will win in Vienna, although I cannot say whether it will be by enough goals to win the tie.

BOBBY CHARLTON: We set off as if we were feeling the effects of Monday but then we really got into our stride and I think we should have had more goals. But if three isn't enough, I don't know what is.

DENIS LAW: I didn't hear the whistle on either occasion for my two offside goals, but I am not arguing with the decisions. I was marked tightly, but they were very fair.

RIGHT: *Fuchsbichler (second from left) remonstrates with his defence after a United goal*

BELOW: *Willie Morgan (second from right) scores United's second goal in the first leg match against Rapid Vienna*

ABOVE: *Charlton (second from right) tries a powerful shot which ends up going just wide*

The Times, March 5, 1969

RAPID VIENNA	0
MAN. UTD.	0

1968-69 EUROPEAN CUP, QUARTER FINAL, SECOND LEG, MANCHESTER UNITED WIN 3-0 ON AGGREGATE

Command performance by champions

From Geoffrey Green, Football Correspondent
VIENNA, MARCH 5

Manchester United, the European champions, are into the semi-final of this powerful competition for the fifth time in their history and the third in the last four years. By an aggregate of 3-0, their goals having been scored at Old Trafford in the first leg, they overstepped Rapid Vienna, the Austrian champions, whom they held to a goalless draw here tonight.

With Benfica left behind in the shadows, United remain alone from last season's semi-final. To have done this, after their fourth hard tie in 10 days, shows the extent of their spirit and stamina. They might have been lost in the Vienna woods. They might have been diminished in the great Prater Stadium here before a roaring 60,000 crowd, where these Austrians have been beaten only once in 15 European Cup ties. But they were not.

United did a man's job and the scoreline is a lying jade. But for the acrobatic and brave goalkeeping of Fuchsbichler – not to mention a number of desperately near things – they might well have won by six goals or so. They played like true champions, who have again found their voice.

Rapid's tactics were clear from the start. So often in these ties the first 20 minutes or so can be crucial and the Austrians immediately started to rain hammer blows at the United defence. They were supported in the background by a continuous roar, deep and hopeful, and by a veritable barrage of coloured rockets that cut the night with their smoke trailers.

Yet United held their line firmly, following the thread of Rapid's complicated pattern weaving, as they tried to break through. Here Crerand was the master as he read each move; young James, clearly growing in stature, dominated the middle; and here, too, was Sadler, in place of the injured Law, filling in the midfield with mobile positional play – now as a second centre half, now as a support for attack.

Bit by bit, the bloom was knocked off Rapid, and by the interval Fuchsbichler had made three magnificent saves from Charlton, from one of which he turned a thunderbolt shot onto his own crossbar, thankfully to collect the rebound in his arms. But if Fuchsbichler had become the busier man by half-time, it was Stepney, at the other end, with a blistering save close in at the foot of the post from Kaltenbrunner, who probably broke the Austrian hearts.

It was the sort of save he made in the final at Wembley last year from Eusebio, of Benfica, in the dying minutes of normal time that denied the Portuguese victory. In the second half United, seeing which way the tide was flowing, calmed the tempo to suit themselves and proceeded to give us a command performance.

This was the United of old, playing at the top of their voices. Now they were richly endowed again. One saw, once more, the calibre of the side. The only thing that did not flatter them was the score.

Having refused to surrender in the early stages, when Rapid had put all their eggs in one basket to force a breakthrough by all-out attack, United after that interval sprang back like a conifer. Their football flowed smoothly, with a masterly, and even arrogant, touch as they took control.

Rapid are a fine side, clearly talented, who added to their own graces by playing sportingly and cleanly, but now they excited United's voice and found themselves hushed and left in wonder. They seemed to accept their roles as victims as Charlton, more and more, became the hub of the United attack, which spun out from midfield towards Morgan and Best.

Charlton was denied another three goals by the prehensile Fuchsbichler: and there were near things from the hard-working Kidd, and the rest. By then, United's football had the Austrian crowd virtually waltzing on the terraces with appreciation. The master performer was that virtuoso, Best.

He turned the opposition inside out playing ducks and drakes with them left, right and centre. He played in a kind of radius, drawing each man to him like a magnet and then losing him. It was a superb monologue delivered by a Henry Irving of the game. At the end the whole stadium lost in wonder were chanting "Encore, encore, encore!" Vienna will remember him, Charlton and United for a long time to come.

THE DAILY TELEGRAPH, April 23, 1969

AC MILAN	2
MAN. UTD.	0

1968-69 EUROPEAN CUP, SEMI-FINAL, FIRST LEG,
AC MILAN WIN 2-0

Fitzpatrick sent off as United are well beaten

By Donald Saunders in Milan

Manchester United's lease on the European Cup is likely to run out at Old Trafford three weeks tonight when they resume a semi-final against A.C. Milan that seems to have slipped away from them.

A sad night for English football came to an end before 80,000 jubilant Milanese packed into the noisy San Siro Stadium with the Italian club comfortably ahead and United reduced to 10 men.

The European champions tried desperately hard to fight their way back into the game after conceding goals by Sormani and Hamrin in the 33rd and 48th minutes. But their task became hopeless when they lost Fitzpatrick 15 minutes from time.

This young full-back will take no part at all in the second leg. He was sent off for kicking Hamrin, after the Swedish-born Milan winger had body-checked him, and will now automatically be suspended for the next game.

The referee, Mr. Krnavec, of Czechoslovakia, did not see the incident, since it occured some distance from the scene of play. But after consulting a linesman, he had no hesitation in ordering Fitzpatrick to the dressing room.

So now United must try to score three goals against one of the best club defences in the world, and must not concede one in the process.

You may remember that Celtic went home from San Siro last February with a clean sheet, then were edged out of the competition by the only goal in the return match in Glasgow.

Turning point

When Rivera, the elegant footballer who makes this side tick, limped off for good in the 20th minute with an ankle injury, suffered in a collision with Law, I thought the Italians might sag.

Indeed, they showed some signs of doing so in the 10 minutes immediately following the arrival of Fogli, the substitute.

Then, in the 33rd minute, came the turning point. Sormani lost a heading duel with Foulkes but as the ball broke inside the box, the Milan centre-forward pounced on it and drove an awkward, bouncing shot past Rimmer.

From that moment the Italians were supremely confident. Lodetti took over Rivera's role with great skill, to give them control of the middle of the pitch. The fleet-footed Prati and quick-witted Hamrin caused

FITZPATRICK SENT OFF AS UNITED ARE WELL BEATEN

By DONALD SAUNDERS in Milan
A.C. Milan 2   Manchester United ... 0

MANCHESTER UNITED'S lease on the European Cup is likely to run out at Old Trafford three weeks tonight when they resume a semi-final against A.C. Milan that seems to have

sh football came to an end before packed into the noisy San Siro

LEFT: *Rimmer watches Sormani's shot hit the back of his net for AC Milan's first goal in their first leg match*

1.

ABOVE: *In the thick of it*

all sorts of trouble on the wings and Sormani led the front line with authority.

So it came as no great surprise when Milan scored again three minutes after the interval. This time it was Fogli who started the move, with a quick cross into the penalty box. Sormani cleverly stepped over the ball and Hamrin drove it into the net.

Tremendous pressure

It says much for United's courage that they did not allow the Italians to widen the gap. Though Milan piled on tremendous pressure, Foulkes and his men did not collapse.

United's attempts to narrow the margin, however, had a touch of desperation about them. With Charlton and Crerand out of touch the guidance they needed from midfield simply did not come.

Moreover, Best, so often a match-winner, could not find a way through and more often than not merely ran into trouble. Morgan was rarely in the game and Kidd could not get away from the robust Rosato, who was replaced 10 minutes from time by Maldera.

Stiles, however, came through this testing night with colours flying, though he was given a rougher ride than anyone else on the pitch. Though the crowd constantly whistled at him and occasionally threw fire crackers in his direction, he got through a tremendous lot of work, both as a defender and as the leader of counter attacks.

He took many a nasty bump without flinch-

ing, too, until four minutes from the end, he limped off after a tackle by Hamrin and was replaced by Burns.

Alert Rimmer

Rimmer, playing in his first European Cup-tie, understandly made one or two minor errors, but could not be blamed for either goal. Indeed, his alertness and agility prevented United from falling still further behind.

I am afraid, however, that in the long run that is not going to make much difference — unless Best, Law, Charlton and company rise to great heights at Old Trafford on May 15.

ABOVE: *Morgan (right) heads, Cudicini (No 1) leaps, but it goes over the bar*

DAILY HERALD, May 15, 1969

MAN. UTD.	1
AC MILAN	0

1968-69 EUROPEAN CUP, SEMI-FINAL, SECOND LEG,
AC MILAN WIN 2-1 ON AGGREGATE

United go out – with glory

Peter Lorenzo reports

The champions are out. Manchester United, playing with characteristic heart and commendable all-out aggression, found to their misery last night that their best was not enough.

A magnificently schemed goal by Best, and scored by Charlton 20 minutes from time, maintained United's magnificent European Cup record at Old Trafford.

In 12 years of this competition they have won 19 matches, drawn one, and scored 64 goals against 13.

The question that will never be answered is what might have happened if that Charlton goal had come 20 minutes from the start and not 20 minutes from the end.

In the final analysis, due praise must be given to the Italians, who will now be favourites to regain the prize they held in 1963.

They go forward to meet Ajax of Amsterdam in the Madrid final on May 28 in the knowledge they have beaten the most formidable opposition in the competition – Manchester United, the 1968 champions, and Glasgow Celtic, bosses of 1967.

Perfect

United's task before a capacity crowd of 63,103 was formidable before the game. To pull back two goals against one of the most assured, organised and disciplined defences in European football was asking a lot.

When the pattern of play showed itself so clearly in this second leg the difficulties increased.

United wanted too much from the men they knew had responded so well in the past – Best, Charlton and Law.

This was a night when the professional stranglehold of the Italians on United's big three relaxed only once – after 70 minutes, when Best superbly beat two defenders before laying on a perfect chance for Charlton.

Milan, as expected, were dangerous in breakaways. Hamrin had the ball in the net after 11 minutes but a linesman's flag was up for offside.

Prati, though so often committed to helping his defence, still sprinted away to bring out the best in promising young goalkeeper Rimmer.

This, inevitably, had to be a match when so much United determination and effort was going to be countered by the calm and resilience of an Italian team so practised and experienced in keeping invaders at bay.

Quality

But in the quality and character of one player – Nobby Stiles – much of United's merit was captured. Stiles, playing with an unstable knee and booked for a cartilage operation this summer, never spared himself.

He ran hard, was biting in the tackle, covered any gaps in defence, and was willing to thrust along the flanks and spur his forwards into action.

It was not enough, and United's reign as European kings is over, but there is still pride and, more important, dignity to be taken from the way they went out.

It could be that the era of Sir Matt Busby is now over. Wilf McGuinness assumes the reins on June 1 ... and judged on last night's contribution has many riches to work on.

BELOW: *View from behind Rimmer's goal*

LOOKING BACK WITH DAVID SADLER

Manchester United did not reign for long as champions of Europe.

They started convincingly enough as holders in season 1968-69, but found A C Milan too good for them in the semi-finals.

As David Sadler explains: "The season after winning the European Cup was something of an anti-climax. It shouldn't have been of course, but the club had been such a long time trying for success in Europe that when it eventually came, that seemed to be it and for a while everything stopped.

"Most people felt that the team had peaked, indeed had been slighty over the top winning the European Cup.

"The side which won the championship in 1967 was a fair old side with a good mix of experience and youth, but by the following season it was obvious we were not going to get any better without changes.

"Two or three players were coming towards the end of their careers and it was clear that the team which won the European championship was not going on as a team to do great things.

"They were still great players but as a team we had perhaps lost the edge of hunger which makes all the difference.

"It didn't show early on when we knocked Waterford out 10-2 on aggregate with Denis Law having a fine old time scoring seven of the goals.

"We did well enough against Anderlecht, winning the first leg at home 3-0 so that although we lost 3-1 away we were OK on aggregate.

"The quarter-final was classic European stuff, beating Rapid Vienna 3-0 at Old Trafford and then playing tight away for a goalless draw.

"But the semi-final against A C Milan was a different story. The first leg was away and I remember it well because Alex Stepney and I had both been dropped and we sat together in the stands feeling upset before the game had even started.

"The atmosphere in the San Siro Stadium was frightening with all the rockets and smoke bombs. Fabio Cudicini, their big goalkeeper, was never in difficulty. I remember Paddy Crerand saying after the match: 'Two goals down against any team is bad enough, but against Milan, it's like being four down because they are so good at the back.'

"But we still had a go at Old Trafford. Somebody at the Stretford End threw a missile which hit their goalkeeper which was unfortunate. Little did we know at the time how that kind of hooliganism would escalate into a tragedy which now sees English football banned from Europe.

"Happily the missile was the only sad note on a thrilling night which saw Bobby Charlton score in the 70th minute after a brilliant piece of work by George Best.

"A few minutes later we looked to have scored again to earn a play-off in Brussels of all places. Pat Crerand had chipped into the goalmouth and there was a real scramble on the line.

"The players near the scene swore the ball went over the line and television subsequently suggested it could have been, but the referee didn't give it.

"So we won 1-0 on the night, but went out 2-1 on aggregate. It was the end of an era really. Soon afterwards Sir Matt Busby announced that he was stepping out of the front line to make way for a younger man.

"All the lads had a feeling he would go because he had achieved the ultimate the previous season and he knew that the team had reached a peak and that he would have to make changes.

"Perhaps he didn't relish breaking up a side which had given him the championship of Europe. Anyway he brought Wilf McGuinness in as team coach and we enjoyed a few exciting Cup semi-finals under him.

"But it was the end of Europe for a spell, in fact it took another seven years to qualify for a European competition and by that time I was playing at Preston."

David Sadler made 266 League appearances for United in 11 seasons and played in 16 European ties. He was an ever-present in the team which won the European Cup in 1968.

He played for four years at Preston following his career at Old Trafford which also saw him win amateur caps for England as well as at all professional levels.

Still living in the area he is now secretary of the Manchester United former players' association.

Manchester United fast disappeared from the European arena after winning the championship of champions in 1968 and reaching the semi-finals as holders the following season.

There followed a period in the international wilderness while the club tried to come to terms with the retirement of their famous and successful manager, Sir Matt Busby, knighted soon after the European triumph for his services to football.

It was a traumatic time as United cast wildly around for an appropriate leader to follow in the great man's footsteps.

Wilf McGuinness was promoted from a junior coaching position but didn't quite make the transition, though with hindsight he didn't do badly, taking an ageing team to three Cup semi-finals in two seasons!

In the League the team twice finished eighth, and Frank O'Farrell did no better when he took over in June, 1971, after a brief return to the helm by Busby.

O'Farrell took United to eighth and 18th and did nothing in the Cups. His best moment was signing Martin Buchan from Aberdeen, who went on to become an outstanding player and captain.

Tommy Docherty arrived in January, 1972, and after taking the Reds into and out of the Second Division in double quick time, he marched his team in 1976 to Wembley for the final of the FA Cup against Southampton, losing 1-0, and hoisted them to third in the League.

The Doc ended eight years of European exile with a place in the UEFA Cup and a set of players largely new to the experience. During that 1976-77 season, he also took them to Wembley again, this time beating Liverpool 2-1 with players like Martin Buchan, Stuart Pearson, Jimmy Greenhoff, Steve Coppell and Gordon Hill.

Docherty had also pressed the self-destruct button by falling for the club physiotherapist's wife to leave the board with little option but to ask him to leave.

So he was robbed of the opportunity of a second campaign in Europe. Dave Sexton was appointed his successor to take the team into the Cup Winners Cup of 1977-78.

ABOVE: *Wilf McGuinness (third from right) takes over from Sir Matt Busby (far right), July 1969*

ABOVE: *On the way back up to the first Division . . . the 1975 team with the Second Division trophy*

LEFT: *Stuart Pearson*

THE DAILY TELEGRAPH, September 15, 1976

AJAX AMSTERDAM   1

MAN. UTD.   0

1976-77 UEFA CUP, FIRST ROUND, FIRST LEG, AJAX
AMSTERDAM WIN 1-0

United unlucky to lose but can win return leg

By Denis Lowe

A borderline decision went against Manchester United in Amsterdam's Olympic stadium last night as Ajax, striving to rebuild after their famous European Cup deeds of the early 70s, won this first leg UEFA Cup-tie through a 41st-minute goal from Ruud Krol, the Dutch international defender.

Disappointing though defeat was for United, in a match during which they played well, worked hard and had several scoring opportunities, overall victory should not be beyond Tommy Docherty's men when the teams meet in the return first-round game at Old Trafford on September 29.

Moreover, United who certainly did enough to earn a draw, are convinced that they equalised in the first minute of the second half, only for the linesman nearest the incident to disagree with their claims for a goal.

Fierce shot

Houston, receiving from Macari on the left, put in a fierce, low shot which Schrijvers, off his line, deflected towards the net. The ball looked to be over the line when the goalk-

TOP: *Krol (second from right) scores for Ajax, Stepney (No 1) turns to see the ball in his net*

RIGHT: *On the line but not over – Schrijvers saves as Pearson rushes in*

eeper retrieved it, but Ajax escaped.

Four minutes from half-time the Ajax goal arrived after the Dutchmen, happy to defend for long periods and then break out with speed and determination, had enjoyed their best attacking spell.

Krol's goal, jubilantly received by the Ajax followers in a crowd of about 25,000, should have been prevented, but no United player picked up the defender as he moved up field and linked with Arnesen. Krol moved into the box unchallenged and hit a low shot past Stepney's left hand.

That was a bitter blow for United, back in European competition for the first time since they defended the European Cup in 1968-69. Happily, their defeat was not marked by any crowd disorder in the stadium, a point Mr Docherty had feared rather more than the challenge of Ajax.

Wearing an unfamiliar all-blue strip, United soon stretched Ajax on the wings and might have scored within four minutes. Notten, later booked for a foul on Macari, got back to clear Pearson's shot off the line with Schrijvers beaten following Hill's corner.

Crowded out

Daly and Macari kept the supply lines well primed, with perceptive long and short passes, and Houston, Nicholl and the tenacious Greenhoff were always ready to join in upfield runs in support.

Greenhoff was just crowded out after a burst from inside his own half, and Schrijvers did well to block attempts by McIlroy and Macari after brilliant improvisation on Hill's part.

Pearson, reasonably placed, headed wide from Hill's free-kick before Ajax escaped in the 46th minute, and United maintained the pressure for much of the second half, with Coppell, Hill and Macari trying to get behind the massed Dutch defence.

Hill had a splendid drive turned aside by Schrijvers, put another effort wide, and Macari saw a close range shot deflected against the post.

Ajax, who brought on two substitutes after United had replaced Daly with McCreery, mounted dangerous late raids through Arnesen and Geels, while Krol brought the best out of Stepney when Geels tapped a short free-kick across the penalty area.

Macari was again near in United's final fling, but they should be able to turn the tables in the home leg.

DAILY MAIL, September 29, 1976

| MAN. UTD. | 2 |
| AJAX AMSTERDAM | 0 |

1976-77 UEFA CUP, FIRST ROUND, SECOND LEG,
MANCHESTER UNITED WIN 2-1 ON AGGREGATE

Doc's triumph as Greenhoff wrecks Ajax

By Ronald Crowther

Tommy Docherty produced a stroke of Soccer genius last night to send Manchester United storming into the second round of the UEFA Cup.

His tactical switch involved England defender Brian Greenhoff, who transformed this tie with Ajax in such a spectacular manner that the memory of his effort will make him an Old Trafford idol as long as he lives.

For an hour in the exciting second leg of a tie that began in Amsterdam United lived on a knife edge as they grappled with the subtle skills of the dangerous Dutchmen.

Even an heroic effort by Lou Macari, who shot United into a 43rd minute lead, and four fantastic saves by Alex Stepney, gave them only the prospect of a slender lifeline of extra time.

But then when United needed something to smash the deadlock, they got it from Greenhoff.

Docherty, proving that the Continentals are not the only experts in European strategy, took off Gerry Daly, brought teenager Arthur Albiston into a reshuffled defence, and released Greenhoff from defence to go upfield and attack.

I have never seen a player stamp his personality on a game more than Greenhoff did on a night of sudden magic.

The attack was immediately revitalised, after going into this game without the injured Stewart Pearson. And Greenhoff supplied so much ammunition for his fellow raiders that Dutch international keeper Schrijvers found himself struggling for the first time.

Tormentors

Only five minutes after his switch, it was Greenhoff who rounded the Dutch defence at top speed to supply the low cross for Sammy McIlroy to prod home the second, vital goal that sank the side from Amsterdam.

By that time Ajax, who had threatened to counter-punch their way to success and were unlucky to be a goal down, were in full flight.

And it took half-a-dozen saves by Schrijvers against McIlroy, Macari, Hill and Greenhoff to prevent United from going into Friday's second-round draw with a much bigger margin.

I had to admire the skill with which Ajax used their resilient defence as a springboard for such electrifying breaks.

Ling and Geels were United's tormentors in the first half, and but for veteran Stepney they could have had three goals by half time.

He hurled himself out on one occasion to smother the ball at the feet of Geels. With a one-handed save, he turned a Geels shot on to the bar and later, in a packed goalmouth, he saved from a Geels backheader.

United fans were on edge when these stealthy Ajax strikers threatened. But never more than when Arnesen had a clear run towards goal in the second half, only to be baulked by the courageous, diving Stepney.

Despite these anxious moments, United played with power and perseverance, and Macari was unlucky as early as in the 13th minute, when he burst through to strike a post with a rasping shot.

Dubious

Later Macari, whose fitness had been in doubt until the last minute, got his reward when he pounced to score after Schrijvers had managed only to parry a low drive from Hill.

In a game that was a wonderful advertisement for European Soccer, there was only one booking – a dubious one for a mistimed tackle by Houston.

The new United passed their first big test in Europe with flying colours, with a victory that was well worthy of its place in Old Trafford history.

United-poised on a knife-edge-

MANCHESTER UNITED'S chances of survival in Europe looked no more than paper thin last night after they had wrung a slender lead from the fiery first leg of their UEFA Cup-tie with Juventus.

And even though the Italians, who had infuriated United fans with their furtive tackles, left the field to the chant of 'animals,' they went smiling to their dressing-room, confident of success in Turin in two weeks' time.

For

By RONALD CROWTHER : Manchester United 1, Juventus 0

and often savage Italians and the foul count of 29 by the Juventus men to only eight by United told only part of the story.

After all the pre-match protests of innocence by the Italians they were quick last night to destroy the illusion which they had tried to create.

Skirmish

And the near 60,000 crowd with anger many

booked when he appeared only to be taking evasive action in a skirmish with sweeper Scirea.

Juventus, a team of calculating cunning, had obviously done their homework on United and Pearson was a very heavily marked man from start to finish.

With their off-the-ball nudging and their smother tackles, they always managed somehow to shunt him away from the target area and the manner in which they did so served as a and who go to

tion for the second leg but for Alex Stepney. After one lucky let-off when Causio struck a post in the first half, Stepney needed all his vast experience to cope with a threat by the cunning Boninsegna.

As the Italian leader bore down on him without challenge, the keeper raced out like an athlete leaving his starting blocks to narrow the angle and to turn away his shot one-handed.

Late in the second half, when Juventus still looked menacing on the break, Stepney baulked Boninsegna once more at a time when the veteran international might well

DAILY MAIL, October 20, 1976

| MAN UTD | 1 |
| JUVENTUS | 0 |

1976-77 UEFA CUP, SECOND ROUND, FIRST LEG, MANCHESTER UNITED WIN 1-0

By Ronald Crowther

M anchester United's chances of survival in Europe looked no more than paper thin last night after they had wrung a slender lead from the fiery first leg of their UEFA Cup-tie with Juventus.

And even though the Italians, who had infuriated United fans with their furtive tackles, left the field to the chant of 'animals,' they went smiling to their dressing-room, confident of success in Turin in two weeks' time.

United tried hard enough and shot often enough last night, but Gordon Hill, with a ferocious left-foot volley, was the only man who could penetrate the experienced and ever alert Juventus defence.

It was a stop-at-nothing defensive fight by the cynical and often savage Italians and the foul count of 29 by the Juventus men to only eight by United told only part of the story.

After all the pre-match protests of innocence by the Italians they were quick last night to destroy the illusion which they had tried to create.

Skirmish

And the near 60,000 crowd erupted with anger many times before Causio and Cuccureddu were shown the yellow card by the West German referee for two of the more blatant offences.

Yet even though it seemed at times that the United players over dramatised some of these incidents, some of the worst fouls by the Italians went unpunished.

Three of these were on Stuart Pearson, who, strangely enough, was the first man to be booked when he appeared only to be taking evasive action in a skirmish with sweeper Scirea.

Juventus, a team of calculating cunning, had obviously done their homework on United and Pearson was a very heavily marked man from start to finish.

With their off-the-ball nudging and their smother tackles, they always managed somehow to shunt him away from the target area and the manner in which they did so served as a warning to England who go to Italy next month for their World Cup qualifying game.

The enthusiasm and endeavour of United never flagged after they had set a brisk tempo from the start. But, after some early sorties by Coppell and Hill, the wingers never quite managed to fulful Tommy Docherty's hopes that they could outflank the resilient Juventus defence.

United might have been in a much more precarious position for the second leg but for Alex Stepney. After one lucky let-off when Causio struck a post in the first half, Stepney needed all his vast experience to cope with a threat by the cunning Boninsegna.

As the Italian leader bore down on him without challenge, the keeper raced out like an athlete leaving his starting blocks to narrow the angle and to turn away his shot one-handed.

Late in the second half, when Juventus still looked menacing on the break. Stepney baulked Boninsegna once more at a time when the veteran Italian international might well have equalised with a tricky low drive.

Switch

Hill got the scoring chance which he took with such devastating effect in the 32nd minute from a Nicholl cross which Coppell diverted on to his foot. The mighty Dino Zoff got one hand to the ball, but so great was the power that he couldn't stop it.

Later, however, Zoff showed why he is acknowledged to be one of the world's greatest 'keepers when he made acrobatic saves against Macari, McIlroy, Greenhoff and Coppell.

Yet, for all their effort, United did not show quite enough guile to get to close quarters and most of their shots were at too long a range.

Unable to call on injured Buchan, United switched Houston into the middle of their defence and played young Arthur Albiston at left back, and both men did well to cope with some of the Juventus counter-punch raids.

But I believe the Italians will strike with much greater force in Italy and that United's lead will be far too fragile to see them through into the third round.

Platini shadowed by Moses

Duxbury (left) versus Boniek

THE DAILY TELEGRAPH, October 20, 1976

MAN. UTD.	1
JUVENTUS	**0**

1976-77 UEFA CUP, SECOND ROUND, FIRST LEG,
MANCHESTER UNITED WIN 1-0

Harassed United manage only narrow lead

By Donald Saunders

An angry Old Trafford crowd chanted "animals, animals" at Juventus, last night, after these past masters of skilful, intelligent and, when necessary, cynically brutal defensive football, had restricted Manchester United to a single goal in a tough UEFA Cup-tie.

I doubt whether the Italians found this demonstration unfamiliar or upsetting, as they trotted, smiling into the dressing room, satisfied with a job well done.

They came to Manchester with the primary purpose of ensuring that United would not begin the second leg of this battle, in Turin a fortnight later, with a commanding lead.
Now, having achieved their purpose, they look forward to closing the narrow gap and moving smoothly into the next round of the competition at the Stadio Cummunale next Wednesday week.

Juventus have good reason for confidence. Last month they came to Manchester in the opening round of the same tournament, allowed Manchester City to score only once – and duly won the return leg 2-0.

Although United may pose more problems than their neighbours did, the odds must now be on a relatively comfortable Italian triumph.

Crucial period

When young Hill volleyed home a cross from Nicholl – deflected to him by a defender – on the half hour, I thought this would be a rather happier story.

Alas, they allowed themselves to be dragged into an ill tempered 15 minute battle.

Had Tommy Docherty's men continued to search diligently for goals during this crucial period, they might well have thrown their opponents out of their calm, precise stride and earned comfortable victory.

This objective was forgotten as Hill, Pearson and McIlroy, in particular, became targets for cynical fouls that left them writhing on the turf and ultimately fuming for vengeance.

Pearson, so often sinned against, was shown the yellow card for retaliating against Scirea – an offence that scarcely merited the same punishment as Causio and Cuccureddu received for kicking Hill.

I am surprised Ferdinand Biwerski, the West German referee, did not also book Morini following an outrageous foul on Pearson. Perhaps the referee thought Morini had already been punished sufficiently by the head wound he had suffered earlier.

Herr Biwerski may also have shared my view that United were inclined to complain about fouls rather too often and too histrionically.

Stricter control

Even so, strict control was needed during this ugly period. In its absence, Docherty's men lost their way – and probably the chance of staying in this competition.

Although United, with McCreery replacing Daly in the 58th minute, kept pushing forward in the second half they never seriously threatened to upset the powerful Tardelli in midfield or Morini and Scirea in and around the penalty box.

THE DAILY TELEGRAPH, November 3, 1976

JUVENTUS	**3**
MAN. UTD.	**0**

1976-77 UEFA CUP, SECOND ROUND, SECOND LEG,
JUVENTUS TURIN WIN 3-1 ON AGGREGATE

Lessons for Revie and United as Juventus Dictate

By Donald Saunders

Manchester United's dream of conquering Europe with their ambitious young side was shattered at the Stadio Communale in Turin last night by Roberto Boninsegna and Romeo Benetti, two of the oldest players in the top strata of Italian soccer.

Boninsegna, 32, put Juventus firmly on top by scoring in the 28th and 60th minutes of the second leg of this UEFA Cup-tie, and his colleague Benetti, 30, clinched a well-earned victory with a goal four minutes from the end.

Although United played with greater maturity than I had expected, they would have suffered heavier defeat but for the skill, experience and agility of Stepney, their oldest player.

In defeat, however, Tommy Docherty's young men may have learned much that will be of value to them should they return to Europe in the next few seasons.

Possibly England's manager, Don Revie, also will have benefitted from his visit to this match, just a fortnight before his team take on Italy in a World Cup-tie in Rome.

SENSIBLE MIXTURE

Mr Revie must have noted how fatal it can be to allow these gifted Italian forwards room in which to move, and more than a split second in which to act.

For nearly half an hour last night, United contained their more skilful, experienced opponents with a sensible mixture of watchful defence and enterprising attack.

No doubt they were encouraged by the blow Juventus suffered in the seventh minute when Morini, an accomplished, thoroughly experienced centre-back, limped off with a pulled muscle and was replaced by Spinosi.

At all events, Tommy Docherty's men pushed forward purposefully several times, and Hill almost doubled their 1-0 first-leg lead with a header that flew inches wide.

Even during this period, however, Causio and Tardelli – both members of Italy's current national team – were beginning to take com-

UEFA Cup

LESSONS FOR REVIE AND UNITED AS JUVENTUS DICTATE

By DONALD SAUNDERS

Juventus ... 3   Manchester United ... 0
(Juventus win 3—1 on aggregate)

MANCHESTER UNITED'S dream of conquering Europe with their ambitious young side was shattered at the Stadio Communale in Turin last night by Roberto Boninsegna and Romeo Benetti, two of the oldest players in the top strata of Italian soccer.

Boninsegna, 32, put Juventus firmly on top by scoring in the 28th and 60th minutes of the second leg of this U E F A Cup-tie, and his colleague Benetti, 30, clinched a well-earned victory with a goal four minutes from the end.

Although United played with greater maturity than I had expected, they would have suffered heavier defeat but for the skill, experience and agility of Stepney, their oldest player.

prised when Juventus closed the narrow gap in the 28th minute.

Causio began the move with a pass to Tardelli, who took the ball to the by-line before crossing it low into the penalty box. United's defenders committed the crucial error of concentrating their attention on Bettega—and allowed Boninsegna to race in and hammer the ball into the net.

LEFT: *Boninsegna homes in on Houston (right) in the first leg match between United and Juventus Turin*

BELOW LEFT: *McIlroy (centre) watches as Hill (second from right) tries a header in the second leg match in Turin*

mand in midfield, and Boninsegna and Benetti, also candidates for the Rome game, were causing serious problems for United's defence.

So no-one was particularly surprised when Juventus closed the narrow gap in the 28th minute.

Causio began the move with a pass to Tardelli, who took the ball to the by-line before crossing it low into the penalty box, United's defenders committed the crucial error of concentrating their attention on

Bettega – and allowed Boninsegna to race in and hammer the ball into the net.

Although United did not give up the battle, they never again really looked like reaching the next round.

Mr Docherty replaced McIlroy with McCready in the 55th minute, and pulled off Macari in the 61st, so that he could send on Paterson and push forward Greenhoff. But the switch could not prevent Juventus from taking charge.

DEFIANT STEPNEY

The Italians justly took the lead on aggregate on the hour. United were caught off guard by a free kick which Causio rolled to Tardelli, whose cross was flicked into the net by Boninsegna.

As United risked all in an effort to score the aggregate equaliser that would have earned them victory under the away goals rule, Juventus might well have increased their lead if their shooting had been more accurate – and Stepney less defiant.

Instead, they had to wait until the 86th minute to clinch victory when Benetti collected a pass from Causio and thumped it into the net.

Thanks to Karoly Palotai, a sensible Hungarian referee, the game did not become the tough, physical battle that had been expected after one or two nasty incidents in the first leg.

Both sides soon discovered that they could take no liberties with this strict official, although Benetti, Macari and Furino were shown the yellow card.

Arthur Albiston

▭ LOOKING BACK ▭ WITH ARTHUR ALBISTON

Arthur Albiston is the only survivor from the Juventus tie still playing with Manchester United.

He remembers it well.

"I was only 19 and my full-back partner, Jimmy Nicholl, was a teenager as well. I played in both legs, my first full games in Europe.

"I came into the team because Martin Buchan was injured and Stewart Houston was moved into the centre of defence to let me in at left back.

"Gordon Hill scored our goal at Old Trafford with a typical volley which was really the only way we were going to get through their defence. He got his goal out of nothing. We could have done with another. One goal was not much for such a young side to take to Turin.

"Our substitutes in the second leg who came on were David McCreery and Steve Paterson – and they were even younger than Jimmy and me.

"Tommy Docherty and Tommy Cavanagh told us that we would get a lot of the ball in Turin and that it would be up to the defenders to come through with it because the front men would be tightly marked.

"That's exactly how it happened, but I think we were too inexperienced at the back to take advantage of the situation. We were well hammered.

"What with the racket of the crowd and the general atmosphere, it was quite frightening. It took a lot out of us, mentally as well as physically. I know I was quite exhausted before the end."

Tommy Docherty

◼◼◼ LOOKING BACK WITH TOMMY DOCHERTY ◼◼◼

As Tommy Docherty will tell you . . . he has had more clubs than Jack Nicklaus!

But there is no doubt that the highspot of his well-travelled career was the spell of four and a half years he had as manager of Manchester United.

The Doc occupied the Old Trafford hot-seat at a traumatic time for the club, presiding over their only relegation since the war.

He took over from Frank O'Farrell in the January of 1972 and succeeded in keeping the Reds in the First Division only to go down the following season.

But from then on it was all action . . . winning the Second Division championship at the first attempt and appearing in two F A Cup finals.

In their first season back in the First Division they finished third to qualify for the UEFA Cup and put the Reds back into Europe after an eight-year absence.

It was a short-lived campaign lasting just two rounds, but the experience remains among Docherty's cherished memories.

"We were babes in Europe that season in the UEFA Cup, but I was glad that I had been able to bring back a taste of European action.

"I had taken Chelsea to the semi-finals of the UEFA Cup in my time at Stamford Bridge, but there was always something special about Manchester United's involvement in Europe.

"Our problem at Old Trafford was that we drew two crack teams, starting with Ajax and finishing, literally, with Juventus.

"We were short of experience at that level, though in my time with United I had arranged as many matches as possible to try and keep the players tuned in for European football.

"I used to hang the pennants they presented to us round my office and mentally tick off each country visited. I was also determined to maintain our normal attacking style true to the tradition of adventurous football associated with Manchester United.

"I wanted to bring a smile back into European football and in the first round against Ajax I think we succeeded.

"Not long before, Ajax had been triple European Cup winners, and though some of their great names had departed they were a more than useful side.

"We created a lot of chances in the first leg in Holland, but we lost 1-0 to a goal scored by their sweeper, Rudi Krol, a fine player who had been a star in Holland's World Cup team.

"But I still thought it a good result and as we left the stand I can remember meeting the President of Ajax and saying to him: 'Sorry, my friend, one goal is not enough for you.'

"And that is how it worked out at Old Trafford. Lou Macari equalised for us just before the interval, nicking the ball in after their goalkeeper had only been able to parry a typically stinging drive from Gordon Hill.

"Then half an hour from the end I made one of those tactical changes that makes a manager look either a fool or a hero. I put Arthur Albiston on at fullback, allowing Stewart Houston to take over at centre half so that Brian Greenhoff could replace Gerry Daly in midfield.

"Brian turned the game for us. His strength going forward became the decisive factor. He linked up with Steve Coppell on the right and his centre was flicked in by Sammy McIlroy.

"It was the winner and we felt very optimistic about the next round until we found we had drawn Juventus.

"The first leg was played at Old Trafford and the Italians, who had already knocked Manchester City out, were just too strong for us.

"We won 1-0 with a goal from Gordon Hill who was highly praised by their manager Giovanni Trapattoni but it was never enough, especially as we were missing Martin Buchan from the defence again with injury.

"In the Stadio Communale it was men against boys and it was clear that we still had a lot to learn. We never really tested Dino Zoff while our goalkeeper, Alex Stepney, was one of the busiest men on the park.

"Roberto Boninsegna scored twice and Romeo Benetti got a late one in a 3-0 win.

"Still it was good experience and at least we had had a taste of European football again.

"My biggest disappointment was that in the same season we beat Liverpool at Wembley to win the F A Cup and so qualify for the European Cup Winners Cup.

"I was really looking forward to a second crack at Europe. Unfortunately I wasn't able to do it because along the way I had fallen in love in a situation which led to the sack for me.

"The love of a woman cost me my job and I have no regrets whatsoever except to say that naturally I was sad to leave Manchester United at such a peak of my management there.

"I had to hand over to another man and it was very frustrating, especially when one of United's opponents turned out to be F C Porto, one of my previous clubs.

"But football is full of strange tricks of fate, as I think my career has more than proved!"

Tommy Docherty lives just outside Manchester still and retains an undying loyalty from the fans of that time. He was immensely popular and the crowd still hold him in great affection.

MANCHESTER EVENING NEWS, May 21, 1977

LIVERPOOL	1
MAN. UTD.	2

1977 F.A. CUP FINAL, Manchester United win 2-1

United's Cup After Goal Rush

Pearson, Greenhoff strike

By David Meek

Manchester United today completed another chapter in their fairy-tale success by conquering Liverpool in the FA Cup Final at Wembley.

What an occasion it was for the "Doc," his players and their fans as they clinched a victory which more than made up for the bitter disappointment of last season's Cup Final defeat by Southampton.

Goals by Stuart Pearson and Jimmy Greenhoff gave United a 2-1 victory.

All the goals came in a rush between the 50th and 55th minutes, Jimmy Case having put Liverpool on level terms after Pearson's opener.

Martin Buchan, fighting against injury all week, was tested early. He got up well to head clear in a jump with Keegan, and also broke up the next Liverpool raid as the Anfield men attacked with the help of Smith's free kick.

Stepney collected a high cross confidently, and Albiston made two smothering tackles out on the flank, as Liverpool set the opening pace.

United quickly counter-attacked, with Coppel racing clear down the right wing. The winger pulled the ball back to Nicholl, whose cross was headed on by Jimmy Greenhoff. Pearson just failed to control the ball, which ran out of play.

United stayed on the attack, stringing their football together in an impressive style, for Macari to slam a shot into the side netting.

Buchan stopped Keegan in his tracks, in a Final notable for the way in which the players of both teams settled down without the usual show of nerves.

Both teams quickly struck the high note of performance so eagerly anticipated by the fans.

Warning

There was alarm for Manchester as Heighway robbed Brian Greenhoff, and a few moments later when Case had a shot deflected by Buchan over Stepney's goal.

Kennedy missed a chance for Liverpool in the eighth minute when he failed to get hold of a free kick from Keegan. The ball skidded under his foot out of play, when a touch might have had the ball past Stepney.

United had another escape in the 10th minute, when Johnson failed to hit his shot properly, after Brian Greenhoff and Nicholl had failed to clear.

After the opening quarter of an hour Liverpool began to win an edge in midfield, although United were still looking dangerous on the break.

And it was clearly shown when McIlroy got Hill away and the winger had Clemence in full stretch to tip his shot from the wing over the bar.

Although Liverpool were forcing the pace, United fans had cause to cheer again, when Nicholl stopped Heighway in his tracks.

Then in the 19th minute, Albiston brought off a tremendous tackle to rob Keegan just as the Liverpool star was about to shoot with only Stepney to beat.

At the other end, Pearson got in a shot at Clemence — but not with enough power to beat him — after a sharp attack featuring Hill and McIlory.

Stepney saved from McDermott as Liver-pool continued to dictate the game in midfield through Kennedy, McDermott, and Case, with Macari and McIlroy overpowered at this stage.

A slip by Hughes let in Jimmy Greenhoff, but the United man failed to find Pearson with his pass, and the ball went straight through to Clemence.

Referee Bob Matthewson spoke to Jones after the Liverpool fullback had crash-tackled Macari. But the game was being fought in excellent spirit, competitive but fair, with the accent on creative, attacking football.

Liverpool were showing all the qualities that have won the championship in the last two years, and United's famed forward strength was just not being allowed to get into gear.

Macari and McIlroy were being forced to help out in defence, wingers Coppell and Hill were being pulled back in search of the ball, leaving Jimmy Greenhoff and Pearson frequently on their own up front.

Fortunately for United the defence was playing well with Buchan outstanding and Nicholl facing Heighway with great confidence.

On the other flank Albiston, playing in his first FA Cup tie of the season after replacing the injured Stewart Houston, was also justifying his manager's faith.

RESCUED

Three minutes before the interval, Liverpool almost grabbed the goal they had been threatening.

Case crossed to the far post, where Kennedy beat Nicholl in the air to head the ball down towards a corner of the goal. Stepney rescued the Reds with a brilliant save, bundling the ball round the post with an outstretched fist.

Two minutes after the interval Nicholl came down the right flank on an overlap from

169

ABOVE: *Taking it lying down! Jimmy Greenhoff (on ground) celebrates his goal, Pearson (left) and Coppell (centre) rush to congratulate him while Frank Gray (far right) shows his devastation, as United beat Leeds in the 1977 FA Cup semi-final*

ABOVE: *Triumphant with the FA Cup, having beaten Liverpool in the final, May 1977*

Coppell. And moments later Albiston went on a similar exciting move on the other flank, only to finish with a poor cross.

And United's more positive approach paid off in the 50th minute when Hughes failed to control a bouncing ball midway in his own half. Jimmy Greenhoff nipped in like a flash to head the ball through the narrowest of gaps, for Pearson to brilliantly race clear and score with a tremendous low shot under the diving Clemence.

It was Pearson's first goal in the run to Wembley – just as he had promised. "I have been saving it for Wembley," he said before the match.

United's lead was short-lived though, as just three minutes later Liverpool roared back for Case to score with a blistering shot from just inside the box. He swivelled round and hit such a soaring, thundering, rising drive, that it left Stepney helpless ... even though the keeper got a touch.

United took the blow in their stride, and incredibly came racing straight back to the attack for Jimmy Greenhoff to rob Smith in the Liverpool box.

The ball broke free to Macari, whose shot struck Jimmy Greenhoof and spun past Clemence to put United back in front.

HOPE

Three goals in five minutes had dramatically changed a fine Final. United were now playing with much more conviction and worried Liverpool brought their substitute into the game in the 63rd minute, Callaghan coming on for Johnson.

Cally went in midfield and sent Case up front in the hope of seeing the youngster pull out another of his rocket goals.

Liverpool flung themselves forward in a frenzy of attacking fury, and Stepney had to leap high to hold a back-header from Brian Greenhoff, as the Anfield iron men stepped up the pressure again.

Stepney also had to fling himself full length to save a low snap-shot from Case, but United were also raising their game to tremendous heights.

With nine minutes left United sent on substitute McCreery in place of Hill – a repeat of the move they made in last season's final.

Stepney saved a flurry of shots, most of them prompted by centres from Callaghan on the right flank, as United fought furiously to halt Liverpool's march to a League and Cup double.

DAILY EXPRESS, September 14, 1977

ST. ETIENNE 1

MAN. UTD. 1

1977-78 EUROPEAN CUP WINNERS' CUP, FIRST ROUND, FIRST LEG, DRAW 1-1

Hill Beats Barrier as United go Close to Cracking Record

By Alan Thompson

It was glory all the way for Gordon Hill and Manchester United in the Geoffrey Guichard Stadium last night.

Hill put United in front in the 77th minute after having two earlier efforts disallowed from almost identical moves for offside.

And United came within an ace of being the first foreign team to beat St. Etienne at home. But this Cupwinners' Cup first leg game marked a sad return for Stewart Houston – his first game since breaking an ankle before last season's FA Cup Final.

Houston came on 10 minutes from the end and

Hill beats barrier as United go close to cracking record

By Alan Thompson . St. Etienne 1, Manchester United 1

IT was glory all the way for Gordon Hill Manchester United in the Geoffrey Guichard Sta last night.

Hill put United in front in the 77th minute after two earlier efforts disallowed from almost identical m offside.

And United came within an ace of being the first foreign tea St. Etienne at home. But this Cupwinners' Cup first-leg game sad return for Stewart Houston – his first game since breaking

BELOW: *Barthelemy (second from right) of St Etienne winds his way through the United defence*

THE DAILY TELEGRAPH, October 5, 1977

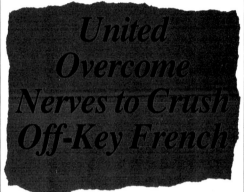

MAN. UTD.	2
ST. ETIENNE	0

1977-78 EUROPEAN CUP WINNERS' CUP, FIRST ROUND, SECOND LEG, MANCHESTER UNITED WIN 3-1 ON AGGREGATE

United Overcome Nerves to Crush Off-Key French

By Donald Saunders

with his first touch deflected the ball to Synaeghel, who accepted the opportunity to keep St. Etienne's record intact.

Despite that, the honours go to United ... and the credit in attack must go to Stuart Pearson and Hill, and in defence, the magnificent Martin Buchan.

United fulfilled their pledge to attack whenever possible and they had the ball in the net in the second minute but Pearson was well off-side.

In the fifth minute Hill began what looked like being a frustrating evening. Pearson and Coppell combined well to get the ball across to Hill at the far post. He stabbed the ball home but was judged offside, though it could have only been by inches.

A similar move in the 65th minute ended in similar fashion. This time Pearson beat two men down the right before putting a low centre to Hill who again stuck the ball home and was again judged just offside.

Hill's luck was to change dramatically in the 77th minute. Pearson again did all the spadework before crossing low across the face of goal. This time Hill ghosted his way round the back of the defence and volleyed fiercely past goalkeeper Curkovic.

CHANCES

The French looked expectantly at the linesman – but this time he kept his flag down.

For a few brief ecstatic minutes it looked as if United might be the side to finally lower St. Etienne's colours in the stadium. But that honour was to be denied them by Synaeghel in the 80th minute.

There were other chances which deserved goals for United. In the 13th minute Nichol sent Coppell away to bring Curkovic to a full length dive.

In the 50th minute the goalkeeper was again at full stretch to tip over a 35-yard shot from Pearson.

St. Etienne hammered United in the last minutes but Stepney earned the praise of everyone when he dived at Revelli's feet five minutes from the end.

Manager Dave Sexton said afterwards: "I am delighted, not just with the result, but with the way we played. We had some injury problems, but we still carried the game to them."

Goal-hero Gordon Hill admitted later: "We had a bit of joke about the disallowed goals, but I came steaming in for the one that counted. Even then I was not sure whether it was going to be allowed."

Manchester United moved peacefully into the second round of the European Cup Winners Cup at Plymouth last night, to the polite applause of a neutral crowd who surely went home wondering why so much fuss is made about "big time" soccer.

A well taken goal by Pearson in the 37th minute, and an even better one from Coppell in the 67th, were sufficient to sweep surprisingly diffident St. Etienne out of the competition and earn United a tie with F.C. Porto, of Portugal.

But United's victory will scarcely rank among their most accomplished or exciting. Like their opponents, they failed utterly to bring this game to life.

With only about 1,000 fully fledged United supporters and some 2,000 from St. Etienne among the crowd, the electric atmosphere these matches usually produce was conspicuously absent.

I suspect that United also were acutely aware that, having drawn the first leg 1-1, they needed to play carefully rather than flamboyantly to clinch success.

So, with St. Etienne rarely showing even a sign of the skilful, enterprising football that had made them such popular campaigners in the European Cup during the previous two seasons, there was little for even the partisans to shout about.

Still United surely will not worry too much about that now. Having been expelled from the competition because of their supporters' misconduct in France three weeks ago, then reinstated on appeal, they are only too pleased to have reached the second round.

Once they had played their way through an unusually nervous early patch, there was never any serious doubt that United would grasp the opportunity the appeal had brought them.

Although Macari did not rule midfield with his usual authority, or McIlroy work with his customary efficiency, they were always comfortably in control in this important sector of the pitch.

Moreover, Pearson, until he was pulled off immediately after scoring, and Jimmy Greenhoff, throughout, looked much more dangerous up front than did the sadly out of touch Rocheteau and Sarramagna.

Even the most nervous among them realised that victory was within comfortable reach when the elder Greenhoff and Pearson combined to put them in front. Greenhoff began the move by sending Coppell speeding down the right flank.

The diving Curkovic failed to cut off Coppell's low cross, Piazza could only deflect it, and Pearson promptly thumped it into the net.

With his job well done, Pearson, who had been suffering from hamstring trouble recently, was quickly replaced by McGrath.

From that moment, St. Etienne seemed to lose all belief in their cause. So, though United missed Pearson's power up front the Frenchmen were firmly brushed aside.

In the 67th minute Coppell moved on to a through pass from Albiston quickly enough to beat the offside trap on which St. Etienne had so long relied, checked, moved inside – and drove home goal No. 2.

So, the match quietly drew to its close, and at the end just one little boy ran on to the pitch – to remind us of the passions this tie had aroused in St. Etienne.

Now, United's major worry, as they prepare to go to Portugal next Wednesday week, will be the behaviour of their supporters – rather than the ability of their opponents.

RIGHT: *Curkovic saves at Greenhoff's feet*

BELOW: *Coppell (right) in duel with Barthenay (left) in the second leg of United's tie against St Etienne*

BELOW: *Pearson (third from left) scores the first goal of the game*

Buchan (mid air left) heads behind St Etienne's Revelli (second from right)

LOOKING BACK

Europe should have heeded the lessons of Manchester United's bitter experience against St Etienne in France.

If UEFA paid more attention to the underlying causes of the crowd trouble it is possible that the tragedy of Heysel Stadium would have been avoided.

For though there was no loss of life or serious injury, United's European Cup Winners Cup preliminary round of 1977-78 spotlighted the problems which led to the disaster on the terraces in Brussels seven years later.

There was inadequate segregation which led to fighting between rival supporters behind one of the goals. The only difference at St Etienne was that their riot police were quickly on the scene, chasing the largely innocent English fans out of the ground, and there was no collapsing wall to bring the crushing deadly chaos of Heysel.

Manchester United secretary Les Olive quickly spotlighted the source of the trouble at St. Etienne.

"UEFA rules say there should be segregation of rival supporters. We repeatedly stressed the importance of this to St Etienne officials when they visited us at Old Trafford.

"But they made no attempt to put Manchester fans together in one special section. They did not have any police on the terraces to try and keep them apart. Our people were in a group surrounded by French supporters who I understand objected to them being there and tried to push them to one side.

"We warned them about the danger they were risking. They kept saying they couldn't make any alterations to the stadium because it was a municipal ground and not their own. They said that in any case they never had any trouble on their own ground.

"Unfortunately they were proved wrong."

UEFA's disciplinary committee reacted to the trouble on the terraces by expelling United from the competition and awarding the tie to St Etienne.

United appealed and after appearing in front of a tribunal in Zurich they succeeded in being reinstated to the tournament, though with the second leg to be played on a neutral ground at least 200 kilometres from Manchester.

The club was also fined £7,500, but the big relief was being allowed to play on. As Sir Matt Busby explains "We had a very fair hearing. The commission were obviously influenced by the fact that there was no segregation of spectators.

"They also noted that there was no problem with United fans who travelled through the official supporters club. I was delighted for our players. For two years they had been the best behaved in the game, winning the Fair Play League, and it would have been grossly unfair to have put them out of the competition for something in which they were entirely innocent."

The late chairman, Louis Edwards, commented at the time: "We asked St Etienne four times for segregation and our pleas were ignored. They also sold tickets on the day of the match to anyone. Under the circumstances we had no chance. With proper arrangements trouble could have been avoided."

After the experience of St Etienne one would have thought that UEFA might have paid more attention to the matter of segregation at the Heysel Stadium where rival supporters were separated only by a flimsy fence, and as the disasterous collapse of the wall indicated, at a stadium in a poor state of repair.

Tragically the signals of danger from St Etienne were soon forgotten.

Despite the distraction of a running battle between police and fans, United drew 1-1 at St Etienne with a 76th minute goal from Gordon Hill. The French team equalised three minutes later.

The second leg was played at Plymouth, a venue chosen deliberately to try to reduce the number of fans travelling from Manchester.

Stuart Pearson scored before limping off with a recurrence of an injury and Steve Coppell clinched the tie in the second half by beating two men to score past Curkovic.

Victory was sweet, but the crowd trouble left a sour note and a hint of more serious consequences for English football in the years to come.

DAILY MAIL, October 20, 1977

FC PORTO	4
MAN. UTD.	**0**

1977-78 EUROPEAN CUP WINNERS' CUP, SECOND ROUND, FIRST LEG, FC PORTO WIN 4-0

United crash on Duda's day

Ronald Crowther
IN OPORTO

A brown-skinned Brazilian bomber with the unlikely name of Duda destroyed Manchester United here in Portugal last night in a disastrous first leg of their Cup-Winners' Cup-tie.

It was Duda's night in almost every way when he rattled up a personal hat-trick in 54 minutes and spearheaded a merciless attack that sank the totally outclassed team from Old Trafford.

United manager Dave Sexton sportingly admitted: 'He is quite obviously a player of enormous talent and it is terribly difficult to contain him.'

And, after such a morale-shattering experience it will now need little short of a miraculous recovery for United to survive on the European trail in the second leg on November 2.

United were in trouble after only eight minutes.

It wasn't so much the quick passing moves between full-back Murca and middle-defender Freitas that made it such a remarkable goal — though that was breathcatching in itself.

But it was a truly fantastic shot by the wily Duda from 25 yards out that baffled Stepney and sent 70,000 Portuguese into ecstasies.

Duda's shot appeared to be going over the bar when, far too suddenly for Stepney, it dropped like a stone into the net because of the crafty flighting.

This disastrous development for United followed an intense battle in midfield in the opening minutes of the game that had started

United against Juventus

Whiteside takes on Everton's Sharp in the FA Cup Final At Wembley 1985

FA Cup Final at Wembley 1985

Unfortunately victory could not lead to another season in Europe because of the ban on English clubs

United crash on Duda's day

A BROWN-SKINNED Brazilian bomber with the unlikely name of Duda destroyed Man-

FROM RONALD CROWTHER

ABOVE: *Porto 'keeper Fonesca captures the ball from in-coming McIlroy in the first leg Cup Winners Cup match in Oporto*

ABOVE: *Fonesca (fourth from right) is beaten, but Simoes heads off the line as United's McCreery (centre left) threatens*

in a peaceful enough atmosphere in the vast bowl of the Estadion Dos Antes.

And it triggered off a savage bombardment on the United goal in which Jimmy Nicholl twice cleared off the line and Stepney made a fine, diving one-handed save against Oliveira.

For a time, however, the fighting qualities of the two little men, Macari and Coppell, began to sustain United.

And in their first raid of note, McGrath had a low shot blocked by the Portuguese 'keeper. Soon, Macari broke through, but the 'keeper made a scrambled save.

Yet United's rally was only short lived and after 26 minutes they were deeper in trouble when Duda scored a second goal.

This one resulted from a corner taken on the left by Octavio. As the ball flew across the penalty area Oliveira beat the United players to the header and steered it along to the Brazilian, who coolly breasted it down and smashed it into the roof of the net.

United's tale of woe didn't end there, for eight minutes later Houston, their second choice centre-half, had to limp out of the game with a leg injury, and Alex Forsyth took over in a reshuffled defence.

But yet again the unstoppable Duda struck in the 54th minute to complete a dazzling hat-trick.

This time it was the swift Seninho who swooped on United's defence to win the ball from Forsyth and to turn it inside.

Swooped

As United's middle defenders converged on Oliveira he craftily stepped over the ball and left the unerring Duda to do the damage.

Six minutes later Porto went even further ahead when Oliveira hit their fourth goal after yet another storming burst by Seninho.

Sexton added: 'Nobody can attempt to take it away from Porto. They played very well indeed. They were undoubtedly the better side. But it was a night on which nothing seemed to be going right for us.

'As for the second leg, it is obviously going to be a very, very difficult task for us now, but there have been turn-ups before, and I refuse to believe that it is impossible in this case.'

One small mercy on a night of misery for the English team was the fact that their fans behaved themselves.

LOOKING BACK WITH STUART PEARSON

Stuart Pearson was signed to shoot Manchester United back into the First Division.

Tommy Docherty paid Hull City £200,000 for him after relegation in season 1973-74, the only major addition to the team which went down.

He made all the difference as the Reds came romping back into the big-time with all guns blazing to make playing with two wingers fashionable again.

It was exciting stuff loved by the fans, but it was a style which didn't always pay off against the sophisticated teams of Europe.

United went only two rounds in the UEFA Cup of season 1976-77 and it was a similar story in the Cup Winners Cup the following year . . . as Pearson explains.

"We came through OK against St Etienne, but came to grief in the next round against F C Porto. The first leg in Portugal waş a horror match.

"Jimmy Greenhoff was missing with a virus. His brother Brian and I were both sitting in the stand, out with injury, as the lads went down 4-0. I am never the best of watchers at football, and I was really squirming in this one.

"We got a real drubbing. We made a bad start and then fell away! The Portuguese were skilful and strong. I remember they had a Brazilian centre forward called Duda who showed all the qualities you associate with Brazil.

"He scored a stunning goal early on, a 25-yard dipping shot which gave Alex Stepney no chance. We were lucky to get away only four goals down.

"No-one gave us much chance of catching up on four goals against such a good team, and indeed we did go out of the competition.

"But what a fight we made of it. We went one better than them and actualy scored five goals. We cut them to pieces with a tremendous display of attacking football.

"It was typical of our cavalier football of those days. Tommy Docherty had encouraged us to throw caution to the wind. He played with two wingers for much of the time, reaching a peak with Steve Coppell on the right and Gordon Hill on the left. By the time of this tie Dave Sexton was manager, but we still played with adventure.

"Unfortunately we often left ourselves open at the back, and that is what happened on this occasion. They scored two breakaway goals so that although we won 5-2, we lost 6-5 on aggregate.

"Stevie Coppell got our first goal and I got the last one, helped in by one of their full-backs as he tried to hook it out.

"We were mugs for getting caught with their goals because we absolutely dominated. But that's the way it went sometimes in those days.

"It was a pleasure to play in though, and I am sure it was tremendously exciting to watch. For instance you don't get many 6-5 results in Europe!

"I was transferred to West Ham at the end of the season and I tasted European football again with the Hammers. But I shall never forget the wonderfully bold football we played in my time at Old Trafford.

"Just think, if we hadn't given those two stupid goals away at Old Trafford, it would have been hailed as one of the great fight-backs of all time."

After playing with West Ham for three seasons, touring South Africa and playing in America, Stuart Pearson returned to Manchester where he hopes to continue in football management and coaching.

Dave Sexton steadied a rocking boat and brought a calm to Old Trafford after the excitement of the Docherty era.

He saw his team beaten by Arsenal in the final of the FA Cup in 1979, but they opened the door back into Europe by finishing a highly creditable second in season 1979-80, just two points behind Liverpool.

By this time Joe Jordan, Gordon McQueen and Ray Wilkins had been signed to stiffen the likes of Sammy McIlroy, Lou Macari and Steve Coppell. Gary Bailey had taken over in goal as the Reds went into the UEFA Cup of 1980-81.

But it was an undistinguished season with the fans growing restive with the rather dull football being served up. The writing was on the wall for Sexton as his team crashed out of European competition in the first round against Widzew Lodz and slipped to eighth in the First Division.

Dave Sexton went at the end of the season and it was another blank year in Europe as Ron Atkinson took over.

Stuart Pearson

DAILY MAIL, November 2, 1977

MAN. UTD.	5
FC PORTO	2

1977-78 EUROPEAN CUP WINNERS' CUP, SECOND ROUND, SECOND LEG, FC PORTO WIN 5-6 ON AGGREGATE

Such glorious failure United

It's a great escape for Porto as supermen hit five

By Ronald Crowther

Fighting hearts, dauntless determination and non-stop aggression were not enough last night to save magnificent Manchester United from failure in the Cup-Winners' Cup.

But this was surely the most glorious failure since the Charge of the Light Brigade when they stormed their way to a 5-2 victory in the second leg only to lose the tie that began two weeks ago in Oporto by 5-6.

So savage was the pounding to which they subjected the panic-stricken Portuguese that there could be no man among Porto players who would not admit, if he were honest, that for the visiting side it was a lucky escape.

Fateful

Rarely in more than 20 years' experience of European soccer have I known a night of bubbling excitement quite like this or seen any side make so many scoring attempts as United did.

But, for all their do-or-die courage, they lived to rue two fateful moments in which a superb, loose-limbed winger by name of Arsenio Seninho cut loose to deliver his killer counter-punches, that made all United's frantic survival effort in vain.

As United's opening assaults reduced the Portuguese to shellshocked jitters, Steve Coppell shot them into the lead after eight minutes and continued to be an inspiration to his side all night.

Caught up in the defensive frenzy Porto's goalkeeper had made a faulty clearance to the feet of McGrath and it was the winger who stabbed the ball straight through to Coppell to give him his chance.

Yet, after one early warning from Seninho of his menace on the break, the winger struck after half an hour to level the scores. It was a tragic moment for United as he cut in from the right, shook off both Albiston and Houston, and then smashed the ball home.

Powered

But again the spirits of the big crowd soared when the combination of a swerving far post centre by Hill and pressure from Pearson caused defender Murca to stab the ball frantically into his own net.

That was in the 40th minute and then, seconds before the interval, Jimmy Nicholl gathered the ball after a corner kick had been only partially cleared and hit goal No. 3 for United.

At the break they still needed three more goals for survival, but nothing, it seemed, was beyond them now. They might have been in an even better position if they had got the penalty award they deserved when Freitas clearly handled the ball.

But they powered their way onto the attack again and McIlroy, Coppell and Hill all went near to breaking down the defence about which manager Dave Sexton's suspicions had been so well-founded.

A victory still seemed to be on when the irrepressible Coppell made it 4-1 following a corner kick by Hill. Even now United found the stamina to keep on attacking.

But, with six minutes left, the hearts of their supporters sank when the stealthy Seninho sped through once more to beat off the combined challenge of Stepney, Buchan, and Albiston and to score a goal just as brilliant as his first-half effort.

Although this was the real killer, gallant United still fought on and seconds from the final whistle Pearson again forced Murca to concede another own goal.

Such glorious failure United

By RONALD CROWTHER

Manchester United 5, FC Porto 2
(Aggregate: 5—6)

It's a great escape for Porto as supermen hit five

FIGHTING hearts, dauntless determination and non-stop aggression were not enough last night to save magnificent Manchester United from failure in the Cup-winners' Cup.

But this was surely the most glorious failure since the Charge of the Light Brigade when they stormed their way to a 5—2 victory in the second leg only to lose the tie that began two weeks ago in Oporto by 5—6.

So savage was the pounding to which they subjected the panic-stricken Portuguese that there could be no man among Porto players who would not admit, if he were honest, that for the visiting side it was a lucky escape.

Fateful

Rarely in more than 20 years' experience of European soccer have I known a night of bubbling excitement quite like this or seen any side make so many scoring attempts as United did.

But, for all their do-or-die courage, they lived to rue two fateful moments in which a superb, loose-limbed winger by name of Arsenio Seninho cut loose to deliver his killer counter-punches, that made all United's frantic survival effort in vain.

As United's opening assaults reduced the Portuguese to shellshocked jitters, Steve Coppell shot them into the lead after eight minutes and continued to be an inspira-

Joe Jordan – powerhouse of the United attack

DAILY MIRROR, September 17, 1980

MAN. UTD.	**1**
RTS WIDZEW LODZ	**1**

1980-81 UEFA CUP, FIRST ROUND, FIRST LEG,
DRAW 1-1

United up the Pole!

By Bob Russell

Manchester United can kiss the UEFA Cup goodbye.

That must be the verdict after a first round first leg lesson in tactical European warfare from the hard, efficient men of Widzew Lodz last night.

Predictably there was the usual frantic Old Trafford finish with the Poles under pressure like never before.

But the fact was that for one of the rare times in my memory United had the mickey taken out of them by foreign opposition.

For a few fleeting early moments it seemed United had been granted the total freedom of Old Trafford.

Three times in as many minutes they threatened to penetrate the Polish defence and on the fourth occasion they succeeded.

Emergency striker Steve Coppell, drifting along the left flank, probed the penalty area and his cross struck already anxious 'keeper Josef Mlynarczyk on the knees.

From the rebound Sammy McIlroy, on the edge of the box, had all the time and space he needed to comfortably steer United into a four-minute lead with his low shot into the corner.

Stunner

But instant ecstasy turned into a stunned silence within seconds as United keeper Gary Bailey unbelievably picked the ball out of the net as the Poles hit back with an unexpected reprisal.

There appeared no danger when East German referee Kurt Scheurell awarded a 30-yard free-kick after Martin Buchan and Arthur Albiston had sandwiched busy little Marek Pieta.

United duly provided the almost statutory five-man wall, but amazingly Krzysztof Surlit found a way round, bending and dipping his shot past the bewildered Bailey.

United responded with all the will in the world but against this composed highly — accomplished Polish side, unbeaten in their own country, it didn't look enough.

Lou Macari flashed a hopeful header wide, Yugoslav defender Nikola Jovanic pushed forward and just failed to get on the end of a Mick Thomas cross and Albiston also rifled a 20-yarder just wide.

More ominously, however, Surlit again sent Bailey full stretch with another "banana" kick, this time from 20 yards, and the 'keeper did well to keep it out.

The Poles, with the arrogant Zbigniew Boniek taking control of the midfield, were only in serious trouble when referee Scheurell warned them for their over-physical approach.

Struggle

United were forced to substitute reserve defender Mike Duxbury for right-back Jimmy Nicholl, who had been struggling with a knee knock.

But they really went all out for another goal.

A cross shot from Coppell fooled 'keeper Mlynarczyk and flicked the bar.

Greenhoff was even closer with a near prod, but with United's luck no better than their touch, the ball hit the inside of a post and rebounded out.

Mlynarczyk was there to be taken, but the fact was that United didn't have the know-how to do it.

The Poles bossed the midfield and despite the industry of Macari and McIlroy United rarely looked like taking charge.

Tlokinski was booked eventually for a scything tackle on Albiston, one of the few moments that really appealed to the 38,000 crowd, in their increasing disenchantment.

RIGHT: *Macari (centre) and Coppell (second from right) in the thick of the Widzew Lodz defence*

THE SUN, September 18, 1980

MAN. UTD.	1
RTS WIDZEW LODZ	1

1980-81 UEFA CUP, FIRST ROUND, FIRST LEG,
DRAW 1-1

Sammy Goes Solo

McIlroy can't believe his luck

By Peter Fitton

Manchester United brought some old-fashioned devil back to Old Trafford and still found themselves fighting for European survival.

Manager Dave Sexton saw his rampaging players give their most passionate performance of this goal-starved season against the Poles of Widzew Lodz.

But he also realised that his ambitions in this UEFA Cup had been seriously dented by the incredible come-back goal of Lodz's hot-shot Krzys Surlit.

United, braving the sly tackles and occasional body checks, pummelled Lodz in a spectacular first-half and discovered that the clever, counter-striking Poles were ready to take it.

Irish ace Sammy McIlroy struck the precious fourth minute goal and almost every other United player had a hard luck story to tell about a goalmouth chance that went missing.

Steve Coppell, Lou Macari and even the raiding Jovanovic had opportunities squeezed off the line of a goalkeeper that was prone to panic and a defence that tended to be reckless under pressure.

But Lodz have class. Their pedigree as leaders of the Polish First Division was demonstrated in their quick counter attacks.

United are clearly going to have plenty of problems when they play behind the Iron Curtain in two weeks time.

But United's jubilation lasted merely seconds. In the fifth minute the terraces were stunned by an equaliser bombed in from 30 yards.

It was a demonstration of the shooting power so feared in Poland as Surlit exploded a free-kick that left United's wall motionless.

Bailey had no hope of pulling off a save.

MANCHESTER EVENING NEWS,
September 18, 1980

MAN. UTD.	1
RTS WIDZEW LODZ	1

1980-81 UEFA CUP, FIRST ROUND, FIRST LEG,
DRAW 1-1

Skidding out!

Inconsistent United run into Europe road block

By David Meek

Manchester United's calamitous, crazy inconsistency near goal has put them on the skids out of Europe.

One match they score three, and then end a six-match scoring famine by running in five. But last night the goals dried up again and the 1-1 draw against Widzew Lodz at Old Trafford looks like the beginning of the end of their UEFA Cup ambitions.

The Poles now are in the driving seat for the return leg in Lodz in a fortnight and naturally are jubilant with the result. Scoring an away goal is particularly valuable when they count double in the event of an aggregate draw.

Not that Widzew will be going for a goalless draw in Poland after their stunning display of swift counter-attacking which would have brought them victory last night but for a superb defensive performance from skipper Martin Buchan.

The Poles on their own ground are going to be a handful. Wlodzimierz Smolarek and Marek Pieta are brilliantly fast raiders and when they are backed up with more support from midfield, they are going to be devastating.

Their talented international, Zbigniew Boniek, was not particularly effective last night, but he is only at half pace with a knee injury.

Power

And the shooting power of Krzysztof Surlit was a revelation, so fierce and accurate. This is the player who once laid out Widzew goalkeeper Jozef Mlynarcyk when he played for another club with a shot that struck him on the chest.

...al red ... but they failed to get the ball away before Poutiniemi swung a hopeful boot to score from a difficult angle.

Liverpool defended grimly in the last 10 minutes to hold on to a draw — no doubt remembering that in the previous two years they have gone out of the competition at this stage.

Manager D... Sex... has been given the boardroom authority to try to negotiate a deal of around £1million later this month when the European future of the two clubs is more certain.

The United chief first approached Forest for Birtles almost a month

...nited chairman Martin Edwards confirmed last night: "Our manager has been back on to Forest. But they have told him they are too heavily committed in Europe to make a positive decision on Birtles at the moment.

"But I expect Forest

...of ...
United or ...ny othe... club offered the straight cash.

And Forest No. 2 Peter Taylor was reported as saying last night that United and Everton have both already gone close to the asking price.

SAMMY GOES SOLO

By PETER FITTON

Man U 1, Wedzew Lodz 1

MANCHESTER UNITED brought some old-fashioned devil back to Old Trafford and still found themselves fighting for European survival.

Manager Dave Sexton saw his rampaging players give their most passionate performance of this goal-starved season against the Poles of Widzew Lodz.

But he also realised

McIlroy can't believe his luck

that his ambitions in this UEFA Cup had been seriously dented by the incredible come-back goal of Lodz's hot-shot Krzys Surlit.

United, braving the sly tackles and occasional body checks, pummelled Lodz in a spectacular first-half and discovered

that the clever, counter-striking Poles were ready to take it.

Irish ace Sammy McIlroy struck the precious fourth minute goal and almost every other United player had a hard luck story to tell about a goalmouth chance that went missing.

Steve Coppell, Lou Macari and even the raiding Jovanovic had opportunities squeezed off the line of a goalkeeper that was prone to panic and a defence that tended to be reckless under pressure.

But Lodz have class.

Their pedigree as leaders of the Polish First Division was demonstrated in their quick counter attacks.

United are clearly going to have plenty of problems when they play behind the Iron Curtain in two weeks time.

But United's jubilation lasted merely seconds. In the fifth minute the terraces were stunned by an equaliser bombed in from 30 yards.

It was a demonstration of the shooting power so feared in Poland as Surlit exploded a free-kick that left United's wall motionless.

Bailey had no hope of pulling off a save.

Ballymena's big boost

Ballymena Utd 2, Vorwaerts 1

THE £10-a-week part-timers of Irish League side Ballymena United bounced back from the shock of an early goal against them to beat East German Army side Vorwaerts in the UEFA Cup last night. Second half goals from Sammy McQuistan and John Sloan knocked out Geyer's fourth minute sickener.

IE HORRIBLE

His free-kick in the fourth minute left Gary Bailey almost as helpless as it rocketed over the defensive wall and went in off the inside of the post.

The 38,000 crowd were just as dumbstruck, for the Widzew goal came only a minute after the Reds had made a dream opening to their European campaign.

Steve Coppell caught the Poles cold with a tricky cross into the goalmouth which Andrzej Grebosz allowed to go through to take Mlynarczyk by surprise. The ball came back off the goalkeeper's legs for a chance which Sammy McIlroy coolly slotted home.

It seemed as if the five-goal mood of the Leicester game was continuing. For even though Widzew bounced straight back to grab an equaliser, United continued to dictate the course of the game.

Boniek, who played the first 10 minutes as a sweeper behind the defence, eventually moved into midfield, but the Reds had a good grip on the game.

It seemed only a matter of time before they scored again. Lou Macari, Jimmy Greenhoff, Nikki Jovanovic and Arthur Albiston all had strikes at goal and at that early stage the inaccuracy just seemed a matter of bad luck.

Breakaways

Surlit bobbed up again in the 24th minute to demonstrate how to combine power with accuracy and only a splendid tip over the bar by Bailey prevented another Widzew goal.

The Poles were mighty dangerous on breakaways, although Buchan was outstanding with the way he covered and closed down the strikers, at times without Jovanovic who was away helping in the general siege of the visitors' goal.

Mike Thomas, Ashley Grimes, Macari again and then a near penalty when Wlodzimierz Zmuda knocked down Thomas gave the Polish goal a charmed life.

United put Mike Duxbury on for the injured Jimmy Nicholl at half-time and the Reds applied

ABOVE: *Bailey in action*

even more pressure. Grimes lobbed just over the bar, a cross from Coppell came off the far post in the 55th minute and a quarter of an hour later Greenhoff prodded a shot against the foot of the post.

United finished the game in a fury of attacking. The shots and headers were coming thick and fast, but when Mlynarczyk turned Coppell's shot round his post in the last minute it was all over.

Even Widzew manager Jacek Machcinski agrees with me: "We were lucky to escape a goal in the second-half, even though I thought our defence played well."

But after allowing for bad luck, the performance does reflect United's erratic record this season of swinging from goal glut to famine.

It could well mean only a short road back to Europe.

Martin Buchan

DAILY STAR, October 1, 1980

RTS WIDZEW LODZ	0

MAN. UTD.	0

1980-81 UEFA CUP, FIRST ROUND, SECOND LEG, DRAW 1-1 ON AGGREGATE, RTS WIDZEW LODZ WIN ON AWAY GOAL

United's agony

From John Wragg

Captain Martin Buchan became the eighth casualty of an injury ravaged season as Manchester United went out of the UEFA Cup with a broken heart last night.

Challenge

Buchan limped out of United's brave attempt to score a vital goal which would have seen them through to the second round.

Facing a sudden challenge from quick raiding Pieta, Buchan looked in immediate pain as he tried to move sharply in the 63rd minute.

Kevin Moran, who has not played for five weeks because of an ankle injury took over and left physio Laurie Brown with the multi-million pound talent of Gordon McQueen, Joe Jordan, Ray Wilkins, Lou Macari, Gary Bailey, Ashley Grimes, Moran and now Buchan on his treatment table.

The succession of injuries have been a tremendous handicap all season and last night bravery and incredible spirit were just not enough to stop the victory bonfires being lit on the Polish terraces.

But Steve Coppell was only an inch or two away from pinching a shock winner in the first half when he hit the post.

But it had needed four saves of international class from Bailey to keep United protected from the attack-conscious Poles.

They only needed this goal-less draw to qualify on the away goal Surlit scored in the 1-1 draw at Old Trafford.

But Lodz knew United were only held together by bandages, sticking plaster and determined spirit.

Bailey's first save came in five minutes when lack of concentration in defence caused a simple high ball to inspire panic, and Bailey dived at Smolarek's feet.

Then the same player set up a cross that Tlokinski headed and Bailey punched over.

No. 3 was about swift thinking and intelligent blocking of another Smolarek shot after Boniek's pass had crept through United.

Sweeping

Bailey's best was saved for the cream of Lodz's football, a sweeping three man move from defence to attack but finished with Bailey stopping the rising shot.

Jimmy Nicholl, for a foul and Mike Thomas for pushing were booked.

DAILY EXPRESS, October 2, 1980

RTS WIDZEW LODZ	0

MAN. UTD.	0

1980-81 UEFA CUP, FIRST ROUND, SECOND LEG, DRAW 1-1 ON AGGREGATE, RTS WIDZEW LODZ WIN ON AWAY GOAL

Agony United

Buchan limps out as Sexton's men slip up

By Derek Potter

Makeshift United suffered all sorts of agonies last night in the vain attempt to score the single goal needed to silence 45,000 Poles.

Apart from their quick exit from the UEFA Cup, skipper Martin Buchan hobbled sadly out of the second leg after 63 minutes with a

Agony United

Buchan limps out as Sexton's men slip up

By Derek Potter

Widzew Lodz 0, Manchester United 0
Aggregate 1—1, Lodz win on away goals

MAKESHIFT UNITED suffered all sorts of agonies last night in the vain attempt to score the single goal needed to silence 45,000 Poles.

Apart from their quick exit from the UEFA Cup, skipper Martin Buchan hobbled sadly out of the second leg after 63 minutes with a pulled hamstring and he could be out for two months.

The United captain slipped and fell awkwardly and the single goal target proved to be beyond their injury-wrecked side.

McQueen, Lou Macari, Ray Wilkins and pre-match casualty Jimmy Greenhoff out

booked early on and Gary Bailey had the 45,000 crowd on their toes with a superb save

pulled hamstring and he could be out for two months.

The United captain slipped and fell awkwardly and the single goal target proved to be beyond their injury-wrecked side.

With the last seconds of injury time ticking away on the electronic scoreboard Widzew survived a final desperate assault by United and the 1-1 draw at Old Trafford saw them through.

It was destined to be a struggle without Gordon McQueen, Lou Macari, Ray Wilkins and pre-match casualty Jimmy Greenhoff out of the side.

On the bonus side, Mike Duxbury, in only his second full game, played impressively and might easily have scored.

But his fierce 25-yard shot went straight at goalkeeper Josef Mlynarczyk.

United had Jimmy Nichol booked early on and Gary Bailey had the 45,000 crowd on their toes with a superb save in the 29th minute when he leaped to his right to save a fierce and well-aimed shot by Tlokinski.

United's chance of saving the tie came in the 37th minute when Steve Coppell broke through, but his shot bounced off the woodwork.

Ron Atkinson breezed into Old Trafford for the start of season 1981-82 and quickly made a resounding impact.

He paid a British record fee of £1.5m for Bryan Robson, and what a bargain it proved to be as the West Bromwich man went on to become England's captain and most influential player.

Remi Moses was bought from West Bromwich as well and Norman Whiteside, the Northern Ireland youngster, was introduced. With Frank Stapleton also signed from Arsenal, the revitalised team ended in third place to go back into the UEFA Cup for season 1982-83 and start a regular run in Europe.

Atkinson spent five and a half years at Old Trafford and had the Reds in European competition for three seasons on the trot before the ban on English clubs taking part.

After the 1982 season in the UEFA Cup, they played in the Cup Winners Cup on the strength of beating Brighton at Wembley. Then it was back into the UEFA Cup after finishing fourth in the League.

Ron Atkinson achieved a high level of consistency and introduced some exciting players. After the initial spending spree involving Robson early in his management reign, he paused for a spell.

Then he went out to buy Gordon Strachan and Jesper Olsen.

But the signing of Alan Brazil had failed and he perhaps rushed his next recruiting drive which brought Peter Davenport, Terry Gibson, Colin Gibson and John Sivebaek to Old Trafford.

The goals dried up in the second half of season 1985-86 as the club hit fierce criticism for the secret way they set about selling top scorer Mark Hughes, the powerful Welsh international who had developed through the junior teams, to Barcelona.

The fortunes had started to dip and the slide gathered speed the following season with the result that the board parted company with their manager in February 1987, in favour of Aberdeen boss Alex Ferguson.

But there is no disputing the excellence of Atkinson's achievements in his five-year reign. His team finished third in his first two seasons and then chalked up three fourths.

He won the FA Cup twice. The 1985 victory over Everton would of course have earned another run in the Cup Winners Cup but for the ban on English clubs in Europe.

Although knocked out in his first European campaign by Valencia in the opening round, he reached the semi-finals of the Cup Winners Cup and the quarter-finals of the UEFA Cup.

Atkinson himself felt that his record had been good enough to have given him more time to overcome his rough patch: it was not to be, but there is no denying that he gave the club some memorable moments, not least in Europe.

DAILY MAIL, September 16, 1982

| MAN. UTD. | 0 |
| VALENCIA CF | 0 |

1982-83 UEFA CUP, FIRST ROUND, FIRST LEG, DRAW 0-0

Back in anger
Missiles rain on Old Trafford pitch

By Peter Johnson

European football and all its frustrations – and nastiness – returned to Old Trafford last night.

After only 40 minutes of this ragged UEFA Cup-tie missiles were raining on to the pitch, while a dozen players jostled and hacked at each other in the Valencia penalty area.

The flashpoint came when a tackle by United's Frank Stapleton on goalkeeper Jose Sempere angered his team-mates who swarmed around the Irish striker.

The Czech referee Dragan Rchnak managed to calm the situation temporarily, but by half-time three men – United's teenager Norman Whiteside and Valencia's Carrete and Saura – had been booked.

The Spaniards had also lost midfield 'ball winner' Arias after a tackle by Ashley Grimes, which had left Valencia seething with resentment.

Grimes, brought in as a last-minute replacement for the injured Arnold Muhren, found most things going against him in his first senior match of the season.

In the first minute a challenge by Gordon McQueen had so unsettled the keeper that his punch steered the ball to Grimes's feet.

It was, admittedly, Grimes's right foot which met the ball, but it was hopelessly and unforgivably wide.

Total, if ugly, defence somehow kept Valencia level through a first half in which the turf in their penalty area was worn almost bare by the pressure they endured.

Defenders queued five abreast to tackle, yet

Back in anger

Missiles rain on
Old Trafford pitch

By PETER JOHNSON: Man. U. 0, Valencia 0

EUROPEAN football and all its frustrations —and nastiness—returned to Old Trafford last night.

After only 40 minutes of this ragged UEFA Cup-tie missiles were raining on to the pitch, while a dozen players jostled and hacked at each other in the Valencia penalty area.

The flashpoint came when a tackle by United's Frank Stapleton on goalkeeper Jose Sempere angered his team-mates who swarmed around the Irish striker.

The Czech referee Dragan Rchnak managed to calm the situation temporarily, but by half-time three men—United's teenager Norman Whiteside and Valencia's Carrete and Saura—had been booked.

The Spaniards had also lost midfield 'ball winner' Arias after a tackle by Ashley Grimes, which had left Valencia seething with resentment.

Grimes, brought in as a last-minute

ANOTHER MISS . . . teenage wonder Norman Whiteside draws a blank with this shot

almost bare by the pressure they endured. Defenders queued five abreast to 'tackle, yet when the

In fact, the only moment of anxiety for United keeper Gary Bailey was a 35-yard drive from Roberto that spun past the post.

Toshack

were invariably in trouble when the ball was in the air.

But United's finishing was never decisive enough to give them the early break they needed.

Arthur Albiston had a shot saved, Bryan Robson a header brilliantly turned aside by Sempere and the unfortunate Grimes was way off target again with another chance.

Valencia buried their Argentinian star Mario Kempes deep in midfield and he was allowed out only once to volley wide from close range.

In fact, the only moment of anxiety for United keeper Gary Bailey was a 35-yard drive from Roberto that spun past the post.

Valencia's restrictive practices slowly but visibly sapped United's speed and stamina.

One Steve Coppell cross was collected and rolled across the face of the goal by Whiteside, but frustrating inches too far ahead of Robson and Stapleton.

Spanish World Cup defender Tendillo was next in the book when he compounded a foul on Stapleton by kicking the ball away. But the Spaniards' organisation was leaving very few doors open to an increasingly desperate United attack.

Daily Mail, September 30, 1982

VALENCIA CF	2
MAN. UTD.	1

1982-83 UEFA CUP, FIRST ROUND, SECOND LEG,
VALENCIA CF WIN 2-1 ON AGGREGATE

Sucker punch floors United

From Peter Johnson

T wo goals in four minutes ended a brave UEFA Cup challenge by Manchester United here last night as violence erupted on the terraces again.

The limitations of Valencia's football showed up starkly when they were asked to do more than park defenders in front of goalkeeper Sempere.

Through the first half there was vastly more composure and inventiveness about United yet those qualities are useless without ruthlessness and steadiness in the last ten yards — and that once again, was what United took so long to find.

Skipper Ray Wilkins was among the culprits. An early Bryan Robson pass, rolled invitingly across the box, left him with time to get more accuracy and power than he did behind an effort that trickled wide.

Remi Moses playing his first game of the season for the injured Steve Coppell and Arthur Albiston both found themselves behind the Spanish defence but with Sempere bearing down on them too quickly.

Challenge

One 'goal' by Robson was disallowed because Norman Whiteside was alleged to have lifted his foot in a challenge on the 'keeper. Sempere somehow managed to keep out a close-range stab from the unhappy Frank Stapleton.

But with the final kick of the first half Wilkins flung the ball across from the left and Robson, arriving in the six-yard box with his customary velocity, leaped above Sempere to head his side into a priceless lead.

Violence, sadly, erupted on the terraces after Valencia equalised in the 71st minute.

Ashley Grimes conceded a penalty which Solsena converted. Worse was to follow in the 75th minute when Fernandez cashed in on a defensive mistake to put his side ahead.

199

Daily Mail, September 30, 1982

VALENCIA CF	2
MAN. UTD.	I

1982-83 UEFA CUP, FIRST ROUND, SECOND LEG,
VALENCIA CF WIN 2-1 ON AGGREGATE

United conned out of the Cup

From Peter Johnson
IN VALENCIA

Manchester United survived Spanish football's brutality only to fall victim to its low cunning last night.

A goal up and in calm control of this UEFA Cup-tie, they were robbed of a place in Europe when yet another naive referee fell for a blatant con-trick.

Valencia's equalising penalty in the 72nd minute was presented to them when their substitute Ribes took a histrionic dive. Within three minutes a disorganised and indignant United defence caved in again to let in Roberto for the winner.

Pressure

The limitations of Valencia's football showed up starkly when they were asked to do more than pack defenders in front of goalkeeper Sempere.

Through the first half there was vastly more composure and inventiveness about United, yet, those qualities are useless without ruthlessness and steadiness in the last ten yards – and that once again, was what United took so long to find.

A goal then, when it was both threatened and deserved, might have spared United the pressure that was to build up around a defence which sometimes found difficulty in coping.

One 'goal' by Robson was disallowed because Norman Whiteside was alleged to have lifted his foot in a challenge on the keeper.

But with the final kick of the first half Wilkins flung the ball across from the left and Robson, arriving in the six yards box with his customary velocity, leaped above Sempere to head his side into a priceless lead.

Fooled

Instead of putting the game beyond Valencia's reach. United found themselves level again in the 72nd minute due entirely to the most outrageous of referee Igma's rulings.

Kevin Moran put in a legitimate-looking block tackle on substitute Ribes who performed an extravagant acrobatic dive which fooled the referee into awarding a penalty.

Solsena blasted it past Bailey and shook United's confidence so badly that within three minutes a cross from the right let in Roberto to give Valencia the lead.

Manager Ron Atkinson claimed: 'It was scandalous. We had everything under control when that penalty came. We had bossed the game in every department and looked to be on the brink of getting three or four.

'Our performance was so good that it was heartbreaking for everybody to have the game taken away from us like this.'

LOOKING BACK

Manchester United did not last long in Europe again in season 1982-83.

Valencia drew 0-0 at Old Trafford in the first leg of the UEFA Cup opening round, and then won 2-1 in Spain.

The tie will be long remembered, though, because it reflected the sad side of European football.

Valencia in Manchester were quite ruthless in their approach, and later UEFA severely reprimanded and fined them £1,000 for "repeated misdemeanours."

· United manager Ron Atkinson called for stronger, more positive action from the European authorities.

He said: The time has come for UEFA to put a stop to those teams which seek to win European matches by consistently breaking every rule in the book. The only way is to kick the offenders out of the competition. I always considered Valencia to be one of the more civilised Spanish teams, but at Old Trafford they fouled continuously. It saddened me to see how low Spanish soccer had sunk."

The second leg in Spain was even more ominous and prompted a dramatic change of policy by Manchester United.

Trouble between United fans and the Spanish police so worried the club that they announced that in future they would actively seek to stop their supporters travelling abroad with them.

It was a depressing conclusion to years of interesting travel to foreign parts by a great many supporters, but something had to be done after years of misbehaviour by English fans generally which had prompted a backlash, bringing retribution from foreign supporters and indeed their police.

The team lost 2-1, despite leading at the interval through a Bryan Robson header from a cross by Ray Wilkins.

But it was events off the field which altered the face of European football for Manchester United followers.

As chairman Martin Edwards explains: "Too many people abroad were trying to incite our supporters. Our people in Valencia got little protection from the local police who subjected parties of United supporters to indiscriminate baton charges."

Edwards then reached the drastic 1982 con-clusion: "I believed our supporters were best off staying at home for their own protection. We could not afford trouble and then a ban on the team taking part in European competition.

"We decided we wouldn't take any allocation of tickets for a match in Europe and wouldn't run any tours. We simply discouraged people from travelling abroad with us."

David Smith, the chairman of the Supporters Club, was even more adamant at the time that there would be no more foreign travel. He announced: "I fear if things are allowed to continue someone is going to lose his life and I cannot take the responsibility.

"As a result of the incidents which occurred in Spain and the real dangers of fatal injury, no further Supporters Club travel will be arranged to matches in Europe until such time as the risks involved have been eliminated.

"United supporters were the victims of unprovoked assaults in Valencia."

Manchester United were still leaving their fans at home when UEFA banned English clubs from Europe following the Heysel disaster.

Bryan Robson

Forewarning . . . crowd trouble when United play West Ham in October 1975, worse was to come in St Etienne and Valencia

Stapleton

Wilkins in action

DAILY MAIL, May 27, 1983

BRIGHTON	0
MAN. UTD.	4

1983 F.A. CUP FINAL, MANCHESTER UNITED WIN
REPLAY 4-0
(FIRST MATCH DRAWN 0-0)

Happy Birthday

United's heroes give Sir Matt the perfect present

Jeff Powell
On a Replay to Remember

Manchester United celebrated the 74th birthday of the man who made them famous with a Wembley victory of historic magnitude.

Not for 80 years, and never in this noble stadium, has the FA Cup been won by four clear, crushing unanswerable goals.

Sir Matt Busby, father of the greatest United team of all, sat among their directors content that Ron Atkinson has begun the creation of a side to compare with his tragic Babes.

Overwhelming

United's red army of supporters turned briefly away from the slaughter of Brighton's seagulls to sing "Happy birthday, Sir Matt". No football man could have wished for a better present. The new United delivered the Cup in the overwhelming style we had expected of them on Saturday.

It was as if Busby's club had waited the five intervening days for the perfect occasion on which to ratify the expanding quality of Atkinson's team.

The extra-time dramatics of the first drawn game gave way to the emotional jubilation of a replay which restored form and order to the 1983 final.

Steve Foster's headband, which had been the symbol of the Cup campaign with which Brighton had relieved their relegation season, waved like a white flag of surrender as the United tide washed over their dream.

Foster, who had dragged through the High Court his vain appeal for the right to appear in Saturday's match, must have wished his suspension had extended to the replay. It was the opposing captain, Bryan Robson of United and England, who proved himself worthy of climbing the step to the Royal Box and lifting the trophy from the hands of Princess Michael of Kent.

Robson scored two of the three first-half goals which left Brighton with little more than the memories of their epic struggle five days earlier.

Then with a penalty offering him the chance to become the first finalist for 30 years to complete a hat-trick, Robson had the humility to leave the honour of United's fourth goal to Dutchman Arnold Muhren.

Class, in every sense, finally told. Still Brighton, the team already condemned to relegation, will be haunted in the Second Division by Gordon Smith's miss in the last minute of Saturday's extra time.

But for that, Robson and teenager Norman Whiteside, two men of unquestioned courage, would not have had last night's chance to endorse United's class.

Jimmy Melia, Brighton's manager, will be left to reflect also on the adjustments made to his defence to accommodate Foster's return. The centre-half may not have deserved the taunts of United's fans — "What a difference Foster's

made", they chanted — but it was inevitable that he would suffer by comparison with the resourcefulness of the Stevens-Gatting partnership which had taken Brighton to a second game.

Foster made some timely interceptions in an opening 25 minutes which kept the faint whiff of a sensation in the night air.

Then United nagged at Gatting's unfamiliarity with his new role at right-back and Brighton's sandcastle fell. Whiteside's shin-high cross was laid back to the edge of the penalty area by young Alan Davies, and Robson swept the first goal low into the far corner of the net.

Four minutes later Davies, an unknown before the final, turned one of Muhren's inswinging corners back into the goalmouth and Whiteside's lunging header made it 2-0.

As if in relief at shaking Brighton from their heels United relaxed and Gary Bailey had to produce an acrobatic save to keep out Case's wickedly deflected shot. Grealish, in a gesture which typified the sportsmanship which never deserted the Final even in its most ferocious moments, was the first to congratulate United's goalkeeper.

Punished

In constrast, Foster's gruesome foul on Whiteside was punished to the full two minutes from half-time. Robson headed on Muhren's resulting free kick and turned to nudge Stapleton's responding header over the line.

Brighton were lucky not to concede one penalty when Whiteside's return pass in the direction of Muhren ran up Foster's arm. But a linesman was perfectly placed to see Stevens, Saturday's hero, wrestle Robson to the ground in the 62nd minute. Robson declined all appeals to embellish his personal triumph and Muhren dispatched the penalty with customary Dutch calm.

Brighton ......(0) 0   Manchester Utd ......(3) 4
Robson 25 and 43 mins
Whiteside 29 Muhren (pen) 62
ATT. 92,000. RECEIPTS: £640,000
REFEREE: MR ALF GREY

JEFF POWELL
ON A REPLAY
TO REMEMBER

Happy birthday

United's heroes give Sir Matt the

MANCHESTER United celebrated the 74th birthday of the man who made them famous with a Wembley victory of historic magnitude.
Not for 80 years, and never in this noble stadium, has the FA Cup been won by four clear, crushing unanswerable goals.
Sir Matt Busby, father of the greatest United team of all, sat among their directors content that Ron Atkinson has begun the creation of a side to compare with his tragic Babes.

DAILY MIRROR, September 15, 1983

| MAN. UTD. | 1 |
| DUKLA PRAGUE | 1 |

1983-84 EUROPEAN CUP WINNERS' CUP, FIRST
ROUND, FIRST LEG, DRAW 1-1

A happier return

*Thanks to birthday present
by Wilkins*

By Derek Wallis

R ay Wilkins threw Manchester United an urgently-needed lifeline in this European Cup Winners' Cup-tie last night, just as the Old Trafford team looked to be drowning in their sorrows.

In the last minute of a first leg that seemed to be beyond United's grasp, Frank Stapleton was pulled down by goalkeeper Karel Stromsik and the referee awarded a penalty unhesitatingly.

In the absence of Arnold Muhren, the usual penalty taker, Wilkins, on his 27th birthday, accepted the responsibility of taking probably the most important deadball kick of his life and drove it in as if he had been doing it all his life.

He struck the ball wide of the offending keeper to give United at least a fragile chance of salvaging the tie in Prague.

But unless United can produce something dramatic and spectacular the first round willies that invariably afflict them in European competition, will destroy their ambitions yet again.

Whatever happens cannot and must not obscure the undeniable fact that in this first leg, United were made to look like European novices.

Aggression

They had neither the wit nor the wisdom to unravel the Czech defence and long before the end of a match they had started so patiently, they resorted to hit and hope passes and the high ball into the middle.

Manager Ron Atkinson called for tempered aggression before the match, but in reality all he saw when United's nerves became frayed was aggressive temper.

Seldom have I seen a United team play with so little thought – poverty stricken in tactics and panic-stricken in attitude towards the end.

The moment when United realised it might not be their night came on the stroke of half-time when Bryan Robson directed a header towards the corner only to be frustrated by an acrobatic save by Stromsik.

As United's anxiety mounted in the second half, they paid the penalty for pushing too many players forward with a breakaway goal in the 60th minute by Tomas Kriz.

When an attack broke down Ladislav Vizek scampered away on the left with Arthur Albiston a lone and stranded defender.

Vizek played the ball into the middle where Kriz ignored the advancing Gary Bailey and scored.

In an attempt to repair the damage United replaced Muhren with Remi Moses and later the injured Robson with John Gidman.

In a fiercely contested match four players were booked – Wilkins and McQueen of United and Vizek and Urban of Dukla.

LEFT: *Wilkins beaten on this occasion in United's first leg match against Dukla Prague*

BELOW: *The Dukla 'keeper watches as Stapleton challenges for the ball*

MANCHESTER EVENING NEWS,
September 27, 1983

DUKLA PRAGUE	2

MAN. UTD.	2

1983-84 EUROPEAN CUP WINNERS' CUP, FIRST ROUND, SECOND LEG, DRAW 3-3 ON AGGREGATE, MANCHESTER UNITED WIN ON AWAY GOALS

It's Czech-mate for Reds

By David Meek

Manchester United reached back into history to revive a proud European tradition as they dazzled and dismayed Dukla Prague in Czechoslovakia last night.

The rampant Reds rolled back the years to the old days of foreign glory as they stormed through to the second round of the European Cup Winners' Cup.

For a decade they have struggled to live with the past and the daring deeds of Sir Matt Busby's teams that conquered the Continent.

Their last two entries into Europe saw them tumbled out in the opening rounds and they faced similar humiliation after managing only a 1-1 draw in the first leg at Old Trafford.

But the team built by Ron Atkinson found the poise and the passion to climb the mountain and emerge worthy winners on the strength of away goals counting double in a 2-2 draw.

In a nail-biting finish the hero was undoubtedly Gary Bailey with a super save of pure reflex when a shot from Peter Rada changed direction off Kevin Moran's boot.

Bailey twisted brilliantly to scoop the ball over the bar.

But it was United's all-out attacking football right from the start that told you that the Manchester United team of today are worthy of comparison with the European masters of 15 years ago.

They took control from the kick-off with a courage and conviction refreshing to see from a British team on the Continent.

By one of those quirks of soccer it was Dukla who scored first, demonstrating as they had done in Manchester, their talent for scoring a breakaway goal.

Well taken

The game was only 11 minutes old when the wily Ladislav Vizek put Stambacher through for a well-taken goal.

It could so easily have crushed United's spirit and ambition, but this team are ready for Europe. They kept their patience and their pattern for Bryan Robson to equalise in the 33rd minute with a stunning 25-yard shot.

The stage was set for a game that produced all that is best in European combat.

Chances were created and either missed or saved at both ends until suddenly in the 78th minute Frank Stapleton ignored a nagging ankle injury to climb high to meet Arthur Albiston's cross for an immaculately headed goal.

United were in front and with the safety net of Dukla needing two goals to win in order to better the visitors' two away goals.

The Czechs were worthy opponents and they were far from beaten as Vaclav Danek showed when he rammed home the equaliser.

They fought superbly for a winner but found Bailey too good to beat.

But don't conclude that because of the desperate finish United only scraped through. They had done more than enough throughout the game to deserve their victory.

From Derek Potter
Dukla Prague 2
Manchester Utd 2

Stapleton wins the battle for United

FRANK STAPLETON dramatically emerged from this Cup Winners' Cup match of personal anguish last night to head United to spectacular victory.

United won on the away goals rule thanks to Stapleton's spectacular header from Arthur Albiston's cross in the 78th minute.

Hero Stapleton battled through more than half the match with his left ankle heavily strapped. "I got hurt early in the first half and poor Norman Whiteside had to battle on his own."

His brilliantly headed goal made the score 2—1 in the Juliska stadium and 3—2 on aggregate and it seemed United would win a memorable match. But eight minutes from the end the brave Czechs struck back when Baclav Danek beat Gary Bailey to toss the tie back onto it's razor edge of action.

"I didn't want to be taken off because we were doing so well and I felt things could go right for me," said the Republic of Ireland striker.

Talking about the goal. Stapleton said "I managed to jump off on my right foot. If it had been my left, I wouldn't have made it."

Bobby Charlton who flew in from Brussels to watch the game said : "This was United of the old days. It was a performance full of guts and brimming with skill."

United had fought brilliantly from the start and for long spells it seemed the Czechs would match them kick for kick and goal for goal.

Masterful

Midfield was the sector where United won the battle. Bryan Robson, Ray Wilkin and Arnold Muhren were three masterful musketeers probing in attack and foraging back in spells when Dukla stormed back at United. And Mike Duxbury and Kevin Moran too, deserve praise.

United could easily have been three goals ahead by the 11th minute when Frantisek Stambacher rapped some casual marking and shot Dukla [...] would be

DAILY EXPRESS, September 28, 1983

DUKLA PRAGUE	2

MAN. UTD.	2

1983-84 EUROPEAN CUP WINNERS' CUP, FIRST ROUND, SECOND LEG, DRAW 3-3 ON AGGREGATE, MANCHESTER UNITED WIN ON AWAY GOALS

It's a knock-out!

Stapleton wins the battle for United

From Derek Potter

Frank Stapleton dramatically emerged from this Cup Winners' Cup match of personal anguish last night to head United to spectacular victory.

United won on the away goals rule thanks to Stapleton's spectacular header from Arthur Albiston's cross in the 78th minute.

Hero Stapleton battled through more than half the match with his left ankle heavily strapped. "I got hurt early in the first half and poor Norman Whiteside had to battle on his own."

His brilliantly headed goal made the score 2-1 in the Juliska stadium and 3-2 on aggregate and it seemed United would win a memorable match. But eight minutes from the end the brave Czechs struck back when Vaclav Danek

It's Czech-mate for Reds

MANCHESTER UNITED reached back into history to revive a proud European tradition as they dazzled and dismayed Dukla Prague in Czechoslovakia last night.

The rampant Reds rolled back the years to the old days of foreign glory as they stormed through to the second round of the European Cup Winners' Cup.

For a decade they have struggled with the

beat Gary Bailey to toss the tie back onto its razor edge of action.

"I didn't want to be taken off because we were doing so well and I felt things could go right for me," said the Republic of Ireland striker.

Talking about the goal Stapleton said: "I managed to jump off on my right foot. If it had been my left, I wouldn't have made it."

Bobby Charlton who flew in from Brussels to watch the game said: "This was United of the old days. It was a performance full of guts and brimming with skill."

United had fought brilliantly from the start and for long spells it seemed the Czechs would match them kick for kick and goal for goal.

Masterful

Midfield was the sector where United won the battle. Bryan Robson, Ray Wilkins and Arnold Muhren were three masterful musketeers probing in attack and foraging back in spells when Dukla stormed back at United. And Mike Duxbury and Kevin Moran too, deserve praise.

United could easily have been three goals ahead by the 11th minute when Frantisek Stambacher rapped some casual marking and shot Dukla into what would have been a decisive 2-1 lead against lesser teams.

Whiteside, McQueen and Albiston had all come frustratingly close to giving United the lead before that jolt from Prague.

Then up popped Robson to provide a flash of the flair England lacked at Wembley last week.

Fierce

The England skipper took a 33rd minute pass from Albiston in his stride, glanced at the goal and hammered in a fierce 20-yarder past goalkeeper Karel Stromsik.

The Czechs fought all the way and several recent lapses have raised question marks about the form of United 'keeper Gary Bailey. He removed them last night with three lightning reflex saves to frustrate Dukla.

United manager Ron Atkinson shook hands and embraced every man in his team and singled out Bailey for a special European salute.

"Gary got us off the hook. He was absolutely brilliant, and Norman Whiteside has never played better. Some of the midfield approach work was as good as anything I've seen anywhere.

"It could have been a 7-6 game if all the chances had gone in, but it was an extravaganza just the same."

DAILY MAIL, September 28, 1983

| DUKLA PRAGUE | 2 |
| MAN. UTD. | 2 |

1983-84 EUROPEAN CUP WINNERS' CUP, FIRST ROUND, SECOND LEG, DRAW 3-3 ON AGGREGATE, MANCHESTER UNITED WIN ON AWAY GOALS

By Jeff Powell

Manchester United showed Europe last night that English clubs still have the fight and determination to succeed at the highest level.

United came from a goal down in this Cup-winners' Cup second leg tie to win on the away goal rule.

There were 12 minutes left when Frank Stapleton put United in front for the first time in the first round tie.

The Irish centre forward rose to meet Arthur Albiston's cross and headed United's second goal of the night.

Though Danek equalised for the Czechs two minutes from time, it was not enough to stop United pulling off an unlikely victory after the 1-1 draw at Old Trafford in the first leg.

Bryan Robson had scored a goal from nowhere to rescue his club from the kind of calamity which overtook his country last week.

England's non-playing captain took devastating aim from fully 25 yards to neutralise the early goal which threatened to resolve this tie in favour of Dukla.

Until then, it seemed as if their desperation to recapture Europe by storm would rebound on them again.

Knocked out in the first round of their last

two seasons in Europe, they were in jeopardy once more by the 10th minute.

The opening charge demanded of them by manager Ron Atkinson in the wake of the 1-1 first leg a fortnight ago, was used by the Czechs as the springboard from which they took the lead on the night and on aggregate.

As at Old Trafford, Ladislav Vizek, the brilliant Czech international, was the architect of the opening goal. He organised a stunning counter attack which ended with him holding off Mike Duxbury and playing a pass of exquisite precision which Frantisek Stambacher controlled in a twinkling and rifled past Gary Bailey in a manner befitting an army captain.

United were dumbfounded. Ray Wilkins, the man whose last-minute penalty in Manchester had brought them to Prague on level terms had set up one good chance which Norman Whiteside had wasted with a header too high.

Yet here they were, behind to a goal of disarming brilliance and falling into the English trap of lobbing the ball into the grateful possession of a Continental sweeper.

Premature celebrations were under way in a stadium carved out of a wooded Prague hillside and within which the noise echoed back off the grey, forbidding walls of the Czech Army headquarters dominating one end of the ground.

The Czechs had some reason to believe that their Army side was on its way to an unchallenged triumph over one of the fabled names in European football.

There appeared no real danger as United bore down on their defence in the 33rd minute. Albiston's pass seemed innocuous enough.

But Robson, who had barely put a foot right hitherto, put United level on aggregate and away goals in spectacular fashion.

The match assumed classic proportions in the last half hour. United, visibly maturing into an intelligent European side, set up Stapleton for two more shots which flew close to the Czech goal.

Dukla, still full of craft on the ball and subtle movement off it, had Bailey leaping in alarm as Stambacher volleyed over, and then diving to his left to finger away a stupendous long shot from Rada.

PAGE 46

EUROPEAN SOCCER

Daily Mail, Thursday, October 20, 1983

United's seaside tonic

By PETER JOHNSON

Spartak Varna 1
Manchester United 2

MANCHESTER UNITED dismissed one of Europe's nonentities last night with the kind of professional disdain to suggest they are ready for far better things.

A goal in each undistinguished half of this Cup-winners' Cup second round first leg tie will surely be a guarantee of a place am...

Robson and Graham book an early passage into the last eight

side of the ground, the huge granite monument to Bulgarian-Russian co-operation glowering on the other.

But the match was rarely worthy of such a stage. The match in the ...

stand. And there was nearly as much deference shown on the field, with Spartak's defence tending to stand back with a respect that was frequently disastrous. ... as earl...

skidded inside Gary Bailey's nearside post.

United survived that without any visible sign of shock.

Their football was never classic, but it was totally dominant and virtually untroubled.

They parcelled up the tie two minutes into the second half when, under physical pressure from Whiteside, the Bulgarian defence failed to clear a header from Frank Stapleton and Arthur Graham's control was good enough to give United a decisive second goal.

...e only real cost of this ...

DAILY MAIL, October 20, 1983

JSK SPARTAK VARNA   1

MAN. UTD.   2

1983-84 EUROPEAN CUP WINNERS' CUP, SECOND ROUND, FIRST LEG, MANCHESTER UNITED WIN 2-1

United's seaside tonic

Robson and Graham book an early passage into the last eight

By Peter Johnson

Manchester United dismissed one of Europe's nonentities last night with the kind of professional disdain to suggest they are ready for far better things.

A goal in each undistinguished half of this Cup-winners' Cup second round first leg tie will surely be a guarantee of a place among the elite in the competition's last eight.

Varna, unheard of in Europe for the last 20 years, looked no better than Third Division standard on their own ground.

One suspects they will find Old Trafford a petrifying place on November 22. The setting here in Varna was spectacular enough, the Black Sea sparkling on one side of the ground, the huge granite monument to Bulgarian-Russian co-operation glowering on the other.

But the match was rarely worthy of such a stage. The pitch in the Yuri Gagarin Stadium was fittingly perhaps as uneven as the surface of the moon.

When that did not disrupt United's rhythm the interfering whistle of the West German referee Walter Eschweiler did.

There was never time – even when the Bulgarians were actually level – that these European beginners looked or felt the equals of United.

The 40,000 all-seater crowd had risen in awe as Bobby Charlton took his place in the stand. And there was nearly as much deference shown on the field, with Spartak's defence tending to stand back with a respect that was frequently disastrous.

It was fatal as early as the ninth minute when Ray Wilkins fed through the ball for Norman Whiteside to force goalkeeper Zafirov into parrying his shot as Bryan Robson, thinking quicker than the covering defence, hammered in the rebound.

Varna's equaliser only two minutes later came in the only way you could see the Bulgarians scoring.

Referee Eschweiler gave Dimov two goes at a 20yd. free-kick and his second effort pierced the defensive wall and skidded inside Gary Bailey's nearside post.

United survived that without any visible sign of shock.

Their football was never classic, but it was totally dominant and virtually untroubled.

They parcelled up the tie two minutes into the second half when, under physical pressure from Whiteside, the Bulgarian defence failed to clear a header from Frank Stapleton and Arthur Graham's control was good enough to give United a decisive second goal.

The only real cost of this victory was the booking of Mike Duxbury and Wilkins, who had been booked in the previous tie against Dukla Prague, and automatically misses the return leg.

United manager Ron Atkinson said: 'Everyone in the side carried out their tasks professionally and with the right attitude.

'Varna may not have looked the greatest of sides, but teams play as well as they are allowed to. We showed a lot of capability tonight.'

LEFT: *Over . . . and in*

BELOW: – *Robson scores United's first goal against Spartak Varna in their first leg match*

DAILY EXPRESS, November 3, 1983

MAN. UTD. 2

JSK SPARTAK VARNA 0

1983-84 EUROPEAN CUP WINNERS' CUP, SECOND ROUND, SECOND LEG, MANCHESTER UNITED WIN 4-1 ON AGGREGATE

Let's be Frank!

United fail to live up to the Stapleton magic

By Derek Potter

Manchester United took only 55 seconds to snuff the spark out of Spartak last night.

A goal of thrilling execution and clinical efficiency by Frank Stapleton looked certain to be the foundation of a landslide victory.

Instead, United's meagre goal margin against modest, but never meek, opponents, merely added to the belief that United lack the killer streak.

That charge will not worry Ron Atkinson. United cruised comfortably into the last eight of a European tournament for the first time in 15 years. And they did it without the wide-ranging talents of Ray Wilkins and Arnold Muhren.

Suicidal

After recent premature departures from such scenes that is a success story in itself for the pioneers of European football.

Hawk-eyed Stapleton spotted that goalkeeper Zafirov had wandered off his line as he pounced on to a suicidal back pass.

Stapleton's lob from 25 yards left Zafirov and his team cold and wide open to a chase towards the record 10 goals against Anderlecht in 1956.

But it took Stapleton until the 31st minute to score the second and despite a multitude of alarms and near misses that was how it ended.

Zafirov made several fine saves, but he could not stop Stapleton's header as he dived at a deflected cross by Arthur Graham.

That goal-producing centre came from the right side and seconds earlier the Scot of the sizzling pace produced a similar opening from the opposite flank.

Atkinson wisely gave Mark Dempsey his first taste of senior action and Mark Hughes a veteran of all of 10 minutes joined him later.

What the faithful following of almost 40,000 wanted most, win apart, was a goal from Gordon McQueen.

McQueen made several long raids to a matador's ovation.

Whatever their short-comings, this was still United's seventh consecutive win in a hectic month of league and cup action – with only one goal, scored by Varna in the first leg, scored against them.

And a total of 146,769 have watched their last four home games in the space of only 18 days.

LOOKING BACK
■ WITH SIR MATT BUSBY ■

Sir Matt Busby, architect of Manchester United's proud tradition in Europe, said about the victory against Barcelona:

"The memories came flooding back. The game took me right back to the time we pulled back two goals against Bilbao at Maine Road for that memorable win in our first season in Europe."

DAILY MIRROR, March 8, 1984

FC BARCELONA	2
MAN. UTD.	0

1983-84 EUROPEAN CUP WINNERS' CUP, QUARTER FINAL, FIRST LEG, FC BARCELONA WIN 2-0

Unbelievable

Hogg own goal shaker — then late Rojo blow

By Bob Russell
IN BARCELONA

Manchester United's dazed reaction to a 2-0 defeat here can be summed up in one word: Unbelievable!

They were still reeling from a Rojo rocket shot for Barcelona in the dying seconds.

It leaves United with what manager Ron Atkinson described as "a mountain to climb," in their European Cup-Winners' Cup return leg at Old Trafford in a fortnight's time.

No wonder they were stunned, for United had recovered from a 35th minute tragic Graeme Hogg own goal to turn in a disciplined show which silenced a 90,000 Nou Camp Stadium crowd.

Atkinson could only gasp: "It's an incredible situation when you look at the way we played." But he immediately insisted: "I still believe we can beat them and go through to the semi-finals."

Gambled

The United boss was also quick to come to the defence of Hogg, the 19-year-old Aberdonian he had gambled on playing in preference to Paul McGrath.

"We're not blaming him for what happened tonight," said Atkinson.

"Kevin Moran was in a position to clear if Graeme had left it, but that's by the way now. Apart from that, the lad did well."

A forlorn Hogg, who lashed a Carrasco cross high into his own net under pressure, said: "I couldn't believe it when it finished up in the back of the net.

"But there was nothing much else I could have done in the circumstances."

Skipper Bryan Robson joined in the "we can't believe it" chorus saying: "It just wasn't our night. Having seen Barcelona with things going for them, we know we are capable of getting through, despite their two-goal lead."

Robson heads United's first goal in their second leg match against Barcelona . . .

Whiteside rises above the Barcelona defence to try a header

ABOVE: *Wilkins (left) takes on Maradona in United's second leg mach against Barcelona*

THE SUN, March 22, 1984

MAN. UTD.	3
BARCELONA	0

1983-84 EUROPEAN CUP WINNERS' CUP, QUARTER FINAL, SECOND LEG, MANCHESTER UNITED WIN 3-2 ON AGGREGATE

Robson glory

Two-goal Bryan sinks Spaniards

By Peter Fitton

Bryan Robson kept his goal vow as Manchester United went on a spectacular rampage in Europe.

The United skipper was heartbroken after his blunders in the Cup Winners' Cup first leg in Barcelona two weeks ago.

And immediately he promised – exclusively in The Sun – that the only way he could repay his bitterly disappointed team mates was with two goals in the return.

His vengeance came sweetly in a packed out Old Trafford stadium when he plundered a brave 50th minute equaliser to add to his first half opener.

Flick

Spanish international Alonso's hastily hit back pass put Barcelona in trouble and in turn Norman Whiteside, Remi Moses and Ray Wilkins added to the panic.

But there was no escape from the prowling Robson as he stabbed the loose ball beneath keeper Urruti.

He might easily have had a hat-trick – but it was Frank Stapleton who put United ahead on aggregate in the 52nd minute after United had waited 20 years to turn round a two-goal deficit.

Raiding full-back Arthur Albiston's cross was directed back by Whiteside and Stapleton jubilantly smashed in United's third goal.

Atkinson had demanded football patience with a punch in United's attempt to shatter the odds stacked against them.

And that's precisely what he got from Robson, the skipper who has carried a goal pledge for a fortnight since his disastrous first leg goal misses.

He struck with the treasured early goal after 22 minutes as United finally added a cutting edge to their pressure.

Dutchman Muhren helped to win a crucial corner that Wilkins dipped into the near post.

A flick of Whiteside's head beat the defenders and there was Robson stooping low to score with a bullet header.

But it wasn't easy exposing gaps in a Barcelona defence that was always alert to triggering the offside trap.

The Spaniards were guilty of just one moment of panic and it might have brought Whiteside the breakthrough after 15 minutes.

A collective blunder by keeper Urruti and the experienced Alesance surrendered the chance. Whiteside flung out a boot but the ball spiralled on top of the bar.

Apart from that the nearest United came to a goal was when Stapleton set up Wilkins for a volley.

LEFT: *Duxbury (right) goes past Moratalla*

LEFT: *Robson (left) is onto Schuster*

BELOW: *Moses (left) goes in to challenge Maradona*

RIGHT: *Wilkins weaving his way between Maradona (left) and Victor (No 5), watched by Muhren*

THE DAILY TELEGRAPH, March 22, 1984

MAN UTD   3

FC BARCELONA   0

1983-84 EUROPEAN CUP WINNERS' CUP, QUARTER
FINAL, SECOND LEG, MANCHESTER UNITED WIN 3-2
ON AGGREGATE

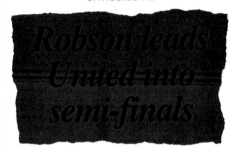

*Robson leads
United into
semi-finals*

By Denis Lowe

Manchester United, on a memorable night
reminiscent of old-time European
occasions at Old Trafford, produced a
marvellous second-leg performance in the Cup
Winners' Cup to overhaul Barcelona's two-goal
lead and reach their first European semi-final
for 15 years.

A full house of 58,350 saw United go
through with two well-taken goals from Bryan
Robson and another coolly driven home by
Frank Stapleton.

So United, deserved 3-2 aggregate victors,
achieved what Ron Atkinson described as the
club's finest team result in his time as manager
and are set for a storming finish to a season in
which they are also contesting the Football
League Championship with Liverpool.

Atkinson danced a jig of delight on the
touchline and hundreds of followers celebrated
on the pitch after this notable victory – only
the third time in their 12 seasons of Continental competition that United have wiped out a
two-goal deficit from the first leg.

They were on top for most of an open,
flowing match which was well controlled by
the Italian referee, Paolo Casarin, and in which
Diego Maradona, Barcelona's Argentine star,
still seemed to be suffering from a recent thigh
injury. Apart from an occasional flourish, he
made little impact.

Sweeping moves

Robson and Wilkins, skilful, decisive and full of
ideas in midfield, led the charge in a splendid
all-round team performance, and the front
runners, Stapleton and Whiteside, worked
tirelessly against a rugged defence which often
relied on the off-side trap.

Other telling contributions came from
Moses, who often clamped down on
Maradona's wiles, and Albiston, and Duxbury,
the over-lapping full-backs, while Moran and
Hogg gave away little in defence and Bailey
made important saves from Julio Alberto,
Maradona and Victor.

United had to be both positive and patient in
the opening stages, when Whiteside was desperately close with an astute lob, but the early
goal they wanted came in the 22nd minute
after the roving Stapleton had forced a corner
on the left.

Wilkins took it, curling the ball in, Whiteside
nodded on and Robson pounced to head past
Urruti.

Wilkins and Marcos were off target with
reasonable chances at either end before
United, full of running and application, launched
themselves into a series of sweeping attacks
which brought goals in the 50th and 52nd
minutes.

Alonso's back pass first put Barcelona in
trouble. Moses won possession to centre from
the right and after Urruti had failed to hold a
shot from Wilkins, Robson scored his second
goal from close range. It was the 15th of the
season for United's captain and his fourth in
European games.

Backed to the full by the capacity crowd,
who paid record club receipts of £180,000,
United once more stunned the Spanish team
two minutes later. Whiteside, causing all kinds
of problems through his aerial power, nodded
Albiston's cross back to the near post where
Stapleton drove powerfully past Urruti. Barcelona looked in vain for an offside flag.

Barcelona replaced Alonso with Clos, who
promptly put wide a half chance, and Hughes
took over from Whiteside as United's substitute.

Robson headed over with a fine chance of a
hat-trick goal.

Schuster, whose skilful control pushed Barcelona forward, and Moratella were booked
for fouls on Wilkins and Hughes during a brief
flash of Spanish temper, and United needed to
keep calm at the back as Barcelona tried
desperately to rally in the last 15 minutes.

Schuster went close with an angled drive,
and Manchester followers had a scare as
Gerardo went down in the box under a
challenge by Hughes. The referee, though,
waved aside the penalty appeal, and United
were assured of their seventh European semi-
final when Bailey rose to hold Maradona's free-
kick in the final minute.

34 *The Daily Telegraph, Thursday, March 22, 1984*

· *All six British clubs stay on the Eur*

ROBSON LEADS
UNITED INTO
SEMI-FINALS

By DENIS LOWE

Manchester Utd ..: 3   Barcelona ... 0
(United win 3—2 on aggregate)

MANCHESTER UNITED, on a memorable
night reminiscent of old-time European
occasions at Old Trafford, produced a
marvellous second-leg performance in the
Cup Winners' Cup to overhaul Barcelona's
two-goal lead and reach their first European
semi-final for 15 years.

A full house of 58,350 saw United go
through with two well-taken goals from Bryan
Robson and another coolly driven home
by Frank Stapleton.

So United, deserved 3—2
aggregate victors, achieved
what Ron Atkinson described
as the club's finest team
result in his time as manager
and are set for a storming
finish to a season in which
they are also contesting the
Football League Champion-
ship with Liverpool.

Atkinson danced a jig of
delight on the touchline and
hundreds of followers celebrated on the pitch after this
... third

when Whiteside was desperately
close with an astute lob, but the
early goal they wanted came in
the 22nd minute after the roving
Stapleton had forced a corner on
the left.

Wilkins took it, curling the ball
in, Whiteside nodded on and
Robson pounced to head past
Urruti.

Wilkins and Marcos were off
target with reasonable chances
at either end before United, full
of running and application,
launched themselves into a series
of sweeping attacks which brought
goals in the 50th and 52nd
minutes.

Alonso's back pass first put
Barcelona in ... Moses won

Bryan Robson dives to head past goalkeeper Uritti and put Manchester United
1—0 ahead against Barcelona.

**ATKINSON'S
'PROUDEST
MOMENT'**

RON ATKINSON, a jubilant
Manchester United manager,
looked back on "a great win
for the club, and one which
I will savour, like the rest of
the team, for a long, long
time to come."

Atkinson, who regarded the
victory as the "proudest

Forest go through
with penalty

By DONALD SAUNDERS in Graz, Austria

Sturm Graz 1   Nottingham Forest ... 1
(Aggregate: 1—2 after extra time)

NOTTINGHAM FOREST moved breathlessly into th
UEFA semi-finals, at the Liebenau National Stadiu
last night, but only after suffering a nast

LEFT: Robson (left) and Schuster

Bryan Robson

LOOKING BACK WITH BRYAN ROBSON

The fans carried Bryan Robson off shoulder high after his match-winning performance against Barcelona in the European Cup Winners Cup.

The Manchester United captain had scored twice in a 3-0 victory, inspiring a remarkable revival after looking dead and buried with a 2-0 defeat in the first leg in Spain.

Robson played like a man with a cause . . . as he reveals now: "I felt I was to blame for coming home two goals down from the first leg in the Nou Camp stadium.

"Big games are all about putting the ball into the back of the net and a player of my experience should have done just that.

"I had two glorious chances and missed them both.

"The first was very early on. I tried to chip over the goalkeeper in a situation which should have seen me give him no chance.

"As it was he tipped the ball over the bar. Then later in the game I should have put a shot away instead of trying to reach Mark Hughes with a pass.

"If we are talking about standards then I let my self and everyone else down. I was more to blame for the defeat than Graeme Hogg who was just unfortunate with his own-goal.

"At least we carved out some chances which was on the credit side and gave us hope for the second leg. It showed that Barcelona were at least vulnerable and that under pressure they might crack."

The return leg did indeed see the Spaniards crack as Robson launched himself into a personal crusade to make amends for what he considered to be lapses on his part.

He struck after 23 minutes following a corner kick and scored his 17th goal of the season hunting in the goalmouth again five minutes after the interval.

"After missing the chances in Barcelona I said that I owed the lads something, and I was just delighted that I did it for them at Old Trafford," he said.

The skipper's performance on the European stage made him an even more attractive target for foreign clubs with the Italians particularly interested.

United slapped what they considered to be a prohibitive transfer fee of £3m on him but speculation about a move abroad was still rife during the summer.

Much to the satisfaction of the supporters, all was resolved in the October of the following season when club and player agreed a new seven-year contract.

Chairman Martin Edwards said at the time: "The length and worth of the contract is a record in Britain. At the same time there is an element of personal financial sacrifice by the player who could have kept himself available for a move to Italy at a later stage.

"We never really wanted to sell him during the summer and we thought the £3m price tag would frighten people off. We came in for quite a lot of hammer but we hope this contract makes it clear that we want to keep our captain and most influential player.

"Bryan has made it just as clear that money is not everything to him either. It's a good contract but modest compared with Italian money. I cannot commend his attitude enough and we are delighted to have him for the next seven years."

THE GUARDIAN, April 11, 1984

MAN. UTD.	1
JUVENTUS TURIN	1

1983-84 EUROPEAN CUP WINNERS' CUP, SEMI-FINAL, FIRST LEG, DRAW 1-1

Davies back in style

By David Lacey

Manchester United's weakened team preserved their unbeaten home record in Europe last night when they drew 1-1 with Juventus in the opening leg of their Cup Winners' Cup semi-final. But clearly United will do well to survive now and the shot from Stapleton which hit the bar in the second half when he ought to have scored may prove costly.

With Wilkins suspended, Muhren unfit and Robson never likely to play after straining a hamstring in training, United could hardly have been more poorly equipped to stop Juventus and Platini running the game. Gidman, at right-back, McGrath, at centre-back and Graham, at winger filled the vacancies.

United had to attack and their opening lacked nothing in determination, with Gidman quick to advance down the right flank in his old manner. But before United had a real chance to establish any sort of pattern they lost Gidman with the week's fashionable injury, another pulled hamstring.

This brought Davies, the young Welsh winger, back into the senior team for the first time since last year's FA Cup final. Since then injuries had reduced his activities to two full games in the reserves. It was hardly the stuff to inspire hope in United's chances and Juventus belaboured the point by taking the lead on the quarter-hour.

Boniek, his pace always a threat, broke away with United committed to attack and ran at a square defence. The Pole slipped the ball inside to Rossi whose shot appeared to take a deflection off Hogg, leaving Bailey flat-footed and helpless to prevent a goal.

Old Trafford roared its optimism as Stapleton met a centre from Graham by laying a low pass back to the incoming McGrath but he was tackled as he shot and nothing came of the corner. A minute earlier Stapleton had dived hopefully over Gentile's lunging foot but a penalty was out of the question.

Juventus were defending with their usual skilful tenacity but 10 minutes before half-time Tacconi proved himself no Zoff and United drew level. Stapleton challenged the goalkeeper for a long high ball from Albiston on the left and Tacconi never looked like getting it. After the ball had come down, Whiteside shot against the 'keeper before Davies gained possession and, showing admirable calm, found the empty net.

BELOW: *Tacconi, the Juventus 'keeper, holds the ball as United's McGrath rushes in*

Platini (far right) on the move

ABOVE: *Moses (right) goes after Rossi of Juventus in their first leg match*

THE GUARDIAN, April 25, 1984

JUVENTUS TURIN 2

MAN. UTD. 1

1983-84 EUROPEAN CUP WINNERS' CUP, SEMI-FINAL,
SECOND LEG, JUVENTUS TURIN WIN 3-2 ON
AGGREGATE

Platini and Rossi floor courageous United

By David Lacey

The strength of purpose and tenacity of spirit which had preserved Manchester United's unbeaten home record in Europe a fortnight earlier just failed to keep them in the Cup Winners' Cup last night. A goal by Paolo Rossi in the final minute of an entertaining and at times remarkable match in Turin gave Juventus the 2-1 victory which took them to their first final in this competition.

After Whiteside, who had replaced Stapleton just past the hour, brought the scores level United, refusing to concede the mastery of Platini, seemed capable not only of forcing the extra half-hour but achieving what would have been an astonishing, not to say illogical win.

In the end, however, they had to drag themselves off the field amid all the fireworks and furore knowing that a jubilant Liverpool still hold a two point lead in the First Division and that for Old Trafford the season's ambitions are fading fast.

Courageously though United played, it has to be said that if Rossi had found his finishing touch earlier, and had Bailey not made a series of excellent saves, Juventus and their supporters would have been spared a nerve racked final 20 minutes.

For two thirds of the game Platini's vision and superbly struck passes looked sufficent to ensure Juventus a place in the final in Basle no matter how doggedly the opposition carried the play back towards the Italian goal.

There were periods when Platini seemed to be playing football in a different atmospheric layer from the rest. Throughout the match Wilkins sprayed passes to left and right opening up the wings for United with another busily inventive performance. But when Platini moved forward and aimed long, curling passes over defenders' heads and directly into the paths of Boniek or Rossi, the game took on a different dimension.

BELOW: *Boniek beats Bailey for Juventus' first goal in their second leg match against United in Turin*

ABOVE: *Rossi scores the second goal for Juventus*

In the continued absence of Robson and Muhren, United were as badly equipped as ever to confront the Frenchman's genius. Until they forced their way back into the game Robson's capacity to drive wedges into the heart of a disciplined defence and steal through on blind side runs was badly missed.

While Duxbury, Albiston and Graham often found space on the wings, too many of their crosses lacked the quality to worry either the Juventus goalkeeper or the tall Brio who dealt as effectively with Stapleton as he had with Wythe of Aston Villa in the European Cup last season.

Ron Atkinson, the Manchester United manager, had caused a few eyebrows to be raised by keeping Hughes in his attack and starting the game with Whiteside on the bench. In fact the young Welsh player gave an outwardly composed performance and came close to scoring in the eighth minute when Tacconi could only push the ball out. McGrath was ready for the rebound but as he shot Tardelli deflected the ball to safety.

This was the sort of start United had wanted but by the quarter hour the artificial fog created by scores of coloured flares welcoming the Juventus players, had lifted, reality had descended and Manchester United were a goal down.

In the 13th minute Bailey brought off the first of his outstanding saves as he blocked a full blooded effort from Rossi after Moran had allowed Platini's lob to reach Italy's hero of the last World Cup. But in the next instant Platini's penetrating through pass sent Boniek clear and the Pole withstood Albiston's challenge before slipping the ball past the advancing goalkeeper.

Juventus had taken the lead a couple of minutes earlier than they had done at Old Trafford and such was the influence of Platini that it did not seem likely they would stop there. Platini suffered an elbow in the face from Moran and a late tackle for which Moses was cautioned, but in no way was his creative appetite weakened.

For a time Bailey stood alone between Juventus and an emphatic victory. And when Whiteside came on for Stapleton, who had hurt an ankle in the first half, in the 63rd minute the change seemed no more than a gesture. But in the 70th minute Graham played the ball to McGrath, who was given a surprising amount of room to turn and shoot. The ball was blocked, but found its way to Whiteside, who scored with gusto.

As Bailey held one of Platini's canny free-kicks, later saving a thunderous shot from Boniek, so United's confidence improved. Juventus, with Prandelli on for the injured Tardelli, suddenly looked vulnerable and fretful.

But in the last minute, following a free-kick just outside the penalty area, Scirea held the ball under pressure and then tried a shot which hit Boniek, the ball rolled straight into the stride of Rossi and he won the match for Juventus with a low shot past Bailey's left hand.

Videoton

Djurgardens

Vase from Ferencvaros

Anderlecht

Crystal glass from Barcelona

The lion of Sporting Lisbon

Ship from FC Porto

Porcelain couple from Valencia

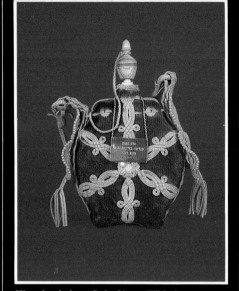

Waterbottle from Raba Vasas ETO Gyor

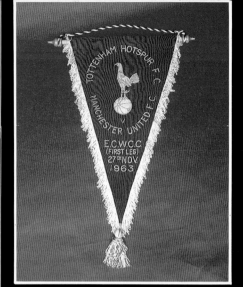

Tottenham Hotspur

Spartak Varna

Statuette from Borussia Dortmund

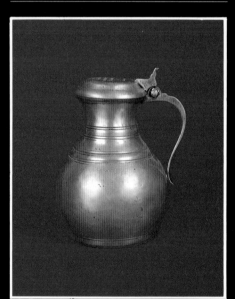

A pewter gift from St Etienne

A carving in coal from Gornik Zabrze

Widzew Lodz

THE PRIDE GUYS!

Rossi shatters dream but Reds were magic

By DAVID MEEK

BITTERLY disappointed of course — but Manchester United can bow out of Europe with their heads held high.

The Reds let no one down against Juventus and came ever so close to climbing the mountain demanded of them in Turin last night.

The Italians' winning goal did not come until 30 seconds from the end, a cruel way to go after so many brave performances and a spirited display against all the odds.

Difficult

A 1-1 draw at Old Trafford in the first leg was always going to make the return difficult in Italy.

And as the red flames of the flares that greeted the arrival of the teams on the pitch obliterated one end of the Stadio Communale with smoke, no one doubted the enormity of United's task.

The din of the fireworks and a near-hysterical Italian crowd sensing victory in their team's favour was nerve-numbing.

Juventus duly got their second-leg 2-1 win, but they

MANCHESTER EVENING NEWS,
April 25, 1984

JUVENTUS TURIN	2
MAN. UTD.	1

1983-84 EUROPEAN CUP WINNERS' CUP, SEMI-FINAL, SECOND LEG, JUVENTUS TURIN WIN 3-2 ON AGGREGATE

The Pride Guys!

Rossi shatters dream but Reds were magic

By David Meek

SO CLOSE — Paul McGrath fires in a shot.

Bitterly disappointed of course — but Manchester United can bow out of Europe with their heads held high.

The Reds let no one down against Juventus and came ever so close to climbing the mountain demanded of them in Turin last night.

The Italians' winning goal did not come until 30 seconds from the end, a cruel way to go after so many brave performances and a spirited display against all the odds.

Difficult

A 1-1 draw at Old Trafford in the first leg was always going to make the return difficult in Italy.

And as the red flames of the flares that greeted the arrival of the teams on the pitch obliterated one end of the Stadio Communale with smoke, no one doubted the enormity of United's task.

The din of the fireworks and a near-hysterical Italian crowd sensing victory in their team's favour was nerve-numbing.

Juventus duly got their second-leg 2-1 win, but they had to wait until those last bitter seconds and, ironically, a stage of the game when United were actually looking the more likely to score.

The killer goal came from ace marksman Paolo Rossi but only with the help of a deflec-

tion — just like the one which lay behind his goal in Manchester when the real damage to United's cause was done.

The Italian sharp-shooter pounced to rip the ball past Gary Bailey only after Zbigniew Boniek's blocked shot had spun fortuitously in his path.

It was a particularly savage blow for Bailey who played the game of his life to keep his team in the hunt right to the end.

Formidable

His brave saves at the feet of players like Rossi and Boniek summed up the character that saw United coolly take the game to their opponents right from the start in a bold bid for the early goal they so desperately needed.

But Juventus are a formidable team, almost beautiful on the break and so deadly.

After 15 minutes, around the time of Rossi's breakaway goal at Old Trafford, Michel Platini suddenly set Boniek accelerating through the middle with a well judged pass.

The Pole was too fast to catch and he clinically put Juventus into the lead.

But just as they did in Manchester, United came back to equalise — and not many teams do that against Juventus.

Unexpected

Norman Whiteside stunned and even silenced the home fans soon after coming on as substitute for the injured Frank Stapleton, who twisted his ankle in the first half and had to call it a day in the 63rd minute.

Paul McGrath superbly opened up the Italian defence with an unexpected twist for Whiteside to smash the equaliser home.

The goal gave the Reds an edge which saw them play some of their best football.

Ray Wilkins was clever and cool throughout the match and gave a team again hit by injuries and missing Bryan Robson, a positive approach from start to finish.

Mark Hughes more than justified his promotion and took instantly to the big game atmosphere. He was shooting into the side-netting after only eight minutes and matched the Italians for neat footwork and a willingness to work the ball.

United's other recent newcomer, McGrath, also responded to the occasion with a fine performance.

It was super game of football and if victory went narrowly to Juventus, the pride and courage can certainly go to Manchester United.

LOOKING BACK WITH RON ATKINSON

Ron Atkinson had five and a half years as manager of Manchester United.

He departed, like his four immediate predecessors, because his team had peaked and he had run out of time, with the League championship looking as elusive as ever.

His record was undoubtedly good . . . never finishing out of the top four and with three Wembley Cup finals.

There were also two exciting seasons in Europe to savour, playing in the Cup Winners Cup in season 1983-84 and the UEFA Cup the following year.

Times had been lean for United in European football and Ron Atkinson can justifiably claim to have restored the tradition for the great occasion in Continental combat.

As he says now: "Europe is a stimulating scene for the big clubs. In the week leading up to a European tie, there is a buzz about the place, and I think it is the same for the fans.

"If for nothing else, I think the 1983-84 season will be long remembered for the great joy and excitement generated by titanic tussles against the cream of European football.

"We played three quality sides in what was a vintage year in the European Cup Winners Cup. Some seasons you get teams which have just got lucky in their domestic Cup competitions.

"But this was a special season, and one of the rare occasions when the Cup Winners tournament was more glamorous than the European Cup.

"We opened against the well-disciplined Dukla Prague team from Czechoslovakia and strangely enough it was our weakest performance. Perhaps we had been too long out of Europe and were nervous.

"I know we only escaped defeat in the first leg at Old Trafford by the skin of our teeth. Ray Wilkins got a late penalty for a 1-1 draw and the Czechs went home confident they would win in Prague.

"Things certainly didn't look very good for us in the second leg when Dukla went ahead again after only 10 minutes.

"But all credit to the character of our players who promptly produced the kind of qualities which were to serve us well for two seasons in Europe.

"They proved themselves to be resilient and courageous, producing probably the best exhibition of football I have seen from an English club playing away from home.

"Goals from Bryan Robson and Norman Whiteside put us in front only for Dukla to respond with an equaliser. Gary Bailey pulled off a superb save in the closing seconds and we

went through on the rule that away goals count double in the event of an aggregate draw.

"We won through comfortably against the Bulgarians, Spartak Varna, in the next round, winning 2-1 away and 2-0 at Old Trafford, to set the stage for a clash against Barcelona.

"I went to watch Barcelona in the Spanish League and came back convinced we could beat them provided we hit top form.

"I must confess I did not feel quite so confident when we lost the first leg 2-0 in the Nou Camp Stadium. Not a lot went right for us. Bryan Robson created a scoring opportunity for himself in the opening minutes through brilliant individual play, but his chip went wide.

"We paid for the miss when Graeme Hogg, performing well on his European debut in the back four, inadvertently put through his own goal trying to deal with a fast cross from Carrasco.

"Barcelona grabbed their second goal with almost the last kick of the match and it was clear that only a superhuman effort could rescue us.

"Happily we were going well on the domestic front. We had just comprehensively beaten Arsenal 4-0 to go top of the First Division and we had Whiteside back in action for the second leg.

"The fans were on song as well. I shall never forget that night with a 58,000 crowd chanting and roaring their encouragement.

"Even so, Barcelona, who of course included the fabulous Diego Maradona, were quite composed and monopolised the early play with well-drilled possession.

We pegged away and got our break-through from a 25th minute corner. Reports from abroad had led me to believe that the Spaniards had been worried about our set-piece plays, and Ray Wilkins exploited their fear with a swinging kick touched on by Graeme Hogg for Bryan Robson to score with a diving header, bravely ignoring the flying boots.

"There was no holding the crowd, nor the players. Robson smashed in a second goal after their goalkeeper had failed to hold a Wilkins shot and within minutes Whiteside had headed a ball down for Frank Stapleton to score.

"It was 3-0 on the night and 3-2 on aggregate. What a turn-round and what an anxious, nail-biting time. Barcelona knew that they only had to score once to win on the away-goals rule, and they showed their class as they opened up to play some fine football.

"They threatened to cut us to pieces and the last 15 minutes seemed an eternity. We were lucky to escape a penalty when Mark Hughes fouled Alonso, but the Italian referee must have

been unsighted.

"Gary Bailey stopped shots from all angles and when the final whistle blew there was a standing ovation for the team to greet a wonderful performance.

"Bobby Charlton, a hero in United's glory nights in Europe in the Sixties and now a director of the club, danced with delight on his seat in the stands!

"The atmosphere was just as electric when Juventus arrived for the first leg of the semi-final with all their stars who had helped Italy win the World Cup, plus Michel Platini and Zbigniew Boniek.

"We were depleted with Bryan Robson and Arnold Muhren injured, and Ray Wilkins suspended. Our midfield had to be hastily assembled round Remi Moses with John Gidman returning after a three-month absence with injury and another defender, Paul McGrath, also switched to the midde of the park.

"I could only say to the lads . . . 'run your guts out and fight for every ball, and then it might just happen for us.'

"Juventus scored after quarter of an hour through Paolo Rossi, a fortunate goal for them with a deflection off Graeme Hogg beating Gary Bailey. Our substitute, Alan Davies, got us an equaliser for a 1-1 result which was never really enough.

"Over there in Italy against a background of smoke bombs and firecrackers, Boniek gave Juventus another early lead. Norman Whiteside came on as substitute to reveal his flair for scoring on the big occasion by grabbing an equaliser.

"It was the first goal the Italians had conceded on their own ground in the competition, and I thought that at that stage we were stronger and fitter. If we had made it to extra time, I think we would have rushed them off their feet.

"But with only a minute to go of normal time, Rossi started a run to finish beautifully and show why he is rated one of the most accomplished goal scorers in the world.

"Juventus went on to win the Cup by beating Porto in the final. I still think that if we had had a full squad for the two legs it would have been us in the final.

"We had certainly gone close and I take great personal satisfaction from restoring the good old days to Manchester United, especially when we put Barcelona to flight.

"I doubt if anything will ever outshine that famous victory which surpassed anything I have experienced in the game. It was even better than winning the F A Cup at Wembley!"

Ray Wilkins

■ LOOKING BACK WITH RAY WILKINS ■

Although Manchester United's quest for European glory in season 1983-84 ended with a 2-1 defeat against Juventus in the Stadio Communale, there was no disgrace.

Goalkeeper Gary Bailey played the game of his life before conceding Paolo Rossi's last-minute winner.

Ray Wilkins, skipper on the night, recalls: "Our 'keeper was fantastic.

"He has had criticism from time to time, especially about one or two moments in big games.

"But his concentration, anticipation and performance in Turin at a game played in a sensational atmosphere were marvellous.

"He deserves a lot of credit and it was certainly no fault of his that we ended up with a 2-1 defeat.

"I thought the difference between the two teams on the night was the one moment of brilliance from Platini when he put Boniek through for their first goal.

"The man is a genius."

THE GUARDIAN, September 20, 1984

MAN. UTD.	3
RABA ETO GYOR	0

1984-85 UEFA CUP, FIRST ROUND, FIRST LEG, MANCHESTER UNITED WIN 3-0

Muhren devours goulash

By Ian Ridley

The Hungarians of Raba Eto Gyor were unable to turn tie or tide at Old Trafford last night, as Manchester United gave another fluid performance which yielded three goals that should make the return leg of the UEFA Cup first round match a formality.

An exquisite performance in midfield by Arnold Muhren, a late replacement for the injured Gordon Strachan, matched by Mark Hughes's sharp display up front, were the jewels in United's crown, one of thorns as far as the visitors were concerned. Each scored well-worked goals, each making one for the other, to add to Bryan Robson's expertly-taken first.

The attendance of 32,537 was low by Old Trafford standards, substantiating the impression that the real business comes on Saturday, when Liverpool visit. The touts outside the ground were even selling tickets for that match rather than last night's.

United, though, gave no impression that they were contemplating ending their un-beaten run, now seven games, the last three with 11 goals scored and one conceded.

After an early period of adjustment to Muhren's presence, United took a 17th-minute lead which began a period of flowing football that Old Trafford has become used to and is becoming used to again.

The Hungarian defence made a goulash of Duxbury's low cross from the right, allowing Robson, with a timely late run, to steer the ball wide of Kovacs from 10 yards.

The second came in the 38th minute, when Hughes played a superb through-pass into the path of Muhren and the Dutchman calmly stroked the ball past Kovacs. It should have been the second of a series but United had to be content with Hughes's far post header from Muhren's delightful curling chip from the left in the 76th minute.

Hughes and his partner up front, Whiteside, were marked man for man with Raba employing a sweeper in Judik but the Welshman and the Ulsterman revelled in it demonstrating the maturity that is coming with international experience. One turn and run by Hughes, which ended with a booking for Judik, was a particular delight.

Raba, runners-up in last season's bribe-ridden Hungarian League after chasing a hat trick of titles, wove some neat midfield patterns but threatened Bailey only when Preszeller shot from 20 yards, and Kurucz headed over the bar. Their neat individual technique, exemplified by Kurucz and their captain Hannich, in midfield, was not matched by a collective determination.

United in contrast created an abundance of chances with Robson's stab, Whiteside's header and Hughes's drive seeming likely to find the net and give the scoreline a more realistic look.

"A good, sound, all-round performance," purred the United manager Ron Atkinson afterwards. It was more than that.

DAILY MAIL, September 20, 1984

MAN. UTD.	3
RABA ETO GYOR	0

1984-85 UEFA CUP, FIRST ROUND, FIRST LEG, MANCHESTER UNITED WIN 3-0

Hero for one night

By Peter Johnson

Dutchman Arnold Muhren, scorer of one goal and creator of another in Manchester United's 3-0 UEFA Cup victory last night, admitted afterwards that he expects to be immediately dropped.

Muhren played his first senior game of the season against the Hungarians of Raba Gyor only because £500,000 signing Gordon Strachan cried off with an ankle injury only hours before the first round tie at Old Trafford.

Miracle

And the 33-year-old midfield man said: 'Even if I did play pretty well tonight I know I'm not sure to keep my place against Liverpool on Saturday. In fact I will be surprised if Gordon is not back in the side.

'If that happens I must accept it. It's the risk you take when you play for a club of this size. Obviously I'm not happy at the prospect of not being in the team – how could I be?

'But the manager has spent £2 million on players during the close season and there would have been no point in spending all that money if he had no intention of playing them.

It's just unfortunate for me that two of them are wide players.'

Muhren's goal in the 38th minute followed one by skipper Bryan Robson 20 minutes earlier. Muhren's pass provided Mark Hughes with the third in the 75th minute.

Though the victory will send United to Hungary in two weeks' time, manager Ron Atkinson cautioned: 'Remember that United once went away with a four-goal lead and lost. We have a useful advantage, but there is still some planning to be done.

'What worried us most tonight was that, in front of a much smaller than average crowd – 32,537 – the atmosphere seemed a bit unreal.

'We were anxious in case some of the players might get lulled into feeling it was too easy, too much like a testimonial. But in the end they kept their discipline well.'

Hero for one night

DUTCHMAN Arnold Muhren, scorer of one goal and creator of another in Manchester United's 3—0 UEFA Cup victory last night, admitted afterwards that he expects to be immediately dropped.

Muhren played his first senior gameo of the season against the Hungarians of Raba Gyor only because £500,000 signing Gordon Strachan cried off with an ankle injury only hours before the first round tie at Old Trafford.

By PETER JOHNSON

Miracle

And the 33 year

£2 million on players during the close season and there would have been no point in spending all that money if he had no intention of playing them. It's just unfortunate for me that two of them are wide players.'

Muhren's goal in the 38th minute followed one by skipper Bryan Robson 20 minutes earlier. Muhren's pass provided Mark Hughes with the third in the 75th minute.

'Thou'

lulled into feeling it was too easy, too much like a testimonial. But in the end they kept their discipline well.'

United, of course, expect to go through, but Wrexham enter the rarified atmosphere of the Estadio das Antas next month sincerely believing in a football miracle.

Delighted

They will step on to Portuguese soil still bearing the anonymity of Fourth Division players but their hearts beating proudly after a historic

Brazil ends the agony!

ALWAYS BEST FOR THE LATE, LAT

| Raba Gyor | 2 |
| Man. U. | 2 |

(Agg: 2—5)

ALAN BRAZIL, the £625,000 ex-Spurs and Ipswich hot-shot, finally broke the ice with Manchester United here tonight.

After nine barren games the Scottish star struck it good after ten minutes of this not-so-easy UEFA Cup second round second leg.

BOB RUSSELL in Hungary

Constantin gave Raba a dubious penalty after a hard shot from striker Szarbo had struck Remi Moses on the arm.

Justice was done when Bailey first blocked international star Hannich's spot-kick and then winger Vagi's follow-up shot.

Raba were virtually dead and buried when Arnold Muhren had the chance to completely finish them after 49 minutes.

But Kovacs again responded brilliantly, blocking a full-blooded 10-yard angled drive after first stopping a...

the archives to regenerate Hungarian enthusiasm and Raba produced one in 51 minutes. There was no apparent danger when Premslier unleashed a 20-yard drive that penetrated the top corner with Bailey beaten.

Eight minutes later came a second magnificent strike from the Hungarians. This time it was crowd idol Hannich who turned so unexpectedly to ride a half-chance through a stable defence and a stricken keeper from 8 yards.

Raba needed five home goals to win the tie but the pressure was suddenly on United.

The situation changed again in 74 minutes when Muhren hit back from the penalty spot after defend-

DAILY MIRROR, October 4, 1984

| RABA ETO GYOR | 2 |
| MAN. UTD. | 2 |

1984-85 UEFA CUP, FIRST ROUND, SECOND LEG,
MANCHESTER UNITED WIN 5-2 ON AGGREGATE

Brazil ends the agony!

By Bob Russell
IN HUNGARY

Alan Brazil, the £625,000 ex-Spurs and Ipswich hot-shot, finally broke the ice with Manchester United here tonight.

After nine barren games the Scottish star struck it good after ten minutes of this not-so-easy UEFA Cup first round second leg.

Despite Brazil's relief United were strangely uncomfortable against the team they beat so smoothly at Old Trafford.

For a team with everything apparently going for them there was surprisingly early uncertainty about United.

Constantin gave Raba a dubious penalty after a hard shot from striker Szarbo had struck Remi Moses on the arm.

Justice was done when Bailey first blocked international star Hannich's spot-kick and then winger Vagi's follow-up shot.

Raba were virtually dead and buried when Arnold Muhren had the chance to completely finish them after 49 minutes.

But Kovacs again responded brilliantly, blocking a full-blooded 10-yard angled drive after first stopping a Mark Hughes blockbuster.

It needed a goal from the archives to regenerate Hungarian enthusiasm and Raba produced one in 51 minutes. There was no

ABOVE: *Moran of Manchester United with a shot in the second leg match against Raba Vasas ETO Gyor in Hungary*

LEFT: *Muhren's penalty goes in for United's second goal*

apparent danger when Preszeller unleashed a 20-yard drive that penetrated the top corner with Bailey beaten.

Eight minutes later came a second magnificent strike from the Hungarians. This time it was crowd idol Hannich who turned so unexpectedly to rifle a half-chance through a static defence and a stricken keeper from 15 yards.

Raba needed five home goals to win the tie but the pressure was suddenly on United.

The situation changed again in 74 minutes when Muhren hit back from the penalty spot after defender Nlaguik had grounded the marauding Moses.

Patrick Barclay—PSV Eindhoven 0, Man Utd 0

Robson, Bailey at their level best

Manchester United took a second half, he failed to make

THE GUARDIAN, October 24, 1984

PSV EINDHOVEN	0
MAN. UTD.	0

1984-85 UEFA CUP, SECOND ROUND, FIRST LEG, DRAW 0-0

Robson, Bailey at their level best

By Patrick Barclay

Manchester United took a long time to come to terms with an able and extremely abrasive PSV in Eindhoven last night but Ron Atkinson's side kept their concentration admirably and well deserved the right to start the second leg level.

They were strenuously tested during a first half in which PSV's Scandinavian strikers, Brylle and Thoresen, gave warning of the threat they will carry on the break at Old Trafford, but after the interval United, with Robson outstanding, had a better share of play.

They might even have snatched victory through efforts by Olsen, whose volley brought an excellent save from Van Breukelen, and Strachan, who beat the goalkeeper with a lob only to see Stevens head off the goal-line.

Apart from Robson, whose command of the match became emphatic as the Dutch frustration grew, United's most important individual contributions came from Moses, unstinting in his appetite for disrupting PSV attacks, and Bailey.

The goalkeeper dealt with three awkward deflected shots from Van Der Kerkhof and (twice) Van Rooy and then excelled himself by touching over a drive from the substitute Wildschut towards the end.

Essentially, however, it was a team performance in which United's back four could be seriously faulted only once. Fortunately for Hogg and Moran, neither of whom picked up Thoresen, providing the Norwegian with a free header from Brylle's cross early in the second half, he failed to make proper contact and floated the ball harmlessly over Bailey's bar.

Though United's approach was anything but defensive, there was a prolonged spell in the first half when they could hardly get a touch of the ball, let alone emerge from their half. But the pace and skill of Brylle came to nothing and Olsen finally managed to break clear in the 26th minute. He cleverly lifted the ball over a defender, Albiston touched it on, and Van Breukelen saved at Robson's feet.

After surviving to the interval United gradually began to show signs of taking control and after one of several cynical Dutch fouls, Robson flighted a free kick to Hughes, whose header Olsen volleyed superbly towards Van Breukelen's bottom left-hand corner, producing a thrilling save.

From then on the match could have gone either way and United's strong finish was further encouragement for the supporters who had travelled, ignoring the club's plea to stay away.

The last of the 1,000 tickets set aside by PSV for people with British passports had been snapped up early in a day that featured a dozen arrests, and outside the stadium local touts were seeking £18 a time from those disappointed. But there was no serious trouble amidst a capacity crowd of 28,500.

BELOW: *Against PSV Eindhoven in the UEFA Cup*

DAILY MAIL, November 8, 1984

MAN. UTD.	1
PSV EINHOVEN	0

1984-85 UEFA CUP, SECOND ROUND, SECOND LEG, MANCHESTER UNITED WIN 1-0 ON AGGREGATE AFTER EXTRA TIME

Strachan's old routine sinks angry Dutch

By Peter Johnson

Featherweight Gordon Strachan bored a hole in an impenetrable Dutch dyke last night and dragged Manchester United through it into Europe.

As this UEFA Cup-tie grumbled into extra time, United had never been in more desperate need of Strachan's dual skill for tempting a defender into a clumsy crime and then punishing him with a penalty.

When, two minutes into overtime, Strachan reached the by-line, Eindhoven seemed as capable of coping as they had been all through the gruelling tie.

Yet the speed of the Scot's wriggling turn forced full-back Berrie van Aerle into a tackle he instantly regretted.

Strachan sprawled, then climbed to his feet to fire in his fifth penalty of the season – four of them for fouls upon himself – while van Aerle and most of his mates waved dismissively at Italian referee Luigi Agnolin.

Relief

It was, on reflection, massive retribution for the niggling, body-checking tactics that had wilfully disrupted the flow of the game.

For long enough Eindhoven had sheltered behind the referee's leniency.

Yet in the dying seconds of that first period of extra time Agnolin was to enrage the Dutch again.

Their Danish striker, Kenneth Brylle, crumpled as he and goalkeeper Gary Bailey went to meet a through ball.

For an instant, the referee appeared to point to the penalty spot.

Then, as the Dutch lept around in relief, his finger changed direction and gave a goal kick.

United never found a rhythm and, apart from some piercing runs from Mark Hughes, the occasional burst by Strachan and Jesper Olsen, the need for caution obviously weighed heavy on their minds.

They were not helped when an early injury took Kevin Moran out of the centre of their defence.

LEFT: *Whiteside (centre) crosses*

D ROUND ACTION

Frank Keatin

Patrick Barclay — Man Utd 2, Dundee Utd 2

Scots build on McAlpine penalty stop

 SOCCER

on and Robson drove past McAlpine; surely now it would be all over.

An invitation to make it so

Robert Armstrong
Spurs 2, Bohemians 0

Stevens safety strike

TOTTENHAM HOTSPUR gave a classic demonstration of how willpower can triumph over superior technique with a rather fortuitous UEFA Cup win against Bohemians Prague at White Hart last ni

Sib:

BOXI

WHEN THE ho came on, the pron alley brawl had alr revealed as an o sweetness and I chivalry.

Having added Kaylor's British monwealth m titles to his own championship with round points win

THE GUARDIAN, November 29, 1984

MAN. UTD.	2
DUNDEE UNITED	2

1984-85 UEFA CUP, THIRD ROUND, FIRST LEG, DRAW 2-2

Scots build on McAlpine penalty stop

By Patrick Barclay

Jokes about Scottish goalkeepers were conspicuous by their absence last night at Old Trafford, where the 36-year-old Hamish McAlpine crowned a brilliant display with a penalty save from Gordon Strachan that turned an extraordinary tie Dundee United's way.

Jim McLean's side will face Manchester United at Tannadice in a fortnight's time with confidence based on equality, an outcome that seemed unthinkable during the first half of last night's encounter.

Then, as the Scots failed miserably to cope with the formidable pace and aggression of a home side who threw McQueen forward to win aerial challenges at will, the question was: How many?

Because of McAlpine, who made excellent saves from Olsen (twice), Gidman and Albiston as the Old Trafford full-backs joined the onslaught, Manchester United were restricted to Strachan's earlier successful attempt to beat the veteran keeper from the spot.

This came after the oddest of episodes, the Bulgarian referee requiring to consult a linesman before changing his mind and giving the award for a blatant offence by Malpas, who got both hands to a header from McQueen and

seemed almost on the point of sticking it up his jumper.

Dundee United, having survived so shakily to the interval, promptly stunned the big crowd by equalising within 90 seconds of the second half through Hegarty, the central defender spearing home his 10th European goal after Gough had headed Bannon's free-kick into a crowded area.

Manchester United's reply took three minutes. Olsen flighted a free-kick into the goalmouth, Hughes touched it on and Robson drove past McAlpine; surely now it would be all over.

An invitation to make it so was scorned 10 minutes later, however. The recurrent threat of McQueen, leaping to a corner, impelled Hegarty to handle and once again Strachan approached the spot, seeking his eighth successive penalty success since arriving from Aberdeen. Once again he placed the ball to McAlpine's left, but the goalkeeper guessed correctly and pushed it away.

Within minutes the advantage swung strongly towards the Scots. They were beginning to show more conviction in attack, where Sturrock had fought a lonely, if skilful battle, but the second equaliser carried its share of fortune.

Though Beedie's pass from the right was cunningly angled it should not have got past Duxbury, who missed the ball, enabling Sturrock to steal in behind and beat Bailey.

By now, Dundee United were looking at least as comfortable as their hosts and they might even have become the first side to win a European tie at Old Trafford but for a smart save by Bailey, who touched Bannon's fierce drive over the bar.

Manchester United now face a difficult task at Tannadice where such sides as Borussia Moenchengladbach and Standard Liege have taken fearful hammerings in recent years.

But last night's almost incredible transformation was a reminder of how little can be taken for granted. After overwhelmingly controlling the match through Robson, Moses, Strachan and Hughes for the best part of an hour, Manchester United will not go north in trepidation.

McQueen (second from right) leaps above
Hughes and two Dundee United defenders in
their first leg UEFA Cup tie

Strachan (centre) amidst the Dundee defence

DAILY EXPRESS, November 28, 1984

MAN. UTD.	2
DUNDEE UNITED	2

1984-85 UEFA CUP, THIRD ROUND, FIRST LEG,
DRAW 2-2

Mac's wall of defiance!

By Derek Potter

Veteran goalkeeper Hamish McAlpine last night carried Dundee United to the threshold of a UEFA Cup triumph.

A series of super saves, climaxed when he beat out a second penalty by Gordon Strachan, made the Scots favourites for the second leg at Tannadice.

Twice Dundee fought back from a goal behind in a game full of exciting vigour, some indifferent finishing by the Manchester attack and McAlpine's antics in his 50th European game.

McAlpine, despite being in his 37th year, was the outstanding personality in a night of high drama watched by almost 50,000 at Old Trafford.

It began to unfold in the ninth minute when Gordon Strachan was given his first chance from the spot after a header by Gordon McQueen was blatantly punched out by Maurice Malpas.

Strachan, the ace marksman, calmly hit his seventh penalty past McAlpine, surprisingly never capped at senior level for his country.

That should have inspired Manchester to a comprehensive, calm, and methodical victory. What it did, in fact, was inspire McAlpine, who in turn lifted the Scots to a peak performance.

Somehow Dundee survived until the second half with McAlpine making courageous saves from Jesper Olsen (twice), John Gidman, and Arthur Albiston.

It took the Scots less than two minutes of the second half to hit back following a free kick. Defender Paul Hegarty saw his shot roll in by the upright to beat Bailey and signal the start of an amazing series of events.

Overdue

Seconds later Hegarty was booked – and an overdue caution it was by the Bulgarian referee. Eight minutes further on Hegarty was in the action again to punch the ball away from the airborne menace of McQueen.

Another penalty . . . but this time McAlpine won the war of wits with Strachan, guessing right and diving to his left to save.

That was United's chance to make it 3-1 and add to the goal Bryan Robson stole in the 49th minute.

Again it was the Dundee hordes at the City end who inspired their heroes to a performance that equals the 2-0 home win against Roma last season.

A careless slip by Mike Duxbury in the 62nd minute let Paul Sturrock through and he beat Bailey to make it 2-2.

Frank Stapleton was thrust into attack in place of Norman Whiteside, whose earlier link ups with the dynamic Mark Hughes had been exciting if non-productive.

It made little difference and it was the Scots who finished on top with Sturrock shooting straight at Bailey.

THE SUN, December 13, 1984

DUNDEE UNITED	2
MAN. UTD.	3

1984-85 UEFA CUP, THIRD ROUND, SECOND LEG,
MANCHESTER UNITED WIN 5-4 ON AGGREGATE

Muhren's a marvel

Arnie seals it

Manchester United had to squirm through another nightmare of self-inflicted torture in Europe at sell-out Tannadice last night.

The favourite fall-guys of football suffered again in the UEFA Cup confrontation with a classic example of soccer suicide.

Twice Ron Atkinson's team were ahead – and twice they threw it away in a second leg of heartache and drama.

Paul Hegarty, the Dundee United skipper who rallied his team to the cause at Old Trafford, proved why he has got 11 goals in Europe with a second equaliser after 55 minutes.

But it was gifted to him by defensive negligence.

As a free-kick curled into the box, Gordon McQueen's header didn't clear the danger and – with Gary Bailey committed – Hergarty looped a header into an unprotected net.

Panic

But Dutchman Arnie Muhren put Big Ron's men ahead again in the 78th minute when he deflected a McQueen shot into the net to put United 5-4 ahead on aggregate.

The curse of keeper McAlpine loomed early for Atkinson's team.

Stapleton was in space and on the run he struck a superb drive – but McAlpine's reflexes were ready for the test.

But 60 seconds later Hughes, the most deadly finisher in the Old Trafford camp, had proved his technique in the box once more to give his team mates the lead.

★ McAlpine can't stop Bryan Robson from scoring Manchester United's second goal, but the Dundee United keeper went on to distinguish himself with a super show.

Mac's wall of defiance!

VETERAN goalkeeper Hamish McAlpine last night carried Dundee United to the threshold of a UEFA Cup triumph.
A series of super saves, made, when he beat out a second penalty by Gordon Strachan, made for the second leg at Tannadice.
Twice Dundee

Hendrie is

SPURS SPRING A SUR
Stevens shock fc
Bohemia

MUHREN'S A MARVEL

Arnie seals it

MANCHESTER UNITED had to squirm through another nightmare of self-inflicted torture in Europe at sell-out Tannadice last night.

The favourite fall-guys of football suffered again in this UEFA Cup confrontation with a classic example of soccer suicide. Twice Ron Atkinson's men

in a second leg of heartache and drama Paul Hegarty, the Dundee United skipper who rallied his team to the cause at Old Trafford proved why he has 11 goals in Europe

team mates the lead. Among Atkinson's men the defensive lapses are now developing into a phobia and only Moses with an agile goal - line failed to

GORDON STRACHAN . . .
set up the first goal

Among Atkinson's men the defensive lapses are now developing into a phobia and only Moses, with an agile goal-line clearance, foiled the equaliser from Hegarty after 23 minutes.

But the Scots skipper had to wait just three minutes and inevitably it was presented by a lack of covering awareness as Sturrock arched a cross to Bailey's far post.

Atkinson then saw his players take the lead for the fourth time in the tie five minutes from half-time.

Dundee United full back McGinnis hung his head in despair as he sacrificed an own goal in attempting to clear a flick-header from Hughes.

Iron Curtain halts United

MANCHESTER UNITED scrambled over a defiant Hungarian barrier last night to take a tentative grip on the UEFA Cup quarter final.

JUVENTUS MOVE INTO TOP GEAR

● LIVERPOOL'S biggest European Cup danger

A goal by Frank Stapleton finally broke down the 10-man barricade by the desperate Hungarian League leaders.

Until Stapleton emerged from a disappointing personal spell, it had been poor picture

Man United 1
Videoton 0

number Peter Disztle who emerged the Hungarian hero with a spellbinding save from Mark Hughes shortly after Stapleton's goal,

The goal came in the 61st

DAILY EXPRESS, March 7, 1985

MAN. UTD.	1
VIDEOTON	**0**

1984-85 UEFA CUP, FOURTH ROUND, FIRST LEG,
MANCHESTER UNITED WIN 1-0

Iron Curtain halts United

By Derek Potter
AT OLD TRAFFORD

Manchester United scrambled over a defiant Hungarian barrier last night to take a tentative grip on the UEFA Cup quarter final.

A goal by Frank Stapleton finally broke down the 10-man barricade by the desperate Hungarian League leaders.

Until Stapleton emerged from a disappointing personal spell, it had been Soccer of poor picture quality thanks to the tactics of the team run by Hungary's TV manufacturers.

Checked

United had created problems for themselves with much wild and untidy pounding of their cowering opponents.

While at the same time Videoton enjoyed huge chunks of luck keeping the rampant reds at bay.

What is starkly evident is that United face a fierce ordeal on Hungarian soil. Videoton kicked, checked and frustrated in best Italian style hoping to sneak a goal with a break from almost non-stop defence.

Videoton's attacking aims were evident from the fact that United keeper, Gary Bailey came under pressure only twice – each time from headers by his team mates.

And ironically the "near misses" came from two of United's top performers – Paul McGrath and John Gidman.

It was Bailey's opposite number Peter Disztle who emerged the Hungarian hero with a spellbinding save from Mark Hughes shortly after Stapleton's goal.

The goal came in the 61st minute when Gordon Strachan waltzed down the right to supply the perfect cross for Stapleton.

But it could prove scant reward for United, who needed a bigger lead for the second leg to keep alive their Cup quest.

Against a less resolute defence, United might have had that safety net.

Gruesome

Stapleton zoomed one first-half shot high over from six yards in the early probing before Norman Whiteside sent a 20-yard shot soaring over the crossbar following a free kick.

Cries for a penalty when Stapleton claimed his shirt was tugged went unheeded by referee Augusto Castillo, a Spanish official who ignored razor-sharp tackling and blatant bodychecks only to punish often, less gruesome offences.

Graeme Hogg and Strachan were booked, so were two Hungarians – the only equal aspect of a disappointing and untidy match.

LEFT: *Stapleton challenging for the ball in United's second leg match against Videoton in Budapest*

Our own faul

VIDEOTON 1

MAN. UTD. 0

1984-85 UEFA CUP, FOURTH ROUND, SECOND LEG, 1-1 DRAW ON AGGREGATE, VIDEOTON WIN 5-4 ON PENALTIES

Our own fault!
Reds crash on night of misses

By David Meek

M anchester United are out of Europe . . . and I don't know whether to laugh or cry.

It's laughable that a team like Videoton, who produced only one real crack at goal in two legs, should now find themselves in the semi-finals of the UEFA Cup.

And it's a crying shame that the Reds should finally lose out in the lottery of a penalty shootout after dominating the two games.

Blame

Yet United must also accept a slice of the blame for this 1-0 defeat in the second leg of their UEFA quarter-final in Hungary which made the penalty drama necessary.

Even with extra-time, United had not been able to score, so the match was level 1-1 on aggregate.

As the always honest Bryan Robson admitted: "It was partly our own fault because we failed to take our chances."

VIDEOTON 1

MAN. UTD. 0

1984-85 UEFA CUP, FOURTH ROUND, SECOND LEG, 1-1 DRAW ON AGGREGATE, VIDEOTON WIN 5-4 ON PENALTIES

Sudden death
United strikers flop in shoot out

By Bob Russell
IN HUNGARY

M anchester United crashed out of the UEFA Cup last night in a cruelly unjust penalty shoot-out.

Spot flops by star strikers Frank Stapleton and Mark Hughes spelled quarter-final KO for Ron Atkinson's braves.

Stapleton's miss was partly nullified by Videoton sub Borsanye firing wide to leave the shoot-out level at 4-4.

Norman Whiteside, Jesper Olsen, Gordon Strachan and John Gidman had scored for United, with Szabo, Burcsa, Vegh and Wittman replying for the Hungarians.

But now it was down to sudden death following more than three and half hours of deadlock over the two legs.

Hughes had United's penalty No. 6 saved by 'keeper Peter Disztl. Videoton scored . . . and United were finished.

Yet just into the second period of extra time the match should have been all over from a far different penalty situation.

Birthday boy Jesper Olsen, going on as substitute for United skipper Bryan Robson, was blatantly tripped by Videoton midfielder Burcsa on his first surging run into the goal-mouth.

Tragically there was to be no 24th birthday present from Swedish referee Erik Frederiksen for the unlucky little Dane, who had been left on the sidelines for 105 minutes through a tactical decision.

Manager Atkinson took a calculated gamble in preferring the power of Norman Whiteside to Olsen's more delicate skills on a glue pot pitch – and there might have been an early pay-off.

The big Irishman, floating away from his wide left-sided attacking role, burst through the Videoton central defence to inch an eight-yard header round the post from a searching Arthur Albiston cross.

Atkinson had declared pre-match his intention of going for an early kill.

But the plan rebounded when the Hungarians rubbed out United's 1-0 first leg lead with their first show of aggression.

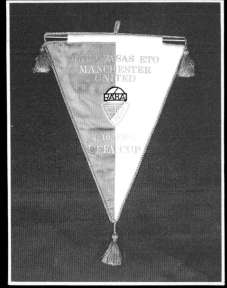

Raba Vasas ETO Gyor pennant

Willem II Tilburg pennant

Pennant from Benfica

Valencia pennant

Waterford

FC Porto pennant

Sporting Club of Lisbon pennant

Raba Vasas ETO Gyor

So it is with very mixed feelings that United bow out of Europe for another year.

There was certainly no doubt about the extent of their domination. They survived a lively opening burst from the Hungarians with the help of some stout defending by Paul McGrath and Graeme Hogg. But they could do nothing about the free-kick awarded in the 19th minute after Robson had tripped Istvan Palkovics.

Geza Wittman's free-kick from just outside the box took a deflection to score low just inside the post, impossible for Gary Bailey to reach.

United's response, in terms of effort and pressure was magnificent. They created a situation where all Videoton could think about was to get behind the goal, pack their penalty area and hope for the best.

Norman Whiteside was inches wide with a header very early on and should possibly have scored in the second half. Frank Stapleton blasted into the side netting from Whiteside in the 38th minute in what was probably the best chance of the match.

McGrath and Mike Duxbury both thumped shots against Peter Disztl, who was in much more convincing form – and needed to be – than he showed in Manchester when Videoton lost 1-0 to a Stapleton goal.

United had no joy either from three penalty claims.

United, despite playing on a swamp of a pitch, drove forward with fury but it was not their scoring night. By this time all Videoton could think about was playing for time.

As Robson says: "In all my years, I have never seen a team deliberately waste time in the hope of a penalty shoot out. I suppose it must have seemed to them like their only chance of winning."

And that, of course, is how it worked out as the luckless Stapleton recorded the first penalty miss by blazing over the bar after Whiteside and Olsen had scored.

Videoton promptly missed one as well to make it 4-4 at the end of the first five penalty phase.

Gordon Strachan and John Gidman were United's other successful scorers.

But in the sudden-death finale, Mark Hughes hit a reasonable shot only to see Disztl move the right way and save it.

This left the coup de grace for Imre Vadasz and the Hungarian hit a stinging shot to win the penalty shootout 5-4 and send the Reds skidding out of the UEFA Cup 6-5 on aggregate.

Gary Bailey

Frank Stapleton – scorer of Manchester's first goal against Videoton in the first leg match

LOOKING BACK WITH GARY BAILEY

Gary Bailey has burning and bitter memories of Manchester United's last campaign in Europe.

Their run in the 1984-85 UEFA Cup came to grief in a quarter-final penalty shoot-out with the goalkeeper naturally the key figure.

And the luckless Bailey dived the wrong way for every one of Videoton's penalties!

Frank Stapleton and Mark Hughes missed their spot-kicks for the Reds, so that was that, and soon afterwards the curtain came down on Europe for all English clubs following the crowd disaster in Brussels.

It was a sad and frustrating exit for the Reds, with no chance of redemption now for the injury-hit Bailey.

"The match has painful recollections for me, particularly now since my knee injury and retirement from football," explained Bailey.

"Penalties are a cruel way to go out of a big competition, though I have got to be honest and say that I cannot think of a better method without inviting all kinds of fixture congestion with replays.

"The problem that upsets players is that though there is tremendous skill in taking the spot-kicks, a lot of luck comes into it as well, and that seems harsh after putting in so much hard work to reach the later stages.

"I mean I went the wrong way for all their kicks, yet I have a fifty per cent save record in my career. So I was particularly disappointed, and it was ironic that our penalty misses were by our two recognised strikers.

"It was galling because we absolutely hammered Videoton over the two legs.

"Frank Stapleton might well have had a couple of penalty awards and we also had two goals disallowed for offside in the first leg at Old Trafford. We won 1-0 with a goal from Frank. We needed a bigger cushion, but the Hungarians had shown so little ability that we really thought we could win the second leg.

"Unfortunately we just didn't get the breaks we needed. We were on top again and we should have won easily. We didn't take our chances, though, and they scored with a deflection from a free kick for a one-goal win on the night and an aggregate draw.

"That sent us into the dreaded penalty shoot-out. It's a situation quite relished by many goalkeepers, and I must admit that you feel you take centre stage with the chance to show what you can do.

"You know it's a great opportunity to become the hero of the whole game, and you put out of your mind the fact that there is also the risk of becoming the villain!

"I missed out on the chance of glory, and I still think it was incredibly bad luck to go the wrong way for every one of their penalties. The only one they missed was when their fellow put it wide.

"So the ultimate dream of making a winning save was not to be, and as far as I am concerned my chance has gone for ever.

"I had to retire. If I had gone on I would have risked aggravating the damage to my knee to the point of perhaps ending up a cripple.

"Naturally as a goalkeeper at the age of 28 I felt my best years for both Manchester United and England were still to come, and I would have liked longer to achieve my ambitions.

"However, I have always been a positive kind of person, and rather than dwell on what might have been, I prefer to be grateful for what I have had, which is 10 fantastic years at Old Trafford.

"United in fact gave me far more than I considered possible, even in my wildest boyhood dreams.

"I think some of my warmest memories will revolve round the players I was lucky enough to play alongside.

"For example I shall never forget Jimmy Greenhoff's goal against Liverpool which took us to the FA Cup final in 1979. Then there was the strength and tenacity of Joe Jordan which took us to a whisker of winning the championship in 1982.

"I will always think admiringly of the organisation of Martin Buchan in the defence in front of me, and the subtle passing skills of Ray Wilkins and Arnold Muhren.

"Probably the best all-round team I played in came together under Bryan Robson in 1985, and reached a peak in the marvellous record club run of 10 wins at the start of season 1985-86.

"Those are the kind of memories which I will use to balance against the bitter disappointment of losing on penalties to Videoton. We all felt we had done the most difficult part by knocking out Raba Gyor, Eindhoven and Dundee United, only to lose to a Hungarian team we knew we should have beaten.

"But that's football, and not a very happy note on which to bow out of Europe."

LOOKING FORWARD WITH ALEX FERGUSON

Alex Ferguson

The ban on English Clubs playing in Europe left a void in football.

Even when I was north of the border still manager of Aberdeen, most people in soccer felt sadness at the absence of teams from England in the various European competitions.

Of course the events at Heysel Stadium were tragic and strong action was necessary.

But for how long must the vast innocent majority suffer for the sins of the few?

I believe the English game has paid its dues, and that the time has come for a return to Europe. The problem of the mindless hooligan is not peculiar to this country.

Other nations have trouble, yet we don't seem to hear about it quite so much. We do appear now rather as scapegoats and in my opinion we have served our time.

Perhaps it would encourage UEFA to lift the ban if the Government would take some positive steps to prevent the trouble-makers travelling to matches on the Continent.

I know the rights of individuals have to be respected, but I'm sure there must be some way in which Government can protect our clubs.

They have got to help us by restricting travel to matches. Football clubs have rights, too!

Certainly I am looking forward to the day when I can lead Manchester United into European action.

I acquired quite a taste for this kind of football when I was with Aberdeen. The highlight at Pittodrie was winning the European Cup Winners Cup in 1983 when we beat mighty Real Madrid 2-1 after extra time in the final in Gothenburg.

We had had a tremendous tussle with Bayern Munich in the quarter-final, and the final was also a fabulous occasion. Happily it was marvellous with the supporters as well.

About 12,000 of our fans went to Sweden and they were terrific ambassadors, good natured and good humoured, enjoying themselves, but with the people of Gothenburg enjoying them, too.

The "St Clair" took a party of about 500. I was at the quayside to see them off, and Mark McGhee and I went back to welcome our "boat people" home after a final which seems now like a dream.

To challenge for European honours with Manchester United will be especially inspiring. I am well aware of the tradition for football in this kind of arena first established by Sir Matt Busby 30 years ago.

I know the Old Trafford supporters are keen for the excitement of Europe again, and that moment cannot come quickly enough for me either.

Statistics

1955-56 LEAGUE CHAMPIONS

SEASON 1956-57

EUROPEAN CHAMPION CLUBS' CUP

Preliminary Round, First Leg
September 12th 1956 (Brussels)
v. ANDERLECHT (Belgium) Won: 2-0
Wood, Foulkes, Byrne, Colman, Jones, Blanchflower, Berry, Whelan, Taylor, Viollet, Pegg.
Scorers: Viollet, Taylor.
Attendance: 35,000

Preliminary Round, Second Leg
September 26th 1956 (Manchester)
v. ANDERLECHT (Belgium) Won: 10-0
Wood, Foulkes, Byrne, Colman, Jones, Edwards, Berry, Whelan, Taylor, Viollet, Pegg.
Scorers: Viollet 4, Taylor 3, Whelan 2, Berry.
Attendance: 43,635

* United won 12-0 on aggregate.

First Round, First Leg
October 17th 1956 (Manchester)
v. BORUSSIA DORTMUND (West Germany) Won: 3-2
Wood, Foulkes, Byrne, Colman, Jones, Edwards, Berry, Whelan, Taylor, Viollet, Pegg.
Scorers: Viollet 2, Burgsmueller (o.g.)
Attendance: 75,598

First Round, Second Leg
November 21st 1956 (Dortmund)
v. BORUSSIA DORTMUND (West Germany) Draw: 0-0
Wood, Foulkes, Byrne, Colman, Jones, McGuinness, Berry, Whelan, Taylor, Edwards, Pegg.
Attendance: 45,000

* United won 3-2 on aggregate.

Second Round, First Leg
January 16th 1957 (Bilbao)
v. ATLETICO BILBAO (Spain) Lost: 3-5
Wood, Foulkes, Byrne, Colman, Jones, Edwards, Berry, Whelan, Taylor, Viollet, Pegg.
Scorers: Taylor, Viollet, Whelan.
Attendance: 45,000

Second Round, Second Leg
February 6th 1957 (Manchester)
v. ATLETICO BILBAO (Spain) Won: 3-0
Wood, Foulkes, Byrne, Colman, Jones, Edwards, Berry, Whelan, Taylor, Viollet, Pegg.
Scorers: Viollet, Taylor, Berry.
Attendance: 65,000

* United won 6-5 on aggregate.

Semi Final, First Leg
April 11th 1957 (Madrid)

v. REAL MADRID (Spain) Lost: 1-3
Wood, Foulkes, Byrne, Colman, Blanchflower, Edwards, Berry, Whelan, Taylor, Viollet, Pegg.
Scorer: Taylor.
Attendance: 135,000

Semi Final, Second Leg
April 25th 1957 (Manchester)
v. REAL MADRID (Spain) Draw: 2-2
Wood, Foulkes, Byrne, Colman, Blanchflower, Edwards, Berry, Whelan, Taylor, Charlton, Pegg.
Scorers: Taylor, Charlton.
Attendance: 61,676

* United lost 3-5 on aggregate

1956-57 LEAGUE CHAMPIONS

SEASON 1957-58

EUROPEAN CHAMPION CLUBS' CUP

Preliminary Round, First Leg
September 25th 1957 (Dublin)
v. SHAMROCK ROVERS (Republic of Ireland) Won: 6-0
Wood, Foulkes, Byrne, Goodwin, Blanchflower, Edwards, Berry, Whelan, Taylor, Viollet, Pegg.
Scorers: Whelan 2, Taylor 2, Berry, Pegg.
Attendance: 46,000

Preliminary Round, Second Leg
October 2nd 1957 (Manchester)
v. SHAMROCK ROVERS (Republic of Ireland) Won: 3-2
Wood, Foulkes, Byrne, Colman, Jones, McGuinness, Berry, Webster, Taylor, Viollet, Pegg.
Scorers: Viollet 2, Pegg.
Attendance: 33,754

* United won 9-2 on aggregate

First Round, First Leg
November 20th 1957 (Manchester)
v. DUKLA PRAGUE (Czechoslovakia) Won: 3-0
Wood, Foulkes, Byrne, Colman, Blanchflower, Edwards, Berry, Whelan, Taylor, Webster, Pegg.
Scorers: Webster, Taylor, Pegg
Attendance: 60,000

First Round, Second Leg
December 4th 1957 (Prague)
v. DUKLA PRAGUE (Czechoslovakia) Lost: 0-1
Wood, Foulkes, Byrne, Colman, Jones, Edwards, Scanlon, Whelan, Taylor, Webster, Pegg.
Attendance: 35,000

* United won 3-1 on aggregate.

Second Round, First Leg
January 14th 1958 (Manchester)
v. RED STAR BELGRADE (Yugoslavia) Won: 2-1
Gregg, Foulkes, Byrne, Colman, Jones, Edwards, Morgans, Charlton, Taylor, Viollet, Scanlon.
Scorers: Charlton, Colman.
Attendance: 60,000

Second Round, Second Leg
February 5th 1958 (Belgrade)
v. RED STAR BELGRADE (Yugoslavia) Draw: 3-3
Gregg, Foulkes, Byrne, Colman, Jones, Edwards, Morgans, Charlton, Taylor, Viollet, Scanlon.
Scorers: Charlton 2, Viollet.
Attendance: 52,000

* United won 5-4 on aggregate.

Semi Final, First Leg
May 8th 1958 (Manchester)
v. AC MILAN (Italy) Won: 2-1
Gregg, Foulkes, Greaves, Goodwin, Cope, Crowther, Morgans, Taylor E., Webster, Viollet, Pearson.
Scorers: Viollet, Taylor E. (pen.)
Attendance: 44,882

Semi Final, Second Leg
May 14th 1958 (Milan)
v. AC MILAN (Italy) Lost: 0-4
Gregg, Foulkes, Greaves, Goodwin, Cope, Crowther, Morgans, Taylor, Webster, Viollet, Pearson.
Attendance: 80,000

* United lost 2-5 on aggregate.

1962-63 FA CUP FINAL

v. LEICESTER CITY (Wembley) Won: 3-1
Gaskell, Dunne, Cantwell, Crerand, Foulkes, Setters, Giles, Quixall, Herd, Law, Charlton.
Scorers: Herd 2, Law.
Attendance: 100,000

SEASON 1963-64

EUROPEAN CUP WINNERS' CUP

First Round, First Leg
September 25th 1963 (Rotterdam)
v. WILLEM II (Netherlands) Draw: 1-1
Gregg, Dunne, Cantwell, Crerand, Foulkes, Setters, Herd, Chisnall, Sadler, Law, Charlton.
Scorer: Herd
Attendance: 20,000

First Round, Second Leg
October 15th 1963 (Manchester)
v. WILLEM II (Netherlands) Won: 6-1
Gregg, Dunne, Cantwell, Crerand, Foulkes, Setters, Quixall, Chisnall, Herd, Law, Charlton.

Scorers: Law 3, Setters, Charlton, Chisnall.
Attendance: 46, 272

* United won 7-2 on aggregate.

Second Round, First Leg
December 3rd 1963 (London)
v. TOTTENHAM HOTSPUR (England)
Lost: 0-2
Gaskell, Dunne, Cantwell, Crerand, Foulkes, Setters, Quixall, Stiles, Herd, Law, Charlton.
Attendance: 57,447

Second Round, Second Leg
December 10th 1963 (Manchester)
v. TOTTENHAM HOTSPUR (England)
Won: 4-1
Gaskell, Dunne, Cantwell, Crerand, Foulkes, Setters, Quixall, Chisnall, Sadler, Herd, Charlton.
Scorers: Herd 2, Charlton 2.
Attendance: 48,639

* United won 4-3 on aggregate.

Quarter Final, First Leg
February 26th 1964 (Manchester)
v. SPORTING CLUB LISBON (Portugal)
Won: 4-1
Gaskell, Brennan, Dunne, Crerand, Foulkes, Setters, Herd, Stiles, Charlton, Law, Best.
Scorers: Law 3 (2 pens.), Charlton.
Attendance: 60,207

Quarter Final, Second Leg
March 18th 1964 (Lisbon)
v. SPORTING CLUB LISBON (Portugal)
Lost: 0-5
Gaskell, Brennan, Dunne, Crerand, Foulkes, Setters, Herd, Chisnall, Charlton, Law, Best.
Attendance: 50,000

* United lost 4-6 on aggregate.

1963-64 LEAGUE CHAMPIONSHIP: FINISHED 2nd

SEASON 1964-65

INTER CITIES FAIRS CUP
First Round, First Leg
September 23rd 1964 (Stockholm)
v. DJURGARDEN (Sweden) Draw: 1-1
Dunne P., Brennan, Dunne A., Crerand, Foulkes, Setters, Connelly, Charlton, Herd, Stiles, Best.
Scorers: Herd
Attendance: 6,537

First Round, Second Leg
October 27th 1964 (Manchester)
v. DJURGARDEN (Sweden) Won: 6-1
Dunne P., Brennan, Dunne A., Crerand, Foulkes, Stiles, Connelly, Charlton, Herd, Law, Best.

Scorers: Law 3 (1 pen.), Charlton 2, Best.
Attendance: 38,437

* United won 7-2 on aggregate.

Second Round, First Leg
November 11th 1964 (Dortmund)
v. BORUSSIA DORTMUND (West Germany) Won: 6-1
Dunne P., Brennan, Dunne A., Crerand, Foulkes, Stiles, Connelly, Charlton, Herd, Law, Best.
Scorers: Charlton 3, Herd, Best, Law.
Attendance: 25,000

Second Round, Second Leg
December 2nd 1964 (Manchester)
v. BORUSSIA DORTMUND (West Germany) Won: 4-0
Dunne P., Brennan, Dunne A., Crerand, Foulkes, Stiles, Connelly, Charlton, Herd, Law, Best.
Scorers: Charlton 2, Law, Connelly.
Attendance: 31,896

* United won 10-1 on aggregate.

Third Round, First Leg
January 20th 1965 (Manchester)
v. EVERTON (England) Draw: 1-1
Dunne P., Brennan, Dunne A., Crerand, Foulkes, Stiles, Connelly, Charlton, Herd, Law, Best.
Scorer: Connelly.
Attendance: 49,075

Third Round, Second Leg
February 9th 1965 (Liverpool)
v. EVERTON (England) Won: 2-1
Dunne P., Brennan, Dunne A., Crerand, Foulkes, Stiles, Connelly, Charlton, Herd, Law, Best.
Scorers: Connelly, Herd.
Attendance: 54,397

* United won 3-2 on aggregate.

Quarter Final, First Leg
May 12th 1965 (Strasbourg)
v. RACING CLUB STRASBOURG (France) Won: 5-0
Dunne P., Brennan, Dunne A., Crerand, Foulkes, Stiles, Connelly, Charlton, Herd, Law, Best.
Scorers: Law 2, Connelly, Herd, Charlton.
Attendance: 28,914

Quarter Final, Second Leg
May 19th 1965 (Manchester)
v. RACING CLUB STRASBOURG (France) 'Draw: 0-0
Dunne P., Brennan, Dunne A., Crerand, Foulkes, Stiles, Connelly, Charlton, Herd, Law, Best.
Attendance: 34,188

* United won 5-0 on aggregate.

Semi Final, First Leg
May 31st 1965 (Manchester)

v. FERENCVAROS (Hungary) Won: 3-2
Dunne P., Brennan, Dunne A., Crerand, Foulkes, Stiles, Connelly, Charlton, Herd, Law, Best.
Scorers: Herd 2, Law (pen.)
Attendance: 39,902

Semi Final, Second Leg
June 6th 1965 (Budapest)
v. FERENCVAROS (Hungary) Lost: 0-1
Dunne P., Brennan, Dunne A., Crerand, Foulkes, Stiles, Connelly, Charlton, Herd, Law, Best.
Attendance: 60,000

* Aggregate scores level, 3-3

Semi Final, Play-off
June 16th 1965 (Budapest)
v. FERENCVAROS (Hungary) Lost: 1-2
Dunne P., Brennan, Dunne A., Crerand, Foulkes, Stiles, Connelly, Charlton, Herd, Law, Best.
Scorer: Connelly.
Attendance: 75,000

* United lost 4-5 on aggregate.

1964-65 LEAGUE CHAMPIONS

SEASON 1965-66

EUROPEAN CHAMPION CLUBS' CUP
Preliminary Round, First Leg
September 22nd 1965 (Helsinki)
v. HELSINKI JK (Finland) Won: 3-2
Gaskell, Brennan, Dunne A., Fitzpatrick, Foulkes, Stiles, Connelly, Law, Herd, Charlton, Aston.
Scorers: Herd, Connelly, Law
Attendance: 15,572

Preliminary Round, Second Leg
October 6th 1965 (Manchester)
v. HELSINKI JK (Finland) Won: 6-0
Dunne P., Brennan, Dunne A., Crerand, Foulkes, Stiles, Connelly, Best, Charlton, Law, Aston.
Scorers: Connelly 3, Best 2, Charlton.
Attendance: 30,388

* United won 9-2 on aggregate.

First Round, First Leg
November 17th 1965 (East Berlin)
v. ASK VORWAERTS (East Germany) Won: 2-0
Gregg, Dunne A., Cantwell, Crerand, Foulkes, Stiles, Best, Law, Charlton, Herd, Connelly.
Scorers: Law, Connelly.
Attendance: 40,000

First Round, Second Leg
December 1st 1965 (Manchester)

v. ASK VORWAERTS (East Germany)
Won: 3-1

Dunne P., Dunne A., Cantwell, Crerand, Foulkes, Stiles, Best, Law, Charlton, Herd, Connelly.
Scorers: Herd 3.
Attendance: 30,082

* United won 5-1 on aggregate.

Second Round, First Leg
February 2nd 1966 (Manchester)
v. SL BENFICA (Portugal) Won: 3-2

Gregg, Dunne A., Cantwell, Crerand, Foulkes, Stiles, Best, Law, Charlton, Herd, Connelly.
Scorers: Herd, Law, Foulkes.
Attendance: 64,035

Second Round, Second Leg
March 9th 1966 (Lisbon)
v. SL BENFICA (Portugal) Won: 5-1

Gregg, Brennan, Dunne A., Crerand, Foulkes, Stiles, Best, Law, Charlton, Herd, Connelly.
Scorers: Best 2, Connelly, Crerand, Charlton.
Attendance: 75,000

* United won 8-3 on aggregate.

Semi Final, First Leg
April 13th 1966 (Belgrade)
v. PARTIZAN BELGRADE (Yugoslavia)
Lost: 0-2

Gregg, Brennan, Dunne A, Crerand, Foulkes, Stiles, Best, Law, Charlton, Herd, Connelly.
Attendance: 60,000

Semi Final, Second Leg
April 20th 1966 (Manchester)
v. PARTIZAN BELGRADE (Yugoslavia)
Won: 1-0

Gregg, Brennan, Dunne A., Crerand, Foulkes, Stiles, Anderson, Law, Charlton, Herd, Connelly.
Scorer: Soskic (o.g.)
Attendance: 62,500

* United lost 1-2 on aggregate.

1966-67 LEAGUE CHAMPIONS

SEASON 1967-68

EUROPEAN CHAMPION CLUBS' CUP
First Round, First Leg
September 20th 1967 (Manchester)
v. HIBERNIANS (Malta) Won: 4-0

Stepney, Dunne, Burns, Crerand, Foulkes, Stiles, Best, Sadler, Charlton, Law, Kidd.
Scorers: Law 2, Sadler 2.
Attendance: 43,915

First Round, Second Leg
September 27th 1967 (Gzira)
v. HIBERNIANS (Malta) Draw: 0-0

Stepney, Dunne, Burns, Crerand, Foulkes, Stiles, Best, Sadler, Charlton, Law, Kidd.
Attendance: 23,217

* United won 4-0 on aggregate.

Second Round, First Leg
November 15th 1967 (Sarajevo)
v. SARAJEVO (Yugoslavia) Draw: 0-0

Stepney, Dunne, Burns, Crerand, Foulkes, Sadler, Fitzpatrick, Kidd, Charlton, Best, Aston.
Attendance: 45,000

Second Round, Second Leg
November 29th 1967 (Manchester)
v. SARAJEVO (Yugoslavia) Won: 2-1

Stepney, Brennan, Dunne, Crerand, Foulkes, Sadler, Burns, Kidd, Charlton, Best, Aston.
Scorers: Aston, Best.
Attendance: 62,801

* United won 2-1 on aggregate.

Quarter Final, First Leg
February 28th 1968 (Manchester)
v. GORNIK ZABRZE (Poland) Won: 2-0

Stepney, Dunne, Burns, Crerand, Sadler, Stiles, Best, Kidd, Charlton, Ryan, Aston.
Scorers: Florenski (o.g.), Kidd
Attendance: 63,456

Quarter Final, Second Leg
March 13th 1968 (Katowice)
v. GORNIK ZABRZE (Poland) Lost: 0-1

Stepney, Dunne, Burns, Crerand, Sadler, Stiles, Fitzpatrick, Kidd, Charlton, Best, Herd.
Attendance: 105,000

* United won 2-1 on aggregate.

Semi Final, First Leg
April 24th 1968 (Manchester)
v. REAL MADRID (Spain) Won: 1-0

Stepney, Dunne, Burns, Crerand, Sadler, Stiles, Best, Kidd, Charlton, Law, Aston.
Scorer: Best.
Attendance: 63,500

Semi Final, Second Leg
May 15th 1968 (Madrid)
v. REAL MADRID (Spain) Draw: 3-3

Stepney, Brennan, Dunne, Crerand, Foulkes, Stiles, Best, Kidd, Charlton, Sadler, Aston.
Scorers: Zoco o.g., Sadler, Foulkes.
Attendance: 125,000

* United won 4-3 on aggregate.

Final
May 29th 1968 (Wembley)

MANCHESTER UNITED 4 (Charlton 2, Best, Kidd)
SL BENFICA (Portugal) 1 (Graca)
MANCHESTER UNITED: Stepney, Brennan, Dunne, Crerand, Foulkes, Stiles, Best, Kidd, Charlton, Sadler, Aston.
SL BENFICA: Henrique, Adolfo, Humberto, Jacinto, Cruz, Graca, Coluna, Augusto, Torres, Eusebio, Simoes.
Attendance: 100,000

* after extra time
score after 90 minutes 1-1.

SEASON 1968-69

1968 WORLD CLUB CHAMPION-SHIP
First Leg
September 25th 1968 (Buenos Aires)
v. ESTUDIANTES (Argentina) Lost: 0-1

Stepney, Dunne, Burns, Crerand, Foulkes, Stiles, Morgan, Sadler, Charlton, Law, Best.
Attendance: 55,000

Second Leg
October 16th 1968 (Manchester)
v. ESTUDIANTES (Argentina) Draw: 1-1

Stepney, Brennan, Dunne, Crerand, Foulkes, Sadler, Morgan, Kidd, Charlton, Law.
Substitute: Sartori for Law.
Scorers: Morgan.
Attendance: 63,500

* United lost 1-2 on aggregate.

EUROPEAN CHAMPION CLUBS' CUP
First Round, First Leg
September 18th 1968 (Dublin)
v. WATERFORD (Republic of Ireland)
Won: 3-1

Stepney, Dunne, Burns, Crerand, Foulkes, Stiles, Best, Sadler, Charlton, Law, Kidd.
Substitute: Rimmer for Stepney.
Scorer: Law 3.
Attendance: 48,000

First Round, Second Leg
October 2nd 1968 (Manchester)
v. WATERFORD (Republic of Ireland)
Won: 7-1

Stepney, Dunne, Burns, Crerand, Foulkes, Stiles, Best, Sadler, Charlton, Law, Kidd.
Scorers: Law 4, Burns, Charlton, Stiles.
Attendance: 41,750

* United won 10-2 on aggregate.

Second Round, First Leg
November 13th 1968 (Manchester)
v. ANDERLECHT (Belgium) Won: 3-0

Stepney, Brennan, Dunne, Crerand, Sadler, Stiles, Ryan, Kidd, Charlton, Law, Sartori.
Scorers: Law 2, Kidd.
Attendance: 51,000

Second Round, Second Leg
November 27th 1968 (Brussels)
v. ANDERLECHT (Belgium) Lost: 1-3
Stepney, Kopel, Dunne, Crerand, Foulkes, Sadler, Fitzpatrick, Stiles, Charlton, Law, Sartori.
Scorer: Sartori.
Attendance: 40,000

* United won 4-3 on aggregate.

Quarter Final, First Leg
February 26th 1969 (Manchester)
v. RAPID VIENNA (Austria) Won: 3-0
Stepney, Fitzpatrick, Dunne, Crerand, James, Stiles, Morgan, Kidd, Charlton, Law, Best.
Scorers: Best 2, Morgan.
Attendance: 61,923

Quarter Final, Second Leg
March 5th 1969 (Vienna)
v. RAPID VIENNA (Austria) Draw: 0-0
Stepney, Fitzpatrick, Dunne, Crerand, James, Stiles, Morgan, Kidd, Charlton, Sadler, Best.
Attendance: 52,000

* United won 3-0 on aggregate.

Semi Final, First Leg
April 23rd 1969 (Milan)
v. AC MILAN (Italy) Lost: 0-2
Rimmer, Brennan, Fitzpatrick, Crerand, Foulkes, Stiles, Morgan, Kidd, Charlton, Law, Best.
Attendance: 90,000

Semi Final, Second Leg
May 15th 1969 (Manchester)
v. AC MILAN (Italy) Won: 1-0
Rimmer, Brennan, Burns, Crerand, Foulkes, Stiles, Morgan, Kidd, Charlton, Law, Best.
Scorer: Charlton.
Attendance: 63,103

* United lost 1-2 on aggregate.

1975-76 LEAGUE CHAMPIONSHIP: FINISHED 3rd

SEASON 1976-77

UEFA CUP
First Round, First Leg
September 15th 1976 (Amsterdam)
v. AJAX (Netherlands) Lost: 0-1
Stepney, Nicholl, Houston, Daly, Greenhoff B., Buchan, Coppell, McIlroy, Pearson, Macari, Hill.
Substitute: McCreery for Daly.
Attendance: 30,000

First Round, Second Leg
September 29th 1976 (Manchester)
v. AJAX (Netherlands) Won: 2-0
Stepney, Nicholl, Houston, Daly, Greenhoff B., Buchan, Coppell, McIlroy, McCreery, Macari, Hill.
Substitutes: Albiston for Daly, Paterson for Hill.
Scorers: Macari, McIlroy.
Attendance: 58,938

* United won 2-1 on aggregate.

Second Round, First Leg
October 20th 1976 (Manchester)
v. JUVENTUS (Italy) Won: 1-0
Stepney, Nicholl, Albiston, Daly, Greenhoff B., Houston, Coppell, McIlroy, Pearson, Macari, Hill.
Substitute: McCreery for Daly.
Scorer: Hill.
Attendance: 59,021

Second Round, Second Leg
November 3rd 1976 (Turin)
v. JUVENTUS (Italy) Lost 0-3
Stepney, Nicholl, Albiston, Daly, Greenhoff B., Houston, Coppell, McIlroy, Pearson, Macari, Hill.
Substitutes: McCreery for McIlroy, Paterson for Macari.
Attendance: 66,632

* United lost 1-3 on aggregate.

1976-77 FA CUP FINAL
v. LIVERPOOL (Wembley) Won: 2-1
Stepney, Nicholl, Albiston, McIlroy, Greenhoff B., Buchan, Coppell, Greenho f, J., Pearson, Macari, Hill.
Substitute: McCreery for Hill
Scorers: Pearson, Greenhoff, J.
Attendance: 100,000

SEASON 1977-78

EUROPEAN CUP WINNERS' CUP
First Round, First Leg
September 14th 1977 (St Etienne)
v. ST ETIENNE (France) Draw: 1-1
Stepney, Nicholl, Albiston, McIlroy, Greenhoff B., Buchan, McGrath, McCreery, Pearson, Coppell, Hill.
Substitutes: Grimes for McIlroy, Houston for Greenhoff B.
Scorer: Hill
Attendance: 33,678

First Round, Second Leg
October 5th 1977 (Plymouth)
v. ST ETIENNE (France) Won: 2-0
Stepney, Nicholl, Albiston, McIlroy, Greenhoff B., Buchan, Coppell, Greenhoff J., Pearson, Macari, Hill.
Substitute: McGrath for Pearson.
Scorers: Coppell, Pearson.
Attendance: 31,634

* United won 3-1 on aggregate.

Second Round, First Leg
October 19th 1977 (Oporto)
v. PORTO (Portugal) Lost: 0-4
Stepney, Nicholl, Albiston, McIlroy, Houston, Buchan, McGrath, McCreery, Coppell, Macari, Hill.
Substitutes: Forsyth for Houston, Grimes for McGrath.
Attendance: 60,000

Second Round, Second Leg
November 2nd 1977 (Manchester)
v. PORTO (Portugal) Won: 5-2
Stepney, Nicholl, Albiston, McIlroy, Houston, Buchan, McGrath, Coppell, Pearson, McCreery, Hill.
Scorers: Coppell 2, Nicholl, Murca 2 (o.g's.)
Attendance: 51,831

* United lost 5-6 on aggregate.

1979-80 LEAGUE CHAMPIONSHIP: FINISHED 2nd

SEASON 1980-81

UEFA CUP
First Round, First Leg
September 17th 1980 (Manchester)
v. WIDZEW LODZ (Poland) Draw: 1-1
Bailey, Nicholl, Albiston, McIlroy, Jovanovic, Buchan, Grimes, Greenhoff J., Coppell, Macari, Thomas.
Substitute: Duxbury for Nicholl
Scorer: McIlroy
Attendance: 38,037

First Round, Second Leg
October 1st 1980 (Lodz)
v. WIDZEW LODZ (Poland) Draw: 0-0
Bailey, Nicholl, Albiston, McIlroy, Jovanovic, Buchan, Grimes, Coppell, Jordan, Duxbury, Thomas.
Substitute: Moran for Buchan.
Attendance: 35,000

* United lost on away goals rule.

1981-82 LEAGUE CHAMPIONSHIP: FINISHED 3rd

SEASON 1982-83

UEFA CUP
First Round, First Leg
September 15th 1982 (Manchester)
v. VALENCIA (Spain) Draw: 0-0
Bailey, Duxbury, Albiston, Wilkins, Buchan, McQueen, Robson, Grimes, Stapleton, Whiteside, Coppell.
Attendance: 46,588

First Round, Second Leg
September 29th 1982 (Valencia)
v. VALENCIA (Spain) Lost: 1-2

Bailey, Duxbury, Albiston, Wilkins, Moran, Buchan, Robson, Grimes, Stapleton, Whiteside, Moses.
Substitutes: Macari for Buchan, Coppell for Moses.
Scorer: Robson.
Attendance: 35,000

* United lost 1-2 on aggregate.

1982-83 FA CUP FINAL REPLAY
v. BRIGHTON AND HOVE ALBION
(Wembley) Won: 4-0

Bailey, Duxbury, Albiston, Wilkins, Moran, McQueen, Robson, Muhren, Stapleton, Whiteside, Davies.
Scorers: Robson 2, Muhren, Whiteside
Attendance: 92,000

SEASON 1983-84

EUROPEAN CUP WINNERS' CUP
First Round, First Leg
September 14th 1983 (Manchester)
v. DUKLA PRAGUE (Czechoslovakia)
Draw: 1-1

Bailey, Duxbury, Albiston, Wilkins, Moran, McQueen, Robson, Muhren, Stapleton, Macari, Graham.
Substitutes: Moses for Muhren, Gidman for Robson.
Scorer: Wilkins (pen.)
Attendance: 39,745

First Round, Second Leg
September 27th 1983 (Prague)
v. DUKLA PRAGUE (Czechoslovakia)
Draw: 2-2

Bailey, Duxbury, Albiston, Wilkins, Moran, McQueen, Robson, Muhren, Stapleton, Whiteside, Graham.
Scorers: Robson, Stapleton.
Attendance: 28,850

* United won on away goals rule.

Second Round, First Leg
October 19th 1983 (Varna)
v. SPARTAK VARNA (Bulgaria) Won: 2-1

Bailey, Duxbury, Albiston, Wilkins, Moran, McQueen, Robson, Muhren, Stapleton, Whiteside, Graham.
Scorers: Graham, Robson.
Attendance: 40,000

Second Round, Second Leg
November 2nd 1983 (Manchester)
v. SPARTAK VARNA (Bulgaria) Won: 2-0

Bailey, Duxbury, Albiston, Moses, Moran, McQueen, Robson, Macari, Stapleton, Whiteside, Graham.
Substitutes: Dempsey for Moran, Hughes for Whiteside.
Scorer: Stapleton 2.
Attendance: 39,079

* United won 4-1 on aggregate.

Third Round, First Leg
March 7th 1984 (Barcelona)
v. BARCELONA (Spain) Lost: 0-2

Bailey, Duxbury, Albiston, Wilkins, Moran, Hogg, Robson, Muhren, Stapleton, Hughes, Moses.
Substitute: Graham for Hughes.
Attendance: 70,000

Third Round, Second Leg
March 21st 1984 (Manchester)
v. BARCELONA (Spain) Won: 3-0

Bailey, Duxbury, Albiston, Wilkins, Moran, Hogg, Robson, Muhren, Stapleton, Whiteside, Moses.
Substitute: Hughes for Whiteside.
Scorers: Robson 2, Stapleton.
Attendance: 58,547

* United won 3-2 on aggregate.

Semi-Final, First Leg
April 11th 1984 (Manchester)
v. JUVENTUS (Italy) Draw: 1-1

Bailey, Duxbury, Albiston, McGrath, Moran, Hogg, Graham, Moses, Stapleton, Whiteside, Gidman.
Substitute: Davies for Gidman.
Scorer: Davies.
Attendance: 58,171

Semi-Final, Second Leg
April 25th 1984 (Turin)
v. JUVENTUS (Italy) Lost: 1-2

Bailey, Duxbury, Albiston, Wilkins, Moran, Hogg, McGrath, Moses, Stapleton, Hughes, Graham.
Substitute: Whiteside for Stapleton.
Scorer: Whiteside.
Attendance: 64,655

* United lost 2-3 on aggregate.

1983-84 LEAGUE CHAMPIONSHIP: FINISHED 4th

SEASON 1984-85

UEFA CUP
First Round, First Leg
September 19th 1984 (Manchester)
v. RABA VASAS ETO GYOR (Hungary)
Won: 3-0

Bailey, Duxbury, Albiston, Moses, Moran, Hogg, Robson, Muhren, Hughes, Whiteside, Olsen.
Scorers: Hughes, Muhren, Robson.
Attendance: 33,119

First Round, Second Leg
October 3rd 1984 (Gyor)
v. RABA VASAS ETO GYOR (Hungary)
Draw: 2-2

Bailey, Duxbury, Albiston, Moses, Moran, Hogg, Robson, Muhren, Hughes, Brazil, Olsen.
Substitute: Gidman for Robson.
Scorers: Brazil, Muhren (pen.)
Attendance: 26,000

* United won 5-2 on aggregate.

Second Round, First Leg
October 24th 1984 (Eindhoven)
v. PSV EINDHOVEN (Netherlands)
Draw: 0-0

Bailey, Gidman, Albiston, Moses, Moran, Hogg, Robson, Strachan, Hughes, Brazil, Olsen.
Attendance: 27,500

Second Round, Second Leg
November 7th 1984 (Manchester)
v. PSV EINDHOVEN (Netherlands) Won: 1-0

Bailey, Gidman, Albiston, Moses, Moran, Hogg, Robson, Strachan, Hughes, Stapleton, Olsen.
Substitutes: Whiteside for Stapleton, Garton for Moran.
Scorer: Strachan (pen.)
Attendance: 39,281

* United won 1-0 on aggregate.

Third Round, First Leg
November 28th 1984 (Manchester)
v. DUNDEE UNITED (Scotland)
Draw: 2-2

Bailey, Gidman, Albiston, Moses, McQueen, Duxbury, Robson, Strachan, Hughes, Whiteside, Olsen.
Substitute: Stapleton for Whiteside.
Scorers: Strachan (pen.), Robson.
Attendance: 48,278

Third Round, Second Leg
December 12th 1984 (Dundee)
v. DUNDEE UNITED (Scotland) Won: 3-2

Bailey, Gidman, Albiston, Moses, McQueen, Duxbury, Robson, Strachan, Stapleton, Hughes, Muhren.
Scorers: Hughes, Muhren, McGinnis (o.g.)
Attendance: 21,821

* United won 5-4 on aggregate.

Fourth Round, First Leg
March 6th 1985 (Manchester)
v. VIDEOTON (Hungary) Won: 1-0

Bailey, Gidman, Albiston, Duxbury, McGrath, Hogg, Strachan, Whiteside, Hughes, Stapleton, Olsen.
Scorer: Stapleton.
Attendance: 35,432

Fourth Round, Second Leg
March 20th 1985 (Szekesfehervar)
v. VIDEOTON (Hungary) Lost: 0-1

Bailey, Gidman, Albiston, Duxbury, McGrath, Hogg, Robson, Strachan, Hughes, Stapleton, Whiteside.
Substitute: Olsen for Robson.
Attendance: 25,000

* United lost 4-5 on penalties, after extra time.

PHOTO CREDITS

AGENCY	PAGE NO(S)	PHOTO	AGENCY	PAGE NO(S)	PHOTO
Allsport Photographic	17	Against Real Madrid	**Associated Newspapers**	65	Against Tottenham Hotspur
	18	Against Real Madrid		67	Against Tottneham Hotspur
	163	Platini/Moses			
	181	Against Juventus	**Colorsport**	10	Matt Busby
	219	Against Barcelona		11	Tommy Taylor
	220	Against Barcelona		12	Duncan Edwards
				13	Jackie Blanchflower
Associated Press	13	Matt Busby with European Cup		24	Jimmy Murphy
	44	Arrival at Belgrade		72	Pat Crerand
	45	Charlton/Cope		86	Nobby Stiles
	49	Crashed plane (middle)		107	Team with European Cup
	52	Matt Busby		122	Bill Foulkes
		Wives visit		134	Brian Kidd
		Blanchflower		158	Martin Buchan
		Hospital staff visit Manchester		164	Against Juventus
	59	Denis Law signs for United		169	Arthur Albiston
	60	Pat Crerand signs for United		182	Against Barcelona
	61	Cantwell with FA Cup		185	Stuart Pearson
	79	Against Strasbourg		187	Gary Bailey
	85	Against Ferencvaros		194	Martin Buchan
	88	Against Helsinki (2)		195	Kevin Moran
	90	Against ASK Vorwaerts		201	Bryan Robson
	93	Against ASK Vorwaerts		206	Frank Stapleton
	98	Against Benfica		207	Ray Wilkins
	99	Against Benfica (2)		222/3	Duxbury/Moratalla
	100	Against Partizan Belgrade		226/7	Action against Barcelona
	104/5	Against Partizan Belgrade		228	Action against Barcelona
	101	Denis Law		230	Bryan Robson
	118	Against Real Madrid		234	Action against Juventus
	119	Team group in Madrid		257	Mark Hughes
	120	Goal against Real Madrid		258	Gary Bailey
		Charlton and fans		259	Frank Stapleton
	125	Best scores against Benfica			
	126	Charlton scores against Benfica	**Contact Photographic Services**	237/8	Pennants/gifts from abroad
		Crerand lies injured		255	Pennants/gifts from abroad
	129	Stepney collects			
	130	Break before extra time	**Daily Mirror**	77	Against Everton (2)
		Sadler with Cup		82/3	Against Ferencvaros
	132	Matt Busby			
	135	Bobby Charlton	**Express Photos**	29	Team boarding plane for Madrid
	139	Nobby Stiles		73	Against Djurgardens
	144	Against Anderlecht (2)		75	Against Borussia Dortmund
	151	Against Rapid Vienna		156/7	Against AC Milan
	155	Against AC Milan			
	166	Against Juventus (bottom)	**S Hale**	182	FA Cup 1985 (2)
	218	Matt Busby		198/9	Robson shoots against Valencia
	254	Against Videoton		210	Against Dukla Prague

PHOTO CREDITS

AGENCY	PAGE NO(S)	PHOTO	AGENCY	PAGE NO(S)	PHOTO
	211	Against Dukla Prague		61	Return with Cup
	224	Against Barcelona		66	Against Tottenham Hotspur
	225	Against Barcelona		68/9	Against Sporting Lisbon
	231	Against Juventus		70	Against Sporting Lisbon
	232/3	Against Juventus		82/3	Against Ferencvaros
				84	Against Ferencvaros
Mail Newspapers	32	Against Real Madrid		87	Against Ferencvaros
	45	Charlton scores		95	Foulkes goal
				96/7	Against Benfica
Manchester Evening News	157	David Sadler		99	Against Benfica (Charlton)
	170	Tommy Docherty		101	Team in Belgrade hotel
	190/1	Against Widzew Lodz		102	Against Partizan Belgrade
	240	Ron Atkinson		102/3	Against Partizan Belgrade
	242	Ray Wilkins		105	Against Partizan Belgrade
	248/9	Against Dundee		114/5	Against Gomik Zabrze
	250	Against Dundee		131	Charlton/Sadler
	251	Against Dundee		143	Anderlecht frustration
	261	Alex Ferguson		148/9	Against Rapid Vienna
				152/3	Against AC Milan
Manchester United FC, Cliff Butler	256	The current team		154	Against AC Milan
				160	Against Ajax (bottom)
				193	Bailey in action
Mirror Group Newspapers, Manchester	12	Harry Gregg			
	16	Against Anderlecht	Photo Source	123	Pennant exchange
	20	Viollet scores		124	Eusebio scores
	21	Schmidt/Byrne		129	Sadler shot
	23	Taylor in flight		130	Charlton lifts the Cup
	26	Against Bilbao		136	Against Estudiantes
	31	Against Real Madrid		170/1	FA Cup Winners 1977
	32	Taylor/Alonso			
	33	Against Real Madrid	Popperfoto	15	Viollet scores
	34	Boarding plane for Ireland		25	Carmelo fists clear
	37	Against Shamrock Rovers		29	Taylor's goal
	39	Taylor/Cadek		45	Team line-up in Belgrade
	40	Pegg scores		46/7	Against Red Star Belgrade
	41	Against Dukla Prague		75	Dunne ready to save
	43	Against Red Star Belgrade		80	Dunne leaps
	48	Jackie Blanchflower		81	Strasbourg 'keeper saves
	49	Boarding plane for Belgrade		106/7	Against Hibernian Valletta (inset)
		Crashed plane			Against Hibernien Valletta
		Newspaper caption		117	Against Real Madrid
	50/1	Scene of crash		125	Law scores
	52	Coffins arrive home		140/1	Against Waterford
		Gregg/nurse		141	Against Waterford (top left)
	55	Against AC Milan		143	Law's goal
	56	Viollet equalises		150	Against Rapid Vienna
	57	Bill Foulkes		160	Against Ajax (top)

NEWSPAPER CREDITS

NEWSPAPER	AUTHOR	PAGE(S)
Daily Express	T Elliott	55, 57
	D Hodgson	78, 106, 108
	D Potter	196, 212, 217, 252, 253
	H Rose	24, 39
	A Thompson	140, 147, 172
	Anon	80
Daily Herald	P Lorenzo	67, 100, 138, 155
	S Richards	68
	Anon	98
Daily Mail	R Crowther	64, 74, 119, 165, 166, 180, 186
	P Johnson	197, 198, 200, 215, 243, 247
	J Powell	208, 213
The Guardian	P Barclay	245, 249
	A Barham	62, 84, 90, 113, 123, 142
	B Crowther	79
	D Lacey	231, 235
	H Mather	58
	An Old International	14, 15, 19, 28, 30, 38, 44
	I Ridley	242
	A Special Correspondent	88
	W R Taylor	22
	E Todd	76, 89
	Anon	72
Manchester Evening News	P Gardner	82
	D Meek	121, 136, 171, 192, 212, 239, 254
Daily Mirror	B Russell	190, 218, 244, 254
	D Wallis	211

NEWSPAPER	AUTHOR	PAGE(S)
News Chronicle	F Taylor	34, 41, 42
Daily Star	J Wragg	196
The Sun	F Clough	74
	P Fitton	192, 221
	L Noad	86, 102
	Anon	252
Daily Telegraph	D Lowe	162, 229
	D Saunders	60, 153, 167, 173
	R H Williams	108, 144
The Times	Association Football Correspondent	64, 71, 95
	G Green	111, 116, 117, 137, 151
	Anon	72, 93